D0667698

About Island Press

Since 1984, the nonprofit organization Island Press has been stimulating, shaping, and communicating ideas that are essential for solving environmental problems worldwide. With more than 1,000 titles in print and some 30 new releases each year, we are the nation's leading publisher on environmental issues. We identify innovative thinkers and emerging trends in the environmental field. We work with world-renowned experts and authors to develop cross-disciplinary solutions to environmental challenges.

Island Press designs and executes educational campaigns in conjunction with our authors to communicate their critical messages in print, in person, and online using the latest technologies, innovative programs, and the media. Our goal is to reach targeted audiences—scientists, policymakers, environmental advocates, urban planners, the media, and concerned citizens—with information that can be used to create the framework for long-term ecological health and human well-being.

Island Press gratefully acknowledges major support of our work by The Agua Fund, The Andrew W. Mellon Foundation, The Bobolink Foundation, The Curtis and Edith Munson Foundation, Forrest C. and Frances H. Lattner Foundation, The JPB Foundation, The Kresge Foundation, The Oram Foundation, Inc., The Overbrook Foundation, The S.D. Bechtel, Jr. Foundation, The Summit Charitable Foundation, Inc., and many other generous supporters.

The opinions expressed in this book are those of the author(s) and do not necessarily reflect the views of our supporters.

The Community Resilience Reader

The Community Resilience Reader

Essential Resources for an Era of Upheaval

Edited by Daniel Lerch

Post Carbon Institute

ISLANDPRESS

Washington | Covelo | London

Copyright © 2017 Post Carbon Institute

Chapter 7, "Systems Literacy": © 2017 Howard Silverman
Chapter 11, "Energy Democracy": © 2017 Denise Fairchild and Al Weinrub

All rights reserved under International and Pan-American Copyright Conventions. No
part of this book may be reproduced in any form or by any means without permission in
writing from the publisher: Island Press, 2000 M St NW, Suite 650, Washington, DC 20036

ISLAND PRESS is a trademark of the Center for Resource Economics.

Library of Congress Control Number: 2017947285

ISBN-13: 978-1-61091-860-2 (paper)
ISBN-13: 978-1-61091-861-9 (electronic)

All Island Press books are printed on environmentally responsible materials.

Manufactured in the United States of America
10 9 8 7 6 5 4 3 2 1

Keywords: Anthropocene, biodiversity, built environment, carrying capacity, climate
change, coal, community resilience, consumption, ecological footprint, ecology, economy,
education, energy, energy democracy, equity, extinction, feedback, food system, fossil
fuels, hydropower, infrastructure, nuclear energy, oil, panarchy, renewable energy,
resilience, social justice, solar power, sustainability, systems thinking, tactical urbanism,
urban planning, walkability, water supply, wind power

Contents

Acknowledgments

Post Carbon Institute is indebted to many people over many years for the ideas that have come together in this book. Transition Network founder Rob Hopkins bears special mention as one of the earliest explorers of how social-ecological system resilience science might be applied to the needs of towns and cities.

Among the staff at the institute, Asher Miller and Richard Heinberg were central to the development of our approach to community resilience and the E^4 crises through years of conversations and writing. Ken White and Marissa Mommaerts contributed greatly through their 2014–2015 work with the Thriving Resilient Communities Collaboratory and a series of interviews and reports that followed. Simone Osborn, Kristin Sponsler, and Bart Anderson have quietly shaped our understanding of community resilience for years as the curators and editors of our website, resilience.org.

Many thanks go to Rebecca Bright and Sharis Simonian from Island Press for helping make this book a reality; to Tim Crownshaw for his research assistance; and to our contributing authors, who were tasked with writing about resilience while the world was suddenly turning upside down in the months surrounding the 2016 presidential election.

Special thanks, as always, go to Post Carbon Institute's stalwart supporters (especially PJ and LH) and to the institute's board of directors and fellows for their years of advice and insight.

Mil gracias a Gloria y Victor por su apoyo y generosidad durante los últimos meses de editar de este libro en su hogar.

Finally, endless thanks go to Judith and Martín for their incredible patience, inspiration, and love.

Daniel Lerch

Introduction

Daniel Lerch

FOR MORE THAN THIRTY YEARS, the world community has tried to resolve the combined challenges of environmental degradation, fossil fuel dependence, economic inequality, and persistent social injustice, largely under the banner of internationally brokered "sustainable development." Despite some partial successes, it is clear today that the pace of these global trends has not been slowed, let alone stopped or reversed. The scale of these trends has grown, and their effects have become so widespread that they now threaten the stability—in some cases, even the existence—of communities around the world. The global sustainability challenges of the past have become the local resilience crises of today.

Resilience is the ability of a system—like a family, a country, or Earth's biosphere—to cope with short-term disruptions and adapt to long-term changes without losing its essential character. A *crisis* is an unstable state of affairs in which decisive change is both necessary and inevitable. We depend on the resilience of all the systems that support us for life and well-being; if these systems falter, we suffer. Today we face four major crises—environmental, energy, economic, and equity—that threaten to overwhelm the resilience of the systems we care about, particularly at the local level.

The failure of international sustainability efforts to thwart these crises means that resilience-building efforts at the community level—working on all issues and systems, not just on climate change and infrastructure—are needed more than ever. The charge to build community resilience, however, raises important questions: Resilience *of* what, exactly? Resilient *to* what, exactly? Building resilience *how*, and benefiting *whom*? *The Community Resilience Reader* aims to answer these questions.

⌒‿

In 2010, Post Carbon Institute produced *The Post Carbon Reader: Managing the 21st Century's Sustainability Crises*. The shocks of the 2008 stock market crash were still reverberating, energy prices were at historic highs, and climate change—although broadly accepted—was still largely seen by mainstream government and business leaders as a manageable future threat.[1] We at the institute, as well as many other observers of modern industrial society's long-term trajectory, were deeply concerned that the end of twentieth-century-style economic growth—coupled with the end of cheap oil and the beginnings of irreversible climate change—could ultimately prove too much for the system to bear. It seemed that humanity's interconnected sustainability challenges were coming to a head and that only deeper understanding of their systemic nature could point to effective responses.

Awareness of these challenges grew quickly in the years that followed, but the responses of the international community ranged from ineffective to counterproductive. The world's major economies, having (barely) stopped a global collapse in 2008, doubled down on efforts to produce short-term growth, but with no serious concurrent effort at fundamental reform. The world's fossil fuel producers, flush with profits from sky-high prices, reinforced society's fossil fuel dependence with investments in more-expensive, more-destructive energy resources like shale gas, tight oil, and tar sands. At one high-profile international conference after another, the world's most powerful nations, although well aware of the threat of climate change, decided to delay effective, coordinated reductions of carbon emissions. In each case, instead of making decisive changes in the face of these challenges, the international community opted for business as usual, both postponing the days when change would no longer be a choice and ensuring that needed actions (whenever they finally got around to them) would be that much more difficult to implement.

Now, at the end of the second decade of the twenty-first century, decisive changes are indeed inevitable, and we have clarity on what this transition from *challenges* to *crises* looks like:

- Ecosystems around the world are being pushed near or past their limits, with impacts like severe topsoil loss, freshwater depletion, biodiversity loss, and climate change being felt worldwide.
- Modern industrial society remains overwhelmingly dependent on fossil fuels, spurring the energy industry to pursue ever-more destructive—and expensive—resource extraction practices like fracking for gas and oil and mountaintop removal for coal.
- Our economies are structured to require constant growth, but the end of cheap fossil fuels and the sheer biophysical limits of the planet are complicating this imperative more and more.
- The broken promises of globalization have helped create the worst economic inequality of the modern era, and institutionalized racism and other forms of bigotry have been allowed to persist. Together, they are now helping fuel a frightening rise in racist, nationalist, authoritarian politics.

Moreover, the effects of these global-scale crises—once isolated to a few unlucky cities and regions—are now threatening the stability (economic, social, or otherwise) of communities everywhere, including in the United States. Economic globalization and corporation-friendly government policies have left cities and towns across the country bereft of decent working-class jobs and civic vitality. Decades of growth-oriented planning and underinvestment have left virtually every American city and town with an insurmountable backlog of infrastructure maintenance and replacement (sometimes with truly dangerous effects, like the lead water crises in Flint, Michigan, and elsewhere). In addition, cities from coast to coast are grappling with the worsening effects of climate change, such as stronger storms and greater temperature and precipitation extremes.

On the bright side, there is now more clarity than in the past about how to understand these crises and most effectively deal with them. When we were developing *The Post Carbon Reader* in 2009, we asked Bill Rees (chapter 6) to write a chapter on the emerging ecosystems management concept of *resilience thinking*; at the time, resilience was otherwise a specialist term mostly found (with varying definitions) in emergency preparedness, engineering, and psychology.[2] Sustainability itself was often a marginalized[3] and even contested[4] idea not very long ago, at least outside of progressive-leaning communities and environmentalist circles. Today the concepts of sustainability and resilience are widely recognized and are being used and explored by countless grassroots activists, local government projects, academic programs, business initiatives, and publications.

And yet, the application of resilience thinking to communities in modern industrial society is still underdeveloped. Urban resilience (as it is commonly called) largely draws on *social-ecological systems resilience science*, an approach that was developed primarily for working with natural resources and the rural communities that directly depend on them. After the unexpected (and very urban) devastation of Superstorm Sandy in October 2012, however, the popular notion took hold that *cities* needed to build their resilience—specifically, to be able to "bounce back" from the future impacts of worsening climate change. Over the next few years, a concept of urban resilience developed that came to include more proactive adaptation to future threats (e.g., "bounce forward") as well as non-climate issues such as economic development and social equity—not least due to the efforts of the Rockefeller Foundation's "100 Resilient Cities" program.[5] This movement is in the right direction, but it is only a start, and the depth of our crises and the insights of resilience science suggest it can go much further.

To help develop this application of resilience to urban settings, Post Carbon Institute produced a report titled *Six Foundations for Building Community Resilience* in 2015. The report characterized the challenges currently facing humanity, and now broadly affecting communities, as *crises*, specifically environmental, energy, economic, and equity crises (the "E⁴ crises"). It then developed the case for responding to these crises by (1) using a deep understanding of social-ecological systems resilience thinking, (2) focusing efforts on the community scale, and (3) prioritizing six "foundation" themes essential to all community resilience work. (The full report, together with responses from various resilience leaders and practitioners, is online at sixfoundations.org.)

This book, *The Community Resilience Reader*, digs deeper into the E⁴ crises, further explores resilience thinking and related tools like systems literacy, and shows how the notion of community resilience building can be applied to specific areas of community concern like energy, food, and consumption. Here are some of the underlying assumptions we build upon throughout this book:

- Approaches to the *E⁴ crises* must be grounded in critical thinking, sober expectations, and acceptance of geophysical realities.
- *Systems literacy* is essential for understanding our systemic, multiscalar, complex challenges and for developing effective responses. (Indeed, there are only responses, not solutions.)
- *Sustainability* and *resilience* are distinct but complementary concepts. As Charles Redman of Arizona State University has put it, "Sustainability prioritizes outcomes; resilience prioritizes process."[6]
- Building resilience means intentionally guiding a system's process of adaptation so as to preserve some qualities and allow others to fade away, all while retaining the essence—or *identity*—of the system. In a human community, identity is essentially determined by what people value about where they live; therefore, the *people* who inhabit a community must be at the heart of the resilience-building process.
- *Communities* are the ideal level of focus for building resilience because the particular powers held at the state and local government levels in the United States make this kind of work possible and because regular people can most effectively be involved at this level.

Chapter 1, "Six Foundations for Building Community Resilience," is an adaptation of the report of the same name mentioned earlier. It is a useful summary of this book's approach, and it presents the "six foundations" that we consider essential for effective community resilience building: people, systems thinking, adaptability, transformability, sustainability, and courage. Watch for those foundational themes as you read through each chapter.

The book then proceeds in three parts:

- Part I, "Understanding Our Predicament," explores the E^4 crises—environmental, energy, economic, and equity—with a view to both current impacts and underlying drivers. The last chapter in this section digs yet deeper, looking to human nature itself to inquire as to why it seems so difficult for us to act on complex, long-term threats like climate change.
- Part II, "Gathering the Needed Tools," packs everything you need to know to get started with systems literacy, sustainability science, and resilience science into just a couple hours of reading. Chapter 10, a transitional chapter, then pulls us down from the cloudy heights of theory to the grounded roots of community.
- Part III, "Community Resilience in Action," shows how the information from part I and the tools from part II can be used to think about seven issues of particular importance to community resilience. The relevance of some of these issues (energy, food) will be obvious; for others (consumption, streets), it might not be as obvious. Through these varied topics, we demonstrate that resilience is not just applicable to structures and services, but also to social and cultural patterns.

Although *The Community Resilience Reader* is not a typical "reader" collecting prepublished material (all but three chapters were written specifically for this book), it is still a book with multiple authors and thus multiple styles and approaches. The authors were asked to write about the things they believed were most important to convey from their fields of expertise as they relate to community resilience. For Leena Iyengar (chapter 2, "The Environmental Crisis"), it meant including personal reflections on biodiversity loss, memory, and meaning. For Howard Silverman (chapter 7, "Systems Literacy"), it meant an essay on enacting "purposeful change." For Rebecca Wodder (chapter 12, "Building

Community Resilience at the Water's Edge"), it meant a systematic exploration of community water issues. For Scott Sawyer (chapter 13, "Food System Lessons from Vermont"), it meant a walk through Vermont's innovative food system resilience initiative.

Perhaps because the writing of these chapters spanned the final months of the raucous 2016 election and the first months of the Trump administration, many of the authors told me they found themselves preoccupied with deep systems change and came to the conclusion that *collaboration* is critical for meeting the challenges of our new political and social reality. That certainly fits well with the bookends of the six foundations: people and courage. *People* is the first foundation, because where else should community resilience start but with the people who live there? *Courage* is the last foundation because, in the end, working with other people—friends, strangers, and even adversaries—on topics that can be threatening, politicized, and deeply personal is not easy.

The work, however, is necessary. Nearly anyone who has collaborated with neighbors to strengthen their community—in the street, in a meeting room, at city hall—will also admit that the work is usually enjoyable, the results rewarding, and the new relationships invaluable.

Building community resilience starts with the courage to collaborate with the people around you to protect the things about your community that you value most. We hope *The Community Resilience Reader* helps support you and your community in shaping a future that is rewarding for everyone.

Notes

1. Two years later, then-ExxonMobil chief executive officer (and as of early 2017, secretary of state under President Donald Trump) Rex Tillerson said of the impacts of climate change, "It's an engineering problem and it has engineering solutions." Matt Daily, "Exxon CEO Calls Climate Change Engineering Problem," June 27, 2012, http://www.reuters.com/article/us-exxon-climate-idUSBRE85Q1C820120627.
2. See William Rees, "Thinking 'Resilience,'" in *The Post Carbon Reader: Managing the 21st Century's Sustainability Crises*, ed. Richard Heinberg and Daniel Lerch (Healdsburg, CA: Watershed Media, 2010), http://www.postcarbon.org /publications/thinking-resilience/. Probably the first significant book to introduce social-ecological systems resilience to nonacademic audiences was Brian Walker

and David Salt, *Resilience Thinking: Sustaining Ecosystems and People in a Changing World* (Washington, DC: Island Press, 2006).

3. In 2007, while researching for my book *Post Carbon Cities*, I attended the national conference of the American Planning Association (APA) (the largest professional organization in the United States for urban planners) in Philadelphia. At that conference, after realizing that I could count the number of sessions (out of hundreds) dealing with sustainability issues literally on one hand, I connected with other members to get the APA to allow an official special-interest division focused on sustainability issues. Over the course of the application process, we were told that there was resistance among some of the national leadership who believed that "sustainability" was no different from well-established environmental planning issues already represented in the APA. A few years later, however, the Sustainable Communities Division was established. Today it is one of the largest and most active of the APA's twenty-one divisions; see http://sustainableplanning.net.

4. For years, sustainability-focused efforts associated (accurately or not) with the United Nations and its various programs and summits have been the target of conspiracy theorists and political disinformation campaigns, including harassment of sustainability advocates and disruption of local government meetings and public processes dealing with sustainability issues. See, for example, Jonathan Thompson, "Fearful of Agenda 21, an Alleged U.N. Plot, Activists Derail Land-Use Planning," *High Country News*, February 6, 2012, http://www.hcn.org/issues/44.2/fearful-of -Agenda-21-an-alleged-united-nations-plot-activists-derail-land-use-planning/.

5. See Rockefeller Foundation, "100 Resilient Cities," accessed April 5, 2017, https:// www.rockefellerfoundation.org/our-work/initiatives/100-resilient-cities/.

6. Charles Redman, "Should Sustainability and Resilience Be Combined or Remain Distinct Pursuits?," *Ecology and Society* 19, no. 2 (2014): 37.

CHAPTER 1

Six Foundations for Building Community Resilience

Daniel Lerch

> How do you know community resilience when you see it? I think you look for the capacity for people to not have to go through extremes ... being knowledgeable and having capacity to do something, to change your circumstances.
> —Doria Robinson, Urban Tilth[1]

> We all need a sense of community. And we all need to believe that we have agency—a sense that we can make choices that will affect our lives.
> —Stuart Comstock-Gay, Vermont Community Foundation[2]

EFFORTS TO BUILD COMMUNITY RESILIENCE often focus on growing the capacity to "bounce back" from disruptions, like those caused by climate change. But climate change is not the only crisis we face, nor is preparing for disruption the only way to build resilience. Truly robust community resilience should do more. It should engage and benefit all community members, and it should consider all the challenges the community faces, from rising sea levels to a lack of living wage jobs. In addition, it should be grounded in resilience science, which tells us how complex systems—like human communities—can adapt and persist through changing circumstances.

What Problem Are We Trying to Solve?

Virtually every American community is part of—and dependent on—a deeply interconnected and highly complex global civilization of nearly two hundred countries, tens of thousands of cities, and more than seven billion people. The prices we pay at the grocery store and the gas station, the investments our businesses make, the regulations our governments set, and even the weather we experience every day are potentially influenced by countless events and decisions made around the world, all to a degree that was barely conceivable just half a century ago.

Although many of the challenges our communities face would exist regardless, this global interconnection is the dominant factor of our modern world and brings us rewards and risks (neither of which are distributed equally) that we cannot ignore. If the aim of community resilience—at minimum—is to safeguard the health and well-being of people in the face of the twenty-first century's many complex challenges, those challenges need to be understood in a global context.

At Post Carbon Institute, we organize those challenges as a set of four distinct but intertwined crises called the "E^4" crises. They influence and multiply one another, and they manifest in myriad ways from the most local to the most global of scales. They are characterized as *crises* because they are pushing us toward decisive changes—tipping points that we may choose to fight, ignore, or take advantage of. The E^4 crises do not encompass all the challenges facing humanity today, but they frame and highlight those that we feel most immediately threaten modern civilization.

1. **The ecological crisis.** Everything we need to survive—to have life, a society, an economy—ultimately depends on the natural world, but

every ecosystem has two important limiting factors: its rate of replenishment and its capacity to deal with wastes and stress. The last two hundred years of exponential economic growth and population growth have pushed ecosystems around the world near or past these limits, with results like severe topsoil loss, freshwater depletion, biodiversity loss, and climate change. Humanity's "ecological footprint" is now larger than what the planet can sustainably handle, and we are crossing key boundaries beyond which human civilization literally may not be able to continue.[3]

2. **The energy crisis.** The era of easy fossil fuels is over, leading the energy industry to resort to extreme measures like tar sands mining, mountaintop removal coal mining, hydrofracturing ("fracking") for shale gas and tight oil, and deepwater drilling. These practices come with significant costs and risks, however, and in most instances, they provide far less net energy than the conventional oil, coal, and natural gas that fueled the twentieth century.[4] Renewable energy is a real but imperfect alternative, as it would take decades and many trillions of dollars to scale up deployment to all sectors of the economy and retrofit transportation and industrial infrastructure accordingly.[5] Declines in the amount of affordable energy available to society threaten to create major environmental, economic, and social impacts as the twenty-first century progresses.[6]

3. **The economic crisis.** Our local, national, and global economies are currently structured to require constant growth, yet with the onset of the Great Recession in 2008, we reached the end of economic growth as we have known it.[7] Despite unprecedented interventions on the part of central banks and governments, economic recovery in the United States and Europe has failed to benefit the majority of citizens.[8] The end of the age of cheap and easy energy, the vast mountains of both private and public debt that we have incurred, and the snowballing costs of climate change impacts are all forcing us into an as-yet-undefined postgrowth economic system, whether we are ready for it or not.

4. **The equity crisis.** Inequity has been a problem throughout recorded human history, and not least in the United States, despite its professed

values of liberty and justice for all. Although social progress since the Civil War has in theory brought political enfranchisement and legal protections to almost everyone, in practice the failure to fully extend both economic opportunity and a functional social safety net—together with the failure to fully address institutionalized racism, sexism, and other forms of prejudice—has led to ongoing inequality of economic, social, and political power. The ecological, energy, and economic crises are together exacerbating inequality, which has become increasingly visible in the rapid concentration of wealth among the ultra-rich and in the increasing violence against people of color.

These four crises shape the many and complex challenges that communities in the United States must wrestle with in the twenty-first century.[9]

Building community resilience is an attempt to keep the community from irrevocably changing for the worse as the result of these crises and, one hopes, change the community for the better. *How* we go about doing this is critical to whether our efforts will succeed and last. To understand why, we need to take a close look at the concept of resilience itself.

What Is Resilience, Really?

Resilience is often thought of as the ability to withstand hard times or "bounce back" from a disaster. For example, a town devastated by a tornado is called resilient when its people and its infrastructure are able to quickly return to how things were before.

In recent years, people working on community sustainability issues have developed a more nuanced view of resilience. A commonly used approach—and the one used in this chapter—comes from the field of ecology, where resilience is understood as the ability to absorb disturbance and still retain basic function and structure, or "identity."[10] In other words, a resilient system can adapt to changes without losing the essential qualities that define what it is and what it does. For example, a maple-beech forest ecosystem might experience wildfire, drought, or infestation. If it is sufficiently resilient, however, it will recuperate from individual incidents and adapt to longer-term changes, all while keeping essentially the same species, patterns, and other qualities that define its identity of "maple-beech forest ecosystem."

In resilience science, a community and the ecosystem it makes use of are together considered a unified social-ecological system. The system's adaptability is a function of general characteristics like diversity, innovation, and feedback as well as its ability to cope with vulnerabilities specific to its situation and make deeper transformations if needed.[11] Importantly, the system is understood to be a "complex adaptive system" that is not static but is constantly adapting to change, change that is often unpredictable.[12] (For a more in-depth discussion of resilience science, see chapter 9.)

When we intervene in a system with the aim of building its resilience, we are intentionally guiding the process of adaptation in an attempt to preserve some qualities and to allow others to fade away, all while retaining the essential nature, or "identity," of the system. Thus, resilience building necessarily starts with decisions about *what we value*. Of course, what a community can be said to "value" is open to interpretation and may not be agreed upon by everyone. It may even reflect ignorance and prejudice; few today would agree with racist and sexist values dominant in many US communities in the 1950s, for example. As we will see later, these core issues of equity and values make a people-centered approach to community resilience especially important.

Resilience science has mostly focused on rural communities and the natural resources they depend on, but new efforts are exploring how it can be applied to nonrural communities and their relationships not only with ecological systems but with economic and social systems as well.[13] We might ask, for example, how a city can address complex challenges like a globalizing economy, more frequent extreme weather, rising health care costs, and uncertainty about the future mix of energy resources.

Applying resilience thinking to a modern city is not fundamentally different from applying it to a small rural community: we are simply considering a broader scope of systems because it is within that community's power to do so. A midsized US city has billions of dollars in infrastructure and social spending to work with over multiple years, not to mention hundreds of thousands of people who can act toward various goals through their economic, civic, and social activities. (Of course, the challenge of facilitating decision making among the larger community's competing interest groups will be more complex than in a smaller community.)

When applied to communities, resilience is sometimes spoken of as the next generation of sustainability; indeed, Post Carbon Institute's definition of community resilience (see below) deliberately incorporates sustainability's nested triad of environment, society, and economy. But the two concepts—*resilience* and *sustainability*—may also be understood as different frameworks for achieving the same goal: organizing how we interact with the world around us and with each other in ways that can continue indefinitely. Sustainability thinking has made important contributions to how we value and steward the resources our communities depend on, although its aspirations have proven difficult to put into meaningful practice at large scales.[14] Resilience thinking offers a complement to sustainability thinking in that it is explicitly focused on the challenges of humans coexisting with ecological systems; after all, it was developed for practical use in the messy, unpredictable real world.[15] As Charles Redman of Arizona State University has put it, "Sustainability prioritizes outcomes; resilience prioritizes process."[16]

Resilience can be a powerful concept for communities, but why bother building resilience at the community level at all when the E[4] crises are ultimately national and global in scale? We will see why in the next section.

Why Communities?

When people speak of a community, they mean something far more than just the physical infrastructure of a human settlement. A community is also the people inhabiting a particular place, defined by their interpersonal relationships, cultural patterns, economic and governance structures, and shared memories and aspirations.

We leave the word *community* loosely defined, envisioned as a place-based group of people who have some meaningful capacity to influence their basic common needs given their particular social and political context. In urban areas, it might be a city of a few million with all its competing interest groups or a close-knit neighborhood of just a few thousand. In rural areas, it might be a village of a few hundred or a 5,000-square-mile county of dispersed towns. Community resilience building can start with whatever scale and set of people the initiators deem appropriate in a given situation, although through discussing needs, aspirations, and capacity (with attention to the six foundations presented in this chapter), it should quickly become apparent if the scale should be expanded or contracted.

The argument for building community resilience—and specifically for doing the work at the community level—is twofold. First, in the United States, community-level resilience building makes practical sense because of how the political system is structured. By design, new ideas typically come to fruition at the federal level slowly, thanks in part to the roles and constraints set by the US Constitution and the procedural hurdles of the US Congress. In contrast, local and state governments often have great flexibility in organizing how public decisions are made as well as significant regulatory and investment power over the issues that most affect everyday life: social services like health care and police, public goods like utilities, civic institutions like schools and courts, land use and transportation planning, and so on.

Indeed, our cities and states are traditionally the country's laboratories for social and economic innovation.[17] One community's experiment can inspire thousands of other experiments, providing valuable insights and best practices and ultimately building support for larger-scale changes. In the first decade of the twenty-first century, while national and international climate efforts languished, many cities across the United States followed early leaders like San Francisco and Seattle and started their own climate initiatives. Using the terminology of resilience science, one could say that cities and states are providers of diversity, openness, and modularity for the resilience of the higher-level national system.

This model of local innovation works as well as it does because it is at the community level where we (as individuals, businesses, organizations) most directly interact with the people and institutions that make up our society. It is where we are most affected by the decisions society makes: what jobs are available to us, what infrastructure is available for our use, and what policies exist that limit or empower us. Critically, it is where the majority of us who do not wield major political or economic power can most directly affect society: as voters, neighbors, entrepreneurs, consumers, activists, and elected officials.[18]

From that observation arises the second part of the argument for building resilience at the community level: it is both ethical and practical for community members to be at the heart of community resilience-building work. (This principle may seem self-evident, but it is not necessarily so; imagine a central government attempting to direct the resilience-building efforts of thousands of communities remotely, relying on uniform indicators, outside managers, and centralized resources.) Using the terminology of sociology, we might say that everyone in a community is a stakeholder, and those stakeholders need the opportunity not only to participate in resilience building, but also to actually have some responsibility for it.

Decades of research underline how important it is for local stakeholders to have real power in decisions that affect them.[19] Some of the central concepts of resilience science tell us why this particularly applies to urban communities. For example, *identity* (as discussed earlier) is the touchstone of a system, and in a democratic society, the members of a community have an inherent right to self-determination; hence, the identity of the community emerges from its members. *Social capital*—people's relationships—is what gets things done in human systems, and it is richest at the local level. Local connections and presence also create more and tighter opportunities for system *feedback*, which is essential for adaptation and innovation.

For us as social animals, identity is tied to community: our relationships to other people and to a place; our sense of shared experience, history and culture; and the smells, sounds, and even the soil that we associate with "home." How else can community members recognize themselves as stakeholders if not by seeing themselves as part of a larger place-based whole?

The ability to put local stakeholders at the heart of resilience-building efforts—plus the practical advantages of community-level government in the United States—makes community resilience building an effective way to respond to the E⁴ crises. Local decision making does not always lead to equitable outcomes, though; indeed, one weakness of decentralization is that parochialism and local prejudice can flourish if unchecked. This suggests two requirements for building community resilience:

1. The **responsibility** for resilience building and the power to decide how it is done must ultimately rest with community members.
2. The **process** of resilience building must equitably address both the particular situation of the community and the broader challenges facing society.

These requirements—in dynamic tension with each other because together they task community members with acting beyond their own self-interest—are the starting point for the six foundations of building community resilience, described in the remainder of this chapter.

The Six Foundations

Although many resilience frameworks and tools for building community resilience are now available, no single approach will likely work for all communities and their varied social and economic contexts. Therefore, we have identified six foundations that, in our view, are essential no matter where or how resilience-building efforts are undertaken or no matter which challenges are of most concern locally: (1) people, (2) systems thinking, (3) adaptability, (4) transformability, (5) sustainability, and (6) courage. To emphasize resilience building as an ongoing process, the foundations support *building* community resilience rather than achieving resilience as a fixed goal.

Foundation 1: People

The power to envision the future of the community and build its resilience resides with community members.

We can try to outsource our problems to a new generation of green engineers, designers, and architects, but we will only see broad,

lasting changes when the people inhabiting these communities create a vision for the future and lead the process for change.
—Phil Myrick, Project for Public Spaces[20]

What It Means

Communities are products of human relationships.[21] What the community is now and what it will be in the future both result from decisions made by people interacting, negotiating, and working together. Trust and deep relationships are crucial to holding communities together year after year and making resilience durable, but they can be challenging to build, especially in diverse communities.[22]

Resilience building cannot turn a blind eye to the political and economic processes that determine what gets done, how it gets done, who decides, and who benefits. People of all interests and means must be able to participate in and benefit from resilience building; indeed, if they are to build true resilience, communities must *embrace* dissent and diversity.

The goals of community resilience-building efforts are best set by and focused on the needs of the people who make up the community, not just the needs of the most politically engaged or powerful individuals, businesses, and external stakeholders. Community members must also collectively have power and responsibility for cultivating the resilience of their community as active participants and leaders rather than only the local government or business leaders holding power and responsibility.

Why It Is Important

IDENTITY

In a democratic society, we might say that the identity of a community arises from its members and represents a shared sense of the community's core qualities. Because we humans have aspirations and free will, we might also say that identity includes a shared vision of what the community should be like in the future. We can try to describe a community's identity by asking people specific questions: What are the values of this community? What defines this community, and why? What do we not want to lose? What do we need to change? These kinds of questions can really only be answered by community members.

Identity is the touchstone of a community's resilience; but, as an expression of values, it also shapes perceptions of what is important and what is worth doing. So, for the work of resilience building, the *way in which* identity is characterized is quite important.[23] Consider the following:

- Systems are defined by their larger context, and human communities exist within larger social, economic, and ecological systems. The voices of outside stakeholders and experts are important to prevent parochialism and include specialist knowledge.[24]
- Systems are also defined by their components, and human communities are aggregates of smaller social groups with varying levels of influence and power. The voices of traditionally disempowered or dissenting groups are not only ethically important to include, but they can also help prevent discrimination and stagnation (although this responsibility is shared by all).
- In human communities, identity is dynamic.[25] It is a function of people existing in a community together, changing as they and the society and environment around them change. University of Colorado professor Bruce Goldstein notes that "identity and community are collaborative achievements, not just entities already out there waiting to be found and dusted off."[26] Those involved in resilience-building efforts should constantly revisit and refine their understanding of what the community's identity is.

In practice, envisioning a shared community identity will be messy, multifaceted, and constantly open to question.[27] To uncover not only inequities and vulnerabilities, but also opportunities and resources, it is essential to open potentially challenging discussions.

Effectiveness

Resilience building is most effective when stakeholders are engaged and invested. In communities, the primary stakeholders are the people who live there. They are the key to the crucial resource of social capital (essentially, the local relationships that make things happen).[28] They are often the most knowledgeable about the community's opportunities and challenges and are best suited to act on them through existing economic, political, and social relationships.[29]

When community members have ownership of and responsibility for resilience building, a sense of agency and support for the work—as well as of fairness and shared effort in what emerges—is created. (Indeed, that is partly why resilience building cannot just be a government project.[30]) Community ownership of resilience building helps with the longer, broader process of social cohesion, the formation of bonds that make us willing and able to cooperate, collaborate, and take care of one another. Social cohesion is essential for helping us get through acute crises like natural disasters,[31] and it makes a community feel enriching and nurturing over the long term.

Social capital accumulates and evolves over time, allowing the community to continually build up its knowledge, skills, and place-based wisdom, things that so many communities have lost.[32] It is more than a renewable resource: the more we use it, the more it grows, and the more it grows, the more it contributes to community resilience.

Foundation 2: Systems thinking

Systems thinking is essential for understanding the complex, interrelated crises now unfolding and what they mean for our similarly complex communities.

> I have seen repeatedly that a too-narrow understanding of the issue—from only limited vantage points or within only one sector for example—leads to poorly framed interventions. Thinking in systems goes beyond any one segment or sector and pushes groups to include those "unlikely bedfellows" that can help find the leverage points for change.
> —Michelle Colussi, Canadian Centre for Community Renewal[33]

What It Means

Our communities are thoroughly integrated subsystems of a single global social-ecological system. They are connected to or influenced by external factors like regional water supplies, national energy policy, and global climate change. Our communities are also complex systems in their own right, with innumerable components constantly changing and interacting with one another, the larger whole, and outside systems. Local economic activity, relationships among different social groups, and local cultural patterns all influence the community from the inside out.

The challenges we face are complex, so we cannot approach them as if they were linear problems. Systems thinking helps us understand the complex E^4 crises as well as how our complex societies and communities work. It is also the basis of resilience science. (For a primer on systems literacy, see chapter 7.)

Why It Is Important

MAKING SENSE OF COMPLEXITY

Systems thinking—simultaneously seeing the parts, the whole, and the relationships within a system[34]—helps us make sense of complexity. Complexity is different from being complicated. Resilience thinkers Brian Walker and David Salt (the authors of chapter 9) describe it this way:

> The mechanism that drives an old-style clock is a set of tiny, intricate cogs and springs, often consisting of many pieces. This is a complicated machine.... However, the individual pieces are not independent of one another; rather, the movement of one depends on another in an unvarying way.... [In contrast,] although a farm might produce just one item (e.g., wheat), the farm is far from simple. The farmer, the farming practices, the crop, the soil it grows on, and the market are all interacting and changing over time. This is a complex adaptive system.[35]

Engineering helps us understand the clock, but it will only get us so far with the farm. Weather, market prices, soil nutrition, government policy, and countless other factors are all in flux and are often unpredictable. Systems thinking gives us concepts that help us model the dynamics and relationships that exist. We can start to think of the farm in terms of "stocks" (resources like the wheat in the storehouse and the nutrients in the soil), "flows" (sales of the wheat, depletion of the soil's nutrients), "feedback loops" (higher demand for grain spurs the farmer to plant more wheat, more cultivation means the farmer needs to replace more lost soil nutrients), and so on.

An essential part of systems thinking is setting a boundary: deciding the limits of what we will consider in detail. By setting a boundary, we are not pretending that everything outside the boundary does not exist; rather, we are choosing one of many possible perspectives and accepting that we cannot know everything we might want to know. Indeed, recognizing that there is more than one way to see things is at the heart of systems thinking. This point is especially important when we are talking about human communities, where there is rarely a lack of diverse views and interests.

If we will never have complete information, it follows that there will always be blind spots. During the run-up to the Iraq War, US Defense Secretary Donald Rumsfeld famously described this as the problem of "known unknowns" and "unknown unknowns."[36] This wording suggests that an open-ended, adaptable response to a problem may be preferable to a static solution. As we will see with the next foundation, adaptability, resilience science gives us tools for anticipating and dealing with uncertainty.

Making the E⁴ crises relevant

Modern industrial society operates today at a global scale, and every community is deeply dependent on resources and processes far beyond its own region.[37] International trade and relations are nothing new, but since World War II, we have created extraordinarily complex interconnections between economic, social, and environmental systems around the world. Building community resilience in the face of the E^4 crises means that we need to think about the myriad challenges (of which only some are predictable) we will face in the foreseeable future.

Consider, for example, American communities' complex relationship with fossil fuels and climate change. Communities currently rely on fossil fuels to provide essential energy services, such as fuel for vehicles, agricultural inputs, heat for buildings and industrial processes, and electricity for communications. Our communities' dependence on fossil fuels, however, is a major driver of climate change, both directly (burning fossil fuels for transportation, electricity, and heat) and indirectly (consuming food and goods manufactured and transported with fossil fuels). Climate change is, in turn, affecting our communities, also directly and indirectly. The direct impacts are obvious and much-discussed: storm surges that damage buildings and infrastructure, droughts that reduce local water supply, extreme heat and cold that endanger vulnerable populations, and more. The indirect impacts are less obvious: drought in one part of the world (or even one part of the country) might hurt agricultural production and cause food prices to rise elsewhere, for example, and climate-driven economic and social unrest in an oil-producing country might disrupt exports, affecting the price or supply of gasoline.

Understanding the E^4 crises can help guide actions at the community level. For example, if we assume that the market will automatically supply affordable energy as long as there is demand, there is no point in worrying about the trend of diminishing cheap-to-produce oil resources. On the other hand, when we understand the basic mechanisms of our energy crisis—that is, that our economy and infrastructure remain extremely dependent on oil, and alternative energy sources are all limited in their capacity to substitute for it[38]—we get a better sense of what to expect in the future and what it might mean for our community.

Systems thinking makes the E^4 crises relevant to communities in one other way: it helps us see that actions even at the relatively small community level play a role in what is happening at the national and global levels. They are all parts of the same system. Building community resilience contributes to the resilience of our global social-ecological system.[39]

Foundation 3: Adaptability

A community that adapts to change is resilient, but because communities and the challenges we face are dynamic, adaptation is an ongoing process.
> In a time of drastic change it is the learners who inherit the future.
> The learned usually find themselves equipped to live in a world
> that no longer exists.
> —Eric Hoffer, *Reflections on the Human Condition*[40]

What It Means

When complex systems are resilient in the face of disruption, it is because they have the capacity to adapt to changing circumstances thanks to system characteristics like diversity, modularity, and openness. In human systems, resilience-building efforts aim (in part) to cultivate such characteristics, but if those efforts themselves do not adapt to changing circumstances, they may unwittingly cultivate the resilience of things that *are not* desired. (Poverty, drought, and authoritarian governments can all be resilient in their own ways.)

Why It Is Important

THE QUALITIES OF RESILIENCE

There are many different ways to think about how resilience is built and how adaptability is supported. In their influential book *Resilience Practice*, Brian Walker and David Salt list "attributes" like *diversity, modularity, openness,* and *reserves.*[41] The Stockholm Resilience Institute identifies "principles" like *manage connectivity* and *broaden participation.*[42] The Rockefeller Foundation lists "qualities" like *robust, redundant, flexible,* and *inclusive.*[43] Although some of these terms and approaches differ, they essentially point to the same ideas. For communities, what matters is that resilience is understood as a quality to continually cultivate by taking on the right patterns, not a goal to be achieved by ticking off a list of characteristics. Andrew Zolli (author of *Resilience: Why Things Bounce Back*) evokes this approach with his "verbs of resilience"—four things that are happening all the time in a resilient community:

1. **Building** regenerative capacity.
2. **Sensing** emerging risks.
3. **Responding** to disruption.
4. **Learning** and transforming.[44]

Initiatives, activists, and politicians come and go, but if resilience building is ingrained in the community culture, it can evolve as the community evolves.

LEARNING

Adaptability is both about responding to change (both external and internal) and learning from the experience. Learning happens through feedback loops. In a model system, feedback loops send information from one part of the system to another so that it can self-regulate; resilience is built by having tight feedback loops. A community lacking in resilience is probably suffering from poor or incomplete feedback loops: perhaps community members do not know what business and government leaders are doing, or perhaps certain groups of people do not have a voice in the community. Effective resilience building aims to identify what types of feedback (and from where and to where) are important, including those that are being overlooked or ignored.

THE PROBLEMS OF COMPLEXITY AND EFFICIENCY

The adaptability of a system is influenced by many things, often not in obvious ways. For example, too much complexity in a system can be a symptom of low resilience: it can reduce flexibility and create resistance to change. In the Northeast blackout of 2003, a few minor problems in Ohio suddenly overwhelmed the electricity distribution system's ability to cope, causing a massive power failure affecting 55 million people. The physical system was no longer able to adapt because it had too much complexity.

One way to potentially reduce excess complexity is to improve efficiency, but that can also have unintended consequences. For example, the post–World War II push to move poor families into oversized, anonymous public housing projects was deemed an efficient way to provide housing cheaply. However, it cut the rich social ties and emotional roots people had in their old neighborhoods, making it easier for crime to flourish and destroying the social capital that might have been tapped to address community challenges.[45] These "planned" social systems were less able to adapt because they had *too little* complexity.

Too much resilience

Communities, their subsystems, and the systems they are part of are constantly changing, often in unpredictable ways. A system that cannot cope with change will ultimately cease to exist. The collapse of the Soviet Union may be the most dramatic example in living memory of a human system whose failure to adapt to both external and internal changes proved fatal.

In contrast, the US political and economic system has been quite resilient, largely because of system characteristics that build resilience, like diversity (competition is encouraged), innovation (financial and social incentives exist for profitable ideas), and reserves (when markets fail, governments have stepped in with bailouts). Resilience can become a problem, however, when the decisions that cultivate resilience-building qualities themselves fail to adapt. The severe market failure of 2008 was essentially brought on by the US system's overdependence on debt and cheap oil (which is a complex function of public-sector policies and private-sector investments).[46] Economic collapse was avoided, but at the cost of actions that ultimately *reinforced* dependence on debt and oil; that is, the system achieved short-term stability but increased its long-term vulnerability. Unless the system can "learn" and truly adapt to the changed reality (i.e., stagnant real economic growth and the end of cheap and easy fossil fuels), it may not get through the next crisis without deep—and likely undesirable—transformation.[47]

Foundation 4: Transformability

Some challenges are so big that it is not possible for the community to simply adapt; fundamental, transformative changes may be necessary.

> The way you maintain the resilience of a system is by allowing it to probe its boundaries.
> —Brian Walker, resilience scientist[48]

If we want things to stay as they are, things will have to change.
—character in *The Leopard* by Giuseppe di Lampedusa[49]

What It Means

Communities generally adapt as the world around them changes. If adaptation happens too slowly or is constrained, however, challenges can outpace the ability to cope and eventually threaten overall resilience. When automobile manufacturing started moving out of the Midwest, for example, many communities were so dependent on the industry that mere adaptation was not an option: they needed to radically rethink their economic basis (and the social and governance implications of radical change) if they hoped to maintain any ability to chart their futures. In other words, these communities needed to change some part of their identity (while retaining their most valued qualities) and transform to a new state that could be resilient under the new circumstances.

Resilience building usually tries to maintain the basic function and structure of a system in the face of disruption. Transformational efforts are *purposefully* disruptive to the system, changing some of its function and structure so that it can build resilience in ways more suited to the new reality.

Why It Is Important

It is hard to get new results from old patterns. Past investments in now-outmoded infrastructure are not easily abandoned, entrenched leaders rely on existing relationships and hold on to outdated assumptions and prejudices, and bureaucracies ossify in decades-old procedures that everybody hates but nobody seems to be able to change.

A system's ability to potentially remake itself—to transform—is a key component of its overall resilience (the other components are its general adaptive capacity and its ability to cope with vulnerabilities specific to its situation).[50] In some situations, it may be necessary for the entire system to transform. In the 1990s, the Austrian community of Güssing transformed itself from a poor agricultural town into a minor industrial center by completely remaking its relationship with energy, going from importing all its (mostly fossil fuel) energy to becoming a net renewable energy producer.[51]

In other situations, it may just be a single but essential part of the system that must transform to achieve greater system resilience. Imagine a community police department with an entrenched culture that disproportionately arrests and harms young black men. This essential subsystem of the community—the law enforcement function—is undermining overall resilience by violently disrupting lives and households, feeding resentment toward local authorities, and raising the chances of social unrest. The police department needs a different culture, different internal policies, and possibly different leaders; it needs to transform into something significantly different from what it currently is.

Community resilience-building efforts can be transformational by tackling those aspects of the community that need fundamental change and sowing the seeds of transformation generally for when change is needed in the future. In resilience science, transformability depends on three attributes:[52]

1. **Getting to acceptance.** Transformation is intentional disruption, so it will not be successful unless the people involved and affected recognize the need for it. Information, transparency, dialogue, and inclusive processes are all important.

2. **Having options for transformational change.** New ideas for dealing with new situations will only be available if there is room for them to be developed and tested. Resilience-building efforts might aim to allow and create space—regulatory, economic, social, and even physical space—for experimentation and novelty within governments, businesses, and neighborhoods as well as seeking out innovations from the margins (which is where transformational change often starts).

3. **Having capacity for transformational change.** As Brian Walker and David Salt describe it, "Transformative change needs support from higher scales and also depends on having high levels of all types of capital—natural, human, built, financial, and social."[53] Support from "higher scales" could mean that state policy makers have good working political relationships with local elected officials or that there is a

solid regional network of charging stations in place to support the city's new electric vehicle program. Of the "high levels" of capital needed, the potential of social capital is particularly compelling; consider, for example, the deep social and cultural relationships that were integral to the success of the 1960s civil rights movement.[54]

Foundation 5: Sustainability

Community resilience is not sustainable if it serves only us and only now; it needs to work for other communities, future generations, and the ecosystems on which we all depend.

> For those who embrace sustainability in the fullest sense—as an environmental, social, economic, and political ideal—we're at a crossroads in our civilization. There are two paths to take: continue with business as usual, ignore the science of climate change, and pretend that our economic system isn't on life support—or, remake and redefine our society along the lines of sustainability.
> —Jeremy Caradonna, *Sustainability: A History*[55]

What It Means

As discussed earlier, sustainability and resilience are distinct concepts that complement each other. Resilience helps us understand the nuts and bolts of how social-ecological systems work and how they might adapt (or fail to adapt) to changes over time. Sustainability helps us understand in a more general sense our extremely complex relationship with the natural world and the consequences of getting that relationship wrong. Where resilience is process-oriented and, in ways, value-neutral, sustainability forces us to confront deep questions and uncomfortable potential futures.

Sustainability is a guiding light for resilience building, where there can be a danger of getting overwhelmed by endless system factors and dynamics. Its tools help us make sense of the torrent of information that systems thinking requires us to explore. The perspective we get from it informs the long-term goals of resilience building, but we also need to be careful in our pursuit of sustainability that we do not mistake what we want for what is actually possible.

Why It Is Important

TOOLS

Sustainability starts with the obvious but still often ignored observations that humanity's actions are ultimately limited by the carrying capacity of our finite planetary biosphere and that we are already running afoul of this limit. In general, it is concerned with exploring how our actions affect the biosphere, how the biosphere in turn affects us, and how our actions need to change over the long term. Community resilience-building efforts will find useful guidance for grappling with the E^4 crises in certain observations and analytical tools that have been developed in sustainability thinking:

- **Limits to growth.** As Post Carbon Institute's Richard Heinberg notes, "In 1972 the now-classic book *Limits to Growth* explored the consequences for Earth's ecosystems of exponential growth in population, industrialization, pollution, food production, and resource depletion.... The underlying premise of the book is irrefutable: At some point in time, humanity's ever-increasing resource consumption will meet the very real limits of a planet with finite natural resources."[56] The related ecological footprint concept shows us how humanity is using Earth's resources faster than it can regenerate them and challenges us to think about whether everyone can and will get a fair share.[57] Community resilience-building efforts may ask: Are we assuming that economic growth will continue? What does our future look like if the natural resources we depend on become scarcer or more expensive?
- **Capital and services.** Environmental and human resources are often thought of as forms of *capital*—namely, natural capital and social capital—when considering the services and benefits we receive from them. Natural capital, perhaps in the form of a forest, can provide services like

cleaning air and filtering water, whereas social capital includes the relationships found within a community and is the basis for organized action. Sustainability thinking can help us think about how these and other resources might be valued against one another—and if it is even possible (or ethical) to do so. This approach has practical implications for communities. For example, if we cut down a nearby forest so that our expanding community has more room for homes and jobs and we offset the loss by building parks elsewhere, is that a defensible trade-off?[58] If gentrification pushes established long-time residents out of a neighborhood but spurs overall community economic growth, is *that* a defensible trade-off?

• **Safe operating space for humanity.** In 2009, Johan Rockström and colleagues proposed a model of nine planetary boundaries within which humanity must remain to avoid catastrophic environmental change.[59] They include limits on climate change, interference with the nitrogen and phosphorous cycles, biodiversity loss, and ocean acidification. Community resilience-building efforts may ask: Are we contributing to humanity pushing past these boundaries? Are we prepared for catastrophic environmental change? What can we do to reduce our impact—and prepare for the unavoidable changes—locally?

• **Seven generations.** The essential aspiration of sustainability is for human civilization to persist on this planet indefinitely.[60] This goal suggests two requirements for community resilience-building efforts that do not necessarily emerge from resilience thinking on its own: they must benefit both present and future generations, and future generations must be able to continue them.

A nonnegotiable yardstick

Of course, sustainability is far more than a suite of useful tools and a theoretical goal to which we should aspire for the sake of future generations: it presents us with a nonnegotiable yardstick against which all our actions, goals, and plans must be measured. Quite simply, each is either sustainable or unsustainable. Rather than face the reality that many of our individual and societal activities—and even our well-intentioned environmental strategies—are incompatible with true sustainability, we have reappropriated the term to refer to practices that are merely more environmentally sound than others.[61]

How can sustainability, as a way of thinking about the world, remain meaningful if it does not seem to be leading us where we urgently need to go?[62] The problem is not the concept of sustainability per se, but rather that we have collectively lacked the courage to engage with it as honestly as needed. We often use sustainability to think critically about the present but only optimistically about the future. In the 1990s, when sustainability was first becoming a household word, it evoked shocking images of disappearing rain forests and stranded polar bears, but inevitably with a hint that tragedy could be reversed if only we each did our small part.[63] Today, with the rain forests still burning and the polar bears still starving, it is clear that a more pragmatic and sober approach is overdue.

Such an approach to sustainability recognizes that if we do not find strategies to keep the human project operating within the limits of the biosphere, that project will ultimately fail. It challenges us to confront a damaged future and, even more important, to learn from our mistakes so that we stop making things even *worse*. Pragmatic, sober sustainability lends urgency and depth to resilience-building efforts at the community level. Indeed, we each need to do our part, and it cannot be small. There is too much at stake.

Foundation 6: Courage

As individuals and as a community, we need courage to confront challenging issues and take responsibility for our collective future.

> More and more I see people who just know the status quo isn't working—they don't have courage, they just know they need some different answers. Accepting the answers may require courage but if they are engaged in cocreating them, there is ownership and commitment.
> —Michelle Colussi, Canadian Centre for Community Renewal[64]

What It Means

Community resilience building is not an engineering problem solvable just by knowledge and skill. It is a social undertaking, involving thousands or even millions of people and their most meaningful relationships, hopes, and fears. It confronts us with the worrying threats of the E^4 crises and compels us to engage with people with whom we may disagree, perhaps quite strongly.

We need motivation and emotional strength to take on such personally challenging work. Individuals need courage to speak out about their views and needs and to make themselves personally vulnerable. Communities, too, need courage to create space for difficult conversations, make far-reaching investments and policy changes, and risk sharing political and economic power.

Courage is the ability to do something you know is difficult, and building community resilience in the face of the E^4 crises can be difficult indeed. Resilience-building efforts need to cultivate courage in both individuals and the community as a whole to confront challenging issues and take responsibility for their collective future.

Why It Is Important

FACING PROBLEMS HEAD-ON

Resilience building makes us grapple with complex problems that do not have easy or obvious answers. It can be overwhelming to try to make sense of the global E^4 crises, not to mention local challenges. Moreover, these challenges literally hit close to home. From the daily injustices of the equity crisis to the existential threat of climate change, the E^4 crises threaten our physical, economic, and emotional well-being as well as some of the things we most hold dear: home, family, friends. They are big, long-lasting problems that will affect our children and grandchildren, as will the actions we take in response to them.

COLLABORATION IS NOT EASY

It is hard enough to work on these issues as individuals and households; it is harder still to work on them as a community, with people who may see things differently. Take, for example, the challenge of finding basic agreement about the "identity" of the community (see above). Should the community aim for growth or stability? Should it preserve the dominant culture, or should it be open to new people and new ideas? There will inevitably be disagreement and even struggle over such questions because social change is always negotiated and contested.

Even finding agreement on which problems are most urgent can be contentious. Urban planner Saharnaz Mirzazad recalls participating in a public meeting about community resilience in Oakland, California, in 2015: "Gentrification, climate change, and fair wages were all part of the discussion. However, community representatives were more concerned about gentrification than climate risks because that was an immediate threat forcing them out of the community."[65]

Talking seriously about the community's future also means talking about the community's past, including how its current trajectory came to be. This discussion can lead to uncomfortable but important conversations about present and past injustices and how power is wielded in the community. Although they can be awkward, such conversations open the door to deliberation about how power can be more equitably shared in the community. In fact, if such discussions about community resilience-building efforts are not challenging, they are probably not going deep enough.

Sticking with the work

We humans form communities in part because we want stability and predictability. We have evolved systems over millennia to provide us with food and water, enable us to move long distances, and interact with one another without constantly fearing for our safety. Those systems—built infrastructure, social institutions, and cultural patterns—are understandably resistant to change. It takes courage to imagine and then do things differently than they have been done before, whether it is adapting current practices or transforming them more fundamentally.

Courage also supports us through the practical challenges of collaboration and public process; logistical obstacles pop up, volunteers disappear, funding runs out, or we simply do not get what we want. It takes courage to collaborate with our neighbors, even on seemingly inconsequential matters. Charla Chamberlain, co-founder of the City Repair Project, told this story about a neighborhood mural project in Portland, Oregon:

> One of the neighbors at the meeting was an artist, and adamant that the colors of the street painting be a certain way. The discussion became strained, and had not been resolved by when she had to leave. A few days after the meeting, one of her neighbors came to her door. The woman timidly showed her a few sets of colors they had chosen after she'd left, and said she and the group had wanted to be sure the artist was OK with what they'd decided. As the artist related this story to me her eyes welled up with tears, and she told me she realized in that moment that her relationship with her neighbor was far more important than whatever color was chosen.[66]

Whether it is organizing a neighborhood street mural, campaigning for energy efficiency, or fighting institutionalized racism, getting involved with your community and making yourself vulnerable to what other people think takes courage.

~

Courage brings us back around to the first foundation, people, because it is the people of the community who will build resilience, and they are the ones who need courage for all the pieces of resilience building:

> Courage to work with other **people** and share in taking responsibility for the community.
> Courage to tackle the complex, **systemic** issues we face.
> Courage to learn from experience and **adapt** our thinking and methods.
> Courage to accept uncertainty and make big **transformations** when necessary.

Courage to commit to far-reaching and long-term resilience building that is truly **sustainable,** for generations to come.

Conclusion

When the Occupy movement shut down Wall Street in 2011 and then Superstorm Sandy shut down Wall Street a year later, it became clear that the twenty-first century poses complex challenges unlike those of the previous century, challenges that reach from the smallest town to the heart of global capitalism. It is no surprise that communities have turned to resilience as the best response; resilience is well suited for grappling with the complexity, uncertainty, and multiple scales of these new challenges.

History is full of communities—even highly complex ones—that persisted for thousands of years: they found ways to be resilient despite natural disaster and internal discord, embedding their wisdom and practices in place-based cultures. Of course, history is also full of communities and civilizations that succumbed to external or internal crises, often far larger than they had any possibility of anticipating. Although we should heed the warnings of that history, we can also consider ourselves fortunate in the modern era to have a broader view of what crises we might face, as well as access to countless examples of community resilience both ancient and contemporary. The frame of the six foundations is meant to help us better understand what made those examples successful and help existing and future resilience-building efforts across the United States be more effective.

This chapter is adapted from a report of the same name published by Post Carbon Institute, available online at sixfoundations.org.

Notes

1. Doria Robinson and Ken White, "Living within a Limit Is OK: Talking Resilience with Doria Robinson," interview with Post Carbon Institute, June 24, 2015, http://www.resilience.org/stories/2015-06-24/talking-resilience-with-doria-robinson.

2. Stuart Comstock-Gay, foreword to *Vermont Dollars, Vermont Sense: A Handbook for Investors, Businesses, Finance Professionals, and Everybody Else*, by Michael Shuman and Gwendolyn Hallsmith (Santa Rosa, CA: Post Carbon Institute, 2015), v.

3. Johan Rockström et al., "A Safe Operating Space for Humanity," *Nature* 461 (September 2009): 24; see also "Specials: Planetary Boundaries," *Nature*, accessed April 7, 2017, http://www.nature.com/news/specials/planetaryboundaries/index.html, and Mathis Wackernagel and William Rees, *Our Ecological Footprint: Reducing Human Impact on the Earth* (Gabriola Island, BC: New Society, 1996).

4. Richard Heinberg, *Searching for a Miracle: "Net Energy" Limits and the Fate of Industrial Society* (San Francisco: International Forum on Globalization, 2009).

5. David Fridley, "Nine Challenges of Alternative Energy," in *The Post Carbon Reader: Managing the 21st Century's Sustainability Crises*, ed. Richard Heinberg and Daniel Lerch (Healdsburg, CA: Watershed Media, 2010), 229–46.

6. Richard Heinberg, "Our Renewable Future, Or, What I've Learned in 12 Years Writing about Energy," Post Carbon Institute, January 21, 2015, http://www.postcarbon.org/our-renewable-future-essay/.

7. Richard Heinberg, *The End of Growth: Adapting to Our New Economic Reality* (Gabriola Island, BC: New Society, 2011).

8. Noah Gordon, "Why Can't People Feel the Economic Recovery?," *Atlantic*, October 14, 2014.

9. See also Richard Heinberg and Daniel Lerch, eds., *The Post Carbon Reader: Managing the 21st Century's Sustainability Crises* (Healdsburg, CA: Watershed Media, 2010); and William Rees, "Cities as Dissipative Structures: Global Change and the Vulnerability of Urban Civilization," in *Sustainability Science: The Emerging Paradigm and the Urban Environment*, ed. Michael P. Weinstein and R. Eugene Turner (New York: Springer, 2012).

10. Brian Walker and David Salt, *Resilience Thinking: Sustaining Ecosystems and People in a Changing World* (Washington, DC: Island Press, 2006), 1. The social-ecological system approach to resilience is prominently explored by the international research community represented at Resilience Alliance (http://resalliance.org) and institutions like the Stockholm Resilience Centre (http://stockholmresilience.org).

11. See chapter 3 of Brian Walker and David Salt, *Resilience Practice: Building Capacity to Absorb Disturbance and Maintain Function* (Washington, DC: Island Press, 2012). Other authors interpret characteristics or principles of resilience differently and for different purposes; see, for example, Reinette Biggs, Maja Schlüter, and Michael L. Schoon, eds., *Principles for Building Resilience: Sustaining Ecosystem Services in Social-Ecological Systems* (Cambridge: Cambridge University Press, 2015).

12. Per Walker and Salt: "In a resilience framework, the concepts of *complex* and *complex systems* carry particular meanings. The three requirements for a complex adaptive system are: it has components that are independent and interacting;

there is some selection process at work on those components and on the results of their interactions; variation and novelty are constantly being added to the system (through components changing over time or new ones coming in)." Walker and Salt, *Resilience Practice*, 5.

13. See, for example, My Sellberg, Cathy Wilkinson, and Garry Peterson, "Resilience Assessment: A Useful Approach to Navigate Urban Sustainability Challenges," *Ecology and Society* 20, no. 1 (2015): 43, http://dx.doi.org/10.5751/ES-07258-200143; Noah Enelow, "The Resilience of Detroit: An Application of the Adaptive Cycle Metaphor to an American Metropolis," *Economics for Equity and Environment*, August 1, 2013, http://www.academia.edu/7973544/The_Resilience_of_Detroit; Rolf Pendall, Kathryn Foster, and Margaret Cowell, "Resilience and Regions: Building Understanding of the Metaphor," *Cambridge Journal of Regions, Economy and Society* 3, no. 1 (2010): 71–84, http://www.academia.edu/10183451/Resilience_and_re gions_building_understanding_of_the_metaphor; and Nathan James Bennett et al., "Communities and Change in the Anthropocene: Understanding Social-Ecological Vulnerability and Planning Adaptations to Multiple Interacting Exposures," *Regional Environmental Change* 16, no. 4 (2016): 907–26, http://link .springer.com/article/10.1007/s10113-015-0839-5.

14. As philosopher John Foster noted, "Mainstreamed as sustainability or sustainable development, environmentalism has failed to reduce, even remotely adequately, the impact of humans on the biosphere." John Foster, *After Sustainability: Denial, Hope, Retrieval* (New York: Routledge, 2015), 2. For an excellent exploration of sustainability thinking, see Jeremy Caradonna, *Sustainability: A History* (Oxford: Oxford University Press, 2014).

15. In his review of a draft of this report, William Rees commented: "Resilience planning, emerging from chaos and catastrophe theory, recognizes that the changes coming may be unprecedented and inherently unpredictable…. The global systems in which humans are interfering are vastly too complicated for the human mind to understand all possible outcomes, so we must be able to (in [resilience scientist] Buzz Holling's famous words) 'manage for surprise.'"

16. Charles Redman, "Should Sustainability and Resilience Be Combined or Remain Distinct Pursuits?," *Ecology and Society* 19, no. 2 (2014): 37.

17. US Supreme Court Justice Louis Brandeis noted how a state may "serve as a laboratory; and try novel social and economic experiments without risk to the rest of the country." *New State Ice Co. v. Liebmann*, 285 U.S. 262 (1932).

18. As theoretical physicist Geoffrey West noted: "One of the great things about being in a city is that there are a lot of crazy people around. I suppose that's another way of saying cities have lots of cognitive diversity…. They provide a landscape that allows the spectrum of ideas to blossom. As the city grows, this makes it more and more multidimensional. Cities seem to open up: the spectrum of functionalities,

job opportunities, connections, etc. That is key to the vitality and the buzz of successful cities." Quoted in Andrew Zolli and Marie Healey, *Resilience: Why Things Bounce Back* (New York: Free Press, 2012), 99.

19. Among many others, see Paul Willis, "Engaging Communities: Ostrom's Economic Commons, Social Capital and Public Relations," *Public Relations Review* 38, no. 1 (March 2012): 116–22.

20. Phil Myrick, "The Power of Place: A New Dimension for Sustainable Development," Project for Public Spaces blog, April 21, 2011, http://www.pps.org/blog/the -power-of-place-a-new-dimension-for-sustainable-development/.

21. As Bruce Goldstein et al. noted: "It is crucial to recognise that urban scales are socially constructed, culturally maintained and politically contested.... Cities are relational accomplishments, which matters profoundly to the theorisation of resilience for urban city regions." Bruce Goldstein et al., "Narrating Resilience: Transforming Urban Systems through Collaborative Storytelling," *Urban Studies* 52, no. 7 (May 2015): 1288.

22. Andrew Zolli noted that "resilience is predicated on trust in a system, allowing potential adversaries to move seamlessly into cooperative mode." Andrew Zolli and Marie Healey, *Resilience: Why Things Bounce Back* (New York: Free Press, 2012), 145.

23. "What is considered as effective and legitimate adaptation depends on what people perceive to be worth preserving and achieving. How to adapt to climate change therefore hinges on the values underlying people's perspectives on what the goals of adaptation should be." In Karen O'Brien and Johanna Wolf, "A Values-Based Approach to Vulnerability and Adaptation to Climate Change," *Wiley Interdisciplinary Reviews: Climate Change* 1, no. 2 (2010): 232.

24. See, for example, Thriving Earth Exchange (http://thrivingearthexchange.org), a project of the American Geophysical Union that makes scientists available to advise communities on climate and natural resource issues.

25. Identity is a complex concept with a long history in the social sciences, including cybernetics; see, for example, Luc Hoebeke, "Identity: The Paradoxical Nature of Organizational Closure," *Kybernetes* 35, no. 1/2 (2006): 65–75.

26. Bruce Goldstein, email message to the author, August 19, 2015.

27. See, for example, the *Vision PDX* undertaking by the City of Portland, Oregon, from 2005 to 2007 (http://www.visionpdx.com). The local government led this multiyear project to develop a community vision for the next twenty years through interviews, surveys, and outreach. See also Goldstein et al., "Narrating Resilience."

28. Of the many conceptualizations of social capital, a commonly used one is from Robert Putnam, author of the classic *Bowling Alone*: "Social capital refers to features of social organization such as networks, norms and trust that facilitate co-ordination and co-operation for mutual benefit." Robert Putnam, *Making Democracy Work:*

Civic Traditions in Modern Italy (Princeton, NJ: Princeton University Press, 1993), 35.

29. As Michael Lewis and Pat Conaty noted: "Centralized, distant, and locally unaccountable power cannot accomplish the transition to low-carbon, ecologically sustainable communities.... Resilience requires a quality of social capital—trust, collaboration, cooperation, and leadership—rooted in the places where people live." Michael Lewis and Pat Conaty, *The Resilience Imperative: Cooperative Transitions to a Steady-State Economy* (Gabriola Island, BC: New Society, 2012), 25. See also Jeffrey Potent, "Employing a Knowledge Systems Approach to Creating a Sustainable Future," State of the Planet blog, Earth Institute, Columbia University, February 21, 2014; http://blogs.ei.columbia.edu/2014/02/21/employing-a-knowledge-systems-approach-to-creating-a-sustainable-future.

30. As Gillian Bristow and Adrian Healy noted, "The networked nature of governance and policy is critical in resilience" (governance being understood as emerging from the interactions of many public and private actors, of which government is but one). Gillian Bristow and Adrian Healy, "Building Resilient Regions: Complex Adaptive Systems and the Role of Policy Intervention," *Raumforschung und Raumordnung* 2 (2014): 97.

31. Trevor Tompson et al., *Resilience in the Wake of Superstorm Sandy* (Associated Press–NORC Center for Public Affairs Research, 2013), http://www.apnorc.org/projects/Pages/resilience-in-the-wake-of-superstorm-sandy.aspx.

32. As Wes Jackson noted: "I think there's a general law: High energy destroys information, of a cultural as well as a biological variety. There's a loss of cultural capacity. And from 1750, the beginning of the Industrial Revolution, the graphical curve for the use of high-energy fossil carbon is increasingly steep." Wes Jackson, "Tackling the Oldest Environmental Problem: Agriculture and Its Impact on Soil," in *The Post Carbon Reader: Managing the 21st Century's Sustainability Crises*, ed. Richard Heinberg and Daniel Lerch (Healdsburg, CA: Watershed Media, 2010), 133.

33. Michelle Colussi, email message to author, August 19, 2015.

34. Many primers on systems thinking exist; a fairly accessible one is Donella Meadows, *Thinking in Systems: A Primer* (White River Junction, VT: Chelsea Green, 2008).

35. Walker and Salt, *Resilience Practice*, 5.

36. "There are known knowns," *Wikipedia*, last modified March 7, 2017, https://en.wikipedia.org/wiki/There_are_known_knowns.

37. Rees, "Cities as Dissipative Structures"; Jennie Moore and William E. Rees, "Getting to One-Planet Living," in *State of the World 2013: Is Sustainability Still Possible?*, ed. Worldwatch Institute (Washington DC: Island Press, 2013), 39–50.

38. Fridley, "Nine Challenges."

39. See C. S. Holling, Lance H. Gunderson, and Garry Peterson, "Sustainability and Panarchies," in *Panarchy: Understanding Transformations in Human and Natural*

Systems, ed. Lance H. Gunderson and C. S. Holling (Washington, DC: Island Press, 2002), 63–102.

40. Eric Hoffer, *Reflections on the Human Condition* (New York: Harper and Row, 1973).

41. Walker and Salt, *Resilience Practice*, 92–98.

42. Biggs, Schlüter, and Schoon, *Principles for Building Resilience*. Stockholm Resilience Institute has a useful summary at http://www.stockholmresilience.org/21/re search/research-news/2-19-2015-applying-resilience-thinking.html.

43. Rockefeller Foundation and Arup, *City Resilience Framework* (London: Arup, December 2015), 5, https://www.rockefellerfoundation.org/report/city-resilience -framework.

44. Andrew Zolli, "The Verbs of Resilience," personal blog, October 28, 2013, http:// andrewzolli.com/the-verbs-of-resilience.

45. Chicago's infamous Cabrini-Green Homes are a textbook example of the social and economic problems that have at times been exacerbated by "efficient" public housing; see https://en.wikipedia.org/wiki/Cabrini-Green_Homes.

46. See, for example, James Hamilton, "Oil Prices and the Economic Recession of 2007–08," Centre for Economic Policy Research blog, June 16, 2009, http://www .voxeu.org/article/did-rising-oil-prices-trigger-current-recession. For a much broader perspective, including the example of the "2008 financial-energy crisis," see Thomas Homer-Dixon et al., "Synchronous Failure: The Emerging Causal Architecture of Global Crisis," *Ecology and Society* 20, no. 3 (2015): 6.

47. Of course, this statement does not imply that this system has been fair or beneficial or that it will be resilient over the long term.

48. Brian Walker, "The Best Explanation to Resilience," Stockholm Resilience Centre TV, uploaded April 3, 2009, 5:33, https://www.youtube.com/watch?v=tXLMeL5n VQk.

49. Giuseppe di Lampedusa, *The Leopard*, trans. Archibald Colquhuon (1958; repr., London: Vintage, 2007), 19.

50. Walker and Salt, *Resilience Practice*, chap. 3.

51. Laurie Guevara-Stone, "A High-Renewables Tomorrow, Today: Güssing, Austria," Rocky Mountain Institute blog, October 8, 2013, http://blog.rmi.org /blog_2013_10_08_high-renewables_tomorrow_today_gussing_austria.

52. These attributes of transformability are drawn from Walker and Salt, *Resilience Practice*, 100–103.

53. Walker and Salt, *Resilience Practice*, 101.

54. See Paul Schmitz, "How Change Happens: The Real Story of Mrs. Rosa Parks and the Montgomery Bus Boycott," *Huffington Post*, December 1, 2014.

55. Jeremy Caradonna, *Sustainability: A History* (Oxford: Oxford University Press, 2014), 5.

56. Richard Heinberg, "Beyond the Limits to Growth," in *The Post Carbon Reader: Managing the 21st Century's Sustainability Crises*, ed. Richard Heinberg and Daniel Lerch (Healdsburg, CA: Watershed Media, 2010), 3–4.

57. Global Footprint Network, http://www.footprintnetwork.org.

58. This question is an example of "strong sustainability" versus "weak sustainability" as understood in the field of ecological economics.

59. Rockström, "A Safe Operating Space"; see also "Specials: Planetary Boundaries."

60. Richard Heinberg, "What Is Sustainability?," in *The Post Carbon Reader: Managing the 21st Century's Sustainability Crises*, ed. Richard Heinberg and Daniel Lerch (Healdsburg, CA: Watershed Media, 2010), 13–24.

61. Heinberg, "What Is Sustainability?"

62. For example, John Foster lambastes "the distracting late-twentieth-century mindset of 'sustainable development,' with its obsessive focus on inherently negotiable futures." Foster, *After Sustainability*, 12.

63. This sentiment was epitomized in the iconic little book by the Earthworks Group, *50 Simple Things You Can Do to Save the Earth* (Berkeley, CA: Earthworks Press, 1989).

64. Michelle Colussi, email message to the author, August 19, 2015.

65. Email message to the author, October 28, 2015.

66. Jenny Leis and Daniel Lerch, eds., *City Repair's Placemaking Guidebook* (Portland, OR: City Repair and Southeast Uplift, 2003), 61.

PART I

Understanding Our Predicament

CHAPTER 2

The Environmental Crisis: The Needs of Humanity versus the Limits of the Planet

Leena Iyengar

In the end, we will conserve only what we love, we will love only what we understand, and we will understand only what we are taught.
—Baba Dioum (1968, New Delhi)[1]

CLIMBING UP THE MIGHTY HIMALAYAS to see the source of the Ganges. Walking the Tibetan plateau, snorkeling the Great Barrier Reef, and hiking the Ngorongoro crater. Experiencing the Gran Sabana and lush Amazonia. Gliding through the Everglades and the Okavango delta. Chasing the aurora borealis and the aurora australis. These and other experiences are penned down in my list of places to go and things to do. They are places that remind me of the beautiful planet we inhabit, places that remind me of forces and processes that have existed for billions of years. They offer a spectacular and awe-inspiring window into a world, a symphony, that humanity is but a small part of, even though we are part of it nonetheless, perhaps even an integral part. We humans definitely did not construct or design this world, and this show of nature and natural events will continue well beyond our lifetimes. But for how much longer?

I grew up near the Western Ghats, a mountain range along the western coast of India that is now recognized as a globally significant "hot spot" of biodiversity. My fond treasure trove of memories from my younger days includes encountering molted snakes' skins and listening for the sound of peacock calls in the far distance; glimpsing the silhouette of a dhole poised perfectly by the full moon high on a rocky clearing; hearing the amateur notes of the Malabar parakeet and the Nilgiri pipit; excitement upon finding possible tracks of a civet; and wondering whether the punctured jackfruit on the tree meant that a wanderoo has been at it.

Such narrative memories define the shape of things to come in life. The very act of living our lives involves developing our own stories and contexts. *Narrative Psychology: The Storied Nature of Human Conduct*, edited by Theodore Sarbin, claims that we make sense of what is going on around us through narratives.[2] To comprehend the abstract and often intangible concepts in our day-to-day work and life, we find inspiration, creativity, passion, drive, and momentum in our narrative of nature.

What We See and What We Know

Connection with nature and natural history—with or without a formal introduction to the subjects—is crucial. We need it to understand the status of our living planet, our inherent interconnectedness, the impacts of disturbing the delicate balance of Earth's biogeophysical systems, and the implications of those impacts for the survival of the human species.

Nature does not simply provide for human needs; it also informs us, and it is important that we pay attention. In his book *Last Child in the Woods*, author Richard Louv narrates a poignant anecdote shared by marine ecologist Paul Dayton:

> What we can't name can hurt us. 'A guy in Catalina sent me photos of a snail he found,' Dayton says. 'The snail is moving north. It's not supposed to be where the guy found it. Something is going on with the snail or its environment.' Global warming? Maybe. 'But if you don't know it's an invasive species, then you detect no change.'[3]

Wildlife in the Western Ghats that has been around for generations and geological millennia is on the decline. The area's richly diverse microcosm is gradually disappearing. Something there is changing, too:

• The majestic dhole (*Cuon alpinus*), the Indian wild dog that captured my imagination, has been listed as endangered on the International Union for Conservation of Nature (IUCN) Red List since 2004.[4]

• The Malabar civet (*Vivera civettina*) is critically endangered since 1996; the most recently assessed data suggest it could be extinct.[5]

• Wanderoo, the lion-tailed macaque (*Macaca silenus*), an Old World monkey endemic to the Western Ghats, is endangered, and its population is in decline.[6]

• The perky Nilgiri pipit (*Anthus nilghiriensis*) is listed as vulnerable with the impending possibility of it becoming an endangered species.[7]

• The Brahminy kite and the Malabar parakeet are listed as "species of least concern," but kite populations have been steadily declining.[8] The most geographically mobile populations are beginning to dwindle and may soon disappear.

The one common and major threat to these species is fragmentation and loss of habitats. Their habitats are being encroached upon to build infrastructure for human habitation, with swaths of forest being cleared for agriculture and plantations. On a global scale, with many such narratives put together, the outlook is stark, and the pressures are piling on.

• The Pamir plateau—the roof of the world that bears the richness of Persian and Tajik cultures, saw Alexander the Great, and inspired Marco Polo—is a recognized United Nations Educational, Scientific and Cultural Organization (UNESCO) World Heritage site and an ecologically unique alpine and tundra region. It is facing multiple environmental pressures,[9] exacerbated by global warming.

• The Ngorongoro Crater in Tanzania is the largest unbroken caldera in the world. Rich and uniquely biodiverse as well as culturally and archaeologically important, this UNESCO World Heritage site is threatened by poorly managed mass tourism and by infrastructure, overpopulation, and overgrazing.[10]

- The spectacular landscape of Venezuela's Gran Sabana is under threat from fossil fuel extraction, mining, logging, infrastructure development, agricultural runoff, and expanding populations encroaching on this unique and fragile ecosystem.[11]

- The meandering, transboundary Okavango River and its biodiverse delta in Botswana face pressures from oil production, violence, and political instability in Angola as well as from river water extraction for energy and agriculture in Namibia.

- Farms, invasive species, dike construction, and urban and industrial expansion have put immense pressure on the fragile ecosystem of Florida's Everglades wetlands.[12] The loss of natural processes in the Everglades, compounded with rising sea levels, is shrinking the expanse and vitality of this "river of grass."

The IUCN Red List of threatened species, published and regularly updated since 1964, is the most comprehensive documentation of the status of nearly 80,000 species and subspecies of flora and fauna of all regions of the world. Currently, IUCN reports that more than 23,000 of these monitored species are threatened with extinction, including 41 percent of amphibians, 34 percent of conifers, 33 percent of reef-building corals, 25 percent of mammals, and 13 percent of birds.[13]

The biennial flagship report of the World Wide Fund for Nature (WWF), the *Living Planet Report*, adds to our understanding of this trend. Since 2002, the *Living Planet Report* has highlighted the status of the planet's biodiversity and its progressive decline as human and environmental pressures encroach on wildlife habitat. It looks closely at the threats pressuring the populations under study: habitat loss and degradation, the overexploitation of species, pollution, invasive species, and disease as well as climate change.[14] The *Living Planet Report 2016* records a 58 percent overall decline in vertebrate population abundance from 1970 to 2012.[15]

The *Living Planet Report* is but one of many scientific publications documenting these worrying trends. The Fifth Assessment Report (2014) of the Intergovernmental Panel on Climate Change (IPCC)—the lead body facilitating the global scientific consensus on climate change—describes the risks associated with a warming world. It notes that many terrestrial, freshwater, and marine species have already shifted their geographic ranges, seasonal activities, migration patterns, and species interactions—and decreased in number—in response to ongoing climate change.[16] The decline in global biodiversity represents a terrible, ongoing loss of our planet's richness that will only worsen in the coming decades. It is also a worrying bellwether of instability in Earth's processes that sustain human civilization and human life.

Earth's System in Crisis

In the 2016 documentary film *Before the Flood*, Anote Tong, the former president of Kiribati, declared, "Crisis is not when whole islands are underwater, it is what happens before."[17] This profound statement is a call to all humanity to heed the signs of debilitating change awaiting Tong's people and acknowledge that the world is in a state of crisis. Reviewing the history of the natural world, and the science that is rapidly collecting evidence, puts the crisis in perspective.

As early as 1974, scientists James Lovelock and Lynn Margulis observed that life on Earth, acting as a single entity, actively interacts with the physical attributes of the planet and is integral in regulating the chemical composition of the atmosphere, oceans, soils, and possibly climate.[18] They called this concept of the close and complex influential relationship of Earth's flora and fauna with its geophysical components—the planet as a whole functioning as a single system, supporting and maintaining life—the Gaia hypothesis.

In the 1980s, the scientific community became increasingly concerned about the possibility that nuclear weapons, ozone-destroying chemicals, and increased emissions of greenhouse gases could radically remake the world.[19] Although there was growing consensus on the stress that humanity was imposing on Earth's biogeochemical and geophysical systems, there was also a perceived need for scientific research to understand and establish causative factors, capture global interest in the matter, and inform environmental management and government decision making. The scientific community ultimately came together and established the International Geosphere-Biosphere Programme (IGBP), institutionalizing the concept of Earth as a system. (The IGBP ran from 1986 until 2015, when it was succeeded by a new international research initiative called Future Earth.) As described by the IGBP:

> The term "Earth system" refers to Earth's interacting physical, chemical, and biological processes. The system consists of the land, oceans, atmosphere, and poles. It includes the planet's natural cycles—the carbon, water, nitrogen, phosphorus, sulphur, and other cycles— and deep Earth processes. Life, too, is an integral part of the Earth system, as it affects the carbon, nitrogen, water, oxygen, and many other cycles and processes.[20]

The IGBP was mandated to "describe and understand the interactive physical, chemical, and biological processes that regulate the total Earth system, the unique environment it provides for life, the changes that are occurring in that system, and the manner in which these changes are influenced by human actions." The program was carried out in structured phases that worked to establish Earth systems science as an interdisciplinary science, garner international scientific cooperation, and filter findings into the policy arena.[21]

In essence, the establishment of the IGBP was recognition that no environmental system or event was isolated. Its interdisciplinary, international, and collaborative work firmly indicated that:

1. There has been a marked acceleration of conditions that are causing environmental adversities around the world.
2. Human activities are unequivocally at the helm of this acceleration.
3. The world is, in fact, facing a global environmental crisis.

The work of the scientific community continues to define the parameters of the global environmental crisis. The indices, models, and indicators born of this work inform policy decisions both globally and locally. Evidence-based scientific studies and tools are crucial to our comprehension of where we came from, how we are faring, and where we are headed, not just as a part of the Earth system, but also as a civilization that has introduced the influence of social and economic systems into the complexity of the Earth system.

From the Holocene to the Anthropocene

Indicators of declining biodiversity, threatened species, and dwindling habitats do not directly represent a global environmental crisis in their own right. They are, however, a red flag: they indicate severe disturbance in a system that has maintained a state of relative stability for more than 11,000 years. Geologists call this period the Holocene (figure 2-1).

The Holocene presented humans with remarkably warmer and more stable climatic conditions compared with what the preceding geologic period offered. It brought "a reliable source of goods and services delivered from a

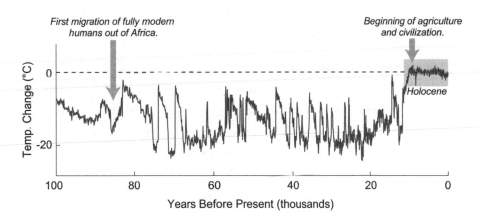

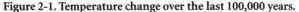

Figure 2-1. Temperature change over the last 100,000 years.
The gray rectangular patch represents the Holocene, the geological time in Earth's history that presented temperatures conducive for human civilizations to thrive. Temperature data based on Greenland ice core research.
Data source: Andrey Ganopolski and Stefan Rahmstorf, "Rapid Changes of Glacial Climate Simulated in a Coupled Climate Model," *Nature* 409 (January 11, 2001): 153–58.

stable equilibrium of forests, savannahs, coral reefs, grasslands, fish, mammals, bacteria, air quality, ice cover, temperatures, freshwater availability, and productive soils."[22] It represented a state of equilibrium between the living world and the geophysical world, creating resource abundance that is vital to the survival of humankind as we know it today.[23] They are conditions that we have become accustomed to and that most of us take for granted. As environmental scientist Johan Rockström (2015) put it, "It's the only state of the planet we know that can support modern societies, and a world population of more than 7 billion people."[24]

Early in the twenty-first century, scientists began warning that this optimal state of the planet seemed to be changing. In 2005, in *Global Change and the Earth System: A Planet Under Pressure*, a team led by climate scientist Will Steffen (executive director of IGBP at the time) noted that

> human activities are so pervasive and profound in their conse-
> quences that they affect the earth in a global scale in complex,
> interactive and apparently accelerating ways; humans now have
> the capacity to alter the Earth system in ways that threaten the very
> processes and components, both biotic and abiotic, upon which the
> human species depends.[25]

Steffen and his team produced a series of graphs (updated in 2015; see figures 2-2 and 2-3) to clearly illustrate these activities and their impacts. The graphs demonstrate "clear evidence for fundamental shifts in the state and functioning of the Earth System that are beyond the range of variability of the Holocene and driven by human activities."[26] This shift is so stark that it has prompted many scientists to declare that we are no longer in the Holocene but rather are in a new geological epoch, commonly called the Anthropocene.

It is easy to notice that every graph in figures 2-2 and 2-3 shows an upward trend. At first glance, the socioeconomic trends in figure 2-2 seem to indicate all-around success in our ability to meet the needs of the growing human population. When viewed in relation to the Earth system trends in

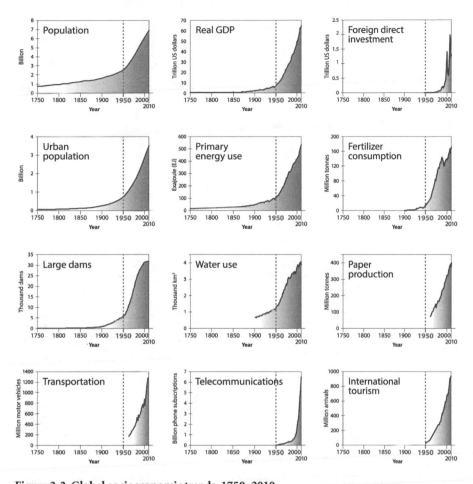

Figure 2-2. Global socioeconomic trends, 1750–2010.
Source: Will Steffen et al., "The Trajectory of the Anthropocene: The Great Acceleration,"
Anthropocene Review 2 (2015), 84.

figure 2-3, however, it would not be unreasonable to question the cost of this perceived success.

Pushing Beyond Earth's Limits

Exponential world population growth is the main driver of the trends shown in figures 2-2 and 2-3. With a current growth rate of 1.18 percent per year, the human population reached 7.3 billion in 2015.[27] The scale at which we have

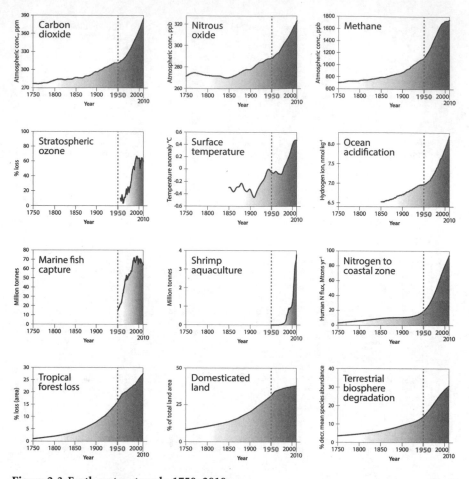

Figure 2-3. Earth system trends, 1750–2010.
Source: Will Steffen et al., "The Trajectory of the Anthropocene: The Great Acceleration," *Anthropocene Review* 2 (2015), 87.

exploited Earth's natural resources—forests, air, land, and water—for the growth and expansion of human enterprise is represented by the ecological footprint metric calculated annually by the Global Footprint Network (figure 2-4).

The ecological footprint concept was developed to demonstrate the principle of *limits to growth* on a finite planet.[28] It is a detailed representative extension of the IPAT equation, which describes the impact (I) on our environment as a function of the total human population (P), per capita affluence (A), and level of technology (T).[29] Global Footprint Network calculates that humanity now

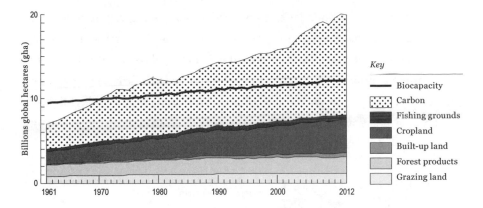

Figure 2-4. Humanity's global ecological footprint compared to world biocapacity, 1961–2012.
Carbon is the dominant component of humanity's ecological footprint (ranging from 43% in 1961 to 60% in 2012), primarily due to the burning of fossil fuels. The line representing world biocapacity shows a slight upward trend as the metric accounts for technological improvements, such as increased productivity in agriculture.
Source: WWF, *Living Planet Report 2016: Risk and Resilience in a New Era* (Gland, Switzerland: WWF International, 2016), 75, http://wwf.panda.org/about_our_earth/all_publications/lpr_2016/.

uses 1.6 Earths' worth of resources annually. This figure is possible because, for example, we emit more carbon dioxide into the atmosphere than our oceans and forests can absorb, and we deplete fisheries and harvest forests more quickly than they can reproduce and regrow.[30]

The ability of the Earth system to provide for the excesses of humanity's resource consumption is diminishing. Even the technological improvements that have extended Earth's natural capacity are targeted to specific outcomes and usually overlook the associated damage. A well-known example is the Green Revolution of the mid-twentieth century in which the introduction to global agriculture of synthetic fertilizers, pesticides, oil-powered machinery (like tractors), and other technological developments brought about a massive increase in global food production. Among other benefits, it helped avoid food crises and provided the conditions for rapid economic growth, especially in developing countries.[31] With these benefits came serious costs to our global ecosystem, however.

In 2009, a group of scientists led by Steffen and Rockström introduced the concept of Planetary Boundaries (figure 2-5), delineating a biophysical "safe operating space" that maintains the relative stability of the Earth system to support humanity. The nine planetary boundaries in part illustrate the detrimental environmental impacts of the Green Revolution—particularly the use of phosphorus and nitrogen in synthetic fertilizers. More generally, they highlight the detrimental uncertainty that awaits when we push against the environmental thresholds that define the Earth system's stability.[32]

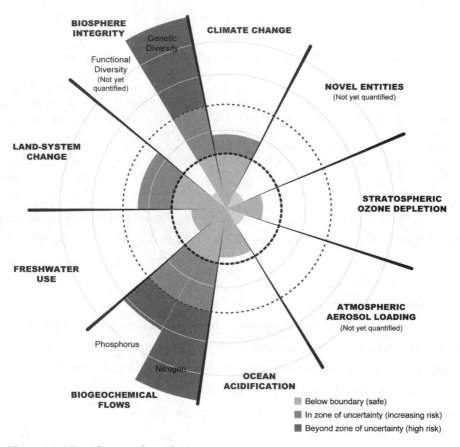

Figure 2-5. Nine planetary boundaries.
The nine planetary boundaries identify the biophysical "safe operating space"—the space inside the bold dotted line in the middle of the diagram—that maintains relative stability of the Earth system to support humanity.
Source: "Planetary Boundaries—An Update," Stockholm Resilience Centre, January 16, 2015, http://www.stockholmresilience.org/research/research-news/2015-01-15-planetary -boundaries---an-update.html. Image credit: Azote Images for Stockholm Resilience Centre.

Cascading Impacts

Cascading impacts are secondary effects in which impacts themselves become part of a chain of drivers of change with influence beyond their original environment and geography.[33] The IPCC's Fifth Assessment Report highlighted how climate change affects the physical attributes and biology of the cryosphere (those areas of Earth's surface covered in ice and snow), the oceans, and the forests, and how those impacts cascade into further effects on other environments and human socioeconomic systems.

Impacts on the cryosphere have especially clear effects because the global system of climate regulation is closely linked to sea ice, permafrost, and vegetation conditions there.[34] For example, cascading impacts from changes in the Arctic have been linked to tropical forests becoming savannahs, monsoons weakening, mangroves collapsing, algae overtaking coral habitats, and the West Antarctica ice sheet collapsing.[35] Outside the polar regions, melting in the Greater Himalayas— the source of the ten largest rivers in Asia—threatens the water supply of more than one billion people and the safety of millions. In 2013, the Gangotri Glacier, the source of the Ganges, caused a flash flood, drowning villages and killing thousands; and in 2016, the Nepalese army conducted a first-of-its-kind draining of a glacial lake due to the anticipated danger of flash floods from melting.

Impacts on the oceans may not be as immediately visible, but they, too, have significant cascading effects. Earth's oceans have been estimated to generate economic benefits worth at least US$2.5 trillion per year. More than two-thirds of the value of oceans for fishing, tourism, transportation, and ecosystem services (such as acting as a carbon sink) rely on healthy ocean conditions.[36] For example, coral reefs—species-rich as well as fascinatingly beautiful—contribute to the economic well-being of more than 500 million people in 109 countries through subsistence fishing and tourism.[37] Reefs are sensitive to a warming climate, however: record-breaking high sea-surface temperatures in 2016, for example, caused a mass bleaching of the 25-million-year-old Great Barrier Reef, the third in just eighteen years.[38] Such events are devastating not only for the myriad species this natural wonder supports, but also for the human communities that rely on the reef for their livelihoods.

In forests, climate change impacts like erratic temperature and precipitation patterns can increase the incidence of droughts, landslides, avalanches, and flash floods.[39] Vegetation is affected—and is predominantly visible in shifting tree lines—which in turn affects wildlife habitats. For example, a study on climate-change-induced shrinking of alpine zones found that 30 percent of the Himalayan snow leopard's habitat could be lost.[40] Moreover, the loss of key species in alpine ecosystems can have cascading effects that include secondary extinctions.[41] These effects, coupled with habitat fragmentation and increasing human activities, are further feeding into the chain of cascading impacts on ecosystems.

It is evident from these indicators, and from actual instances of the world we know, that neither our environment nor our socioeconomic activities function in isolation. Pressures are *cumulative* and *interactive* in their effects, and impacts are not bound by geography. What affects one part of the system affects the other. What happens in one part of the world affects the rest. That is what it means for us to be part of the Earth system.

Making Change

Humanity has come a long way in dealing with the environmental challenges we have created. We have identified the systems and processes that need our attention; we have built up a compelling, evidence-based case for action; we have created international coalitions and institutions to organize our efforts; and we have developed technology to start repairing the damage we have done as well as to better understand the complexity of our situation. The middle years of the 2010s represented a turning point with regard to the most dominant part of our environmental crisis: climate change. The largest global demonstration for action on climate change in history, the People's Climate March, took place in 2014 and included people from all walks of life, from teachers and nurses to bankers and political leaders. In 2015, after twenty-one years of effort, the international community finally agreed to limit global warming to less than 2 degrees Celsius over preindustrial levels in an agreement known as the Paris Accord. In 2016, the level of atmospheric carbon dioxide stayed above 400 parts per million for the first time in millions of years, an unfortunate milestone in the history of the climate crisis. Also in 2016, however, enough national governments ratified the Paris Accord for it to go into effect.[42] Marking the occasion, United Nations Secretary-General Ban Ki-moon said, "What once seemed unthinkable is now unstoppable."[43] Science has delivered, the people have spoken, and the global mechanism to tackle this most difficult of challenges is on course to deliver (with or without the assent of the US federal government).

As global action steams ahead, our individual voices must continue to speak for systemic change that is inclusive and representative as well as for better understanding and respecting the Earth system. That system unceasingly tries to maintain a state of dynamic equilibrium amid the natural biogeophysical chaos, now amplified by human intervention. Although it is almost impossible to wrap our heads around the complexity of this Earth system, we can draw from our personal interests and curiosities to start to make sense of it.

For my part, I am intrigued by the marvelous link between the remnants of an ancient inland sea in North Africa and the lush Amazon rain forest in South America.[44] The Amazon forest relies on soil-fertilizing minerals in dust blown across the Atlantic Ocean from the Bodélé Depression, which rests in the narrow path between two mountain chains northeast of Lake Chad.[45] A delicate balancing of the natural cycle of summer and winter winds, guided by the relief features of the Tibesti and Ennedi mountain chains, carries tens of millions of tons of mineral dust annually over 5,000 miles to settle over the Amazon basin and the Caribbean Sea. By itself, the soil of the Amazon rain forest is nutrient-poor; heavy rains wash out important fertilizing minerals. But the Bodélé dust blown from across the ocean and half of Africa brings the rain forest to life. It is through learning about this and other astounding natural patterns—and experiencing the wonders of nature firsthand, whether as a child, as an adult, or in my dreams for the future—that I begin to understand this beautiful, fragile planet.

Notes

1. Baba Dioum, paper presented at General Assembly of the International Union for the Conservation of Nature and Natural Resources, New Delhi, 1968.

2. Theodore Sarbin, *Narrative Psychology: The Storied Nature of Human Conduct* (New York: Praeger, 1986).

3. Richard Louv, *Last Child in the Woods: Saving Our Children from Nature-Deficit Disorder* (Chapel Hill, NC: Algonquin, 2008).

4. J. F. Kamler et al., *Cuon alpinus*, The IUCN Red List of Threatened Species 2015: e.T5953A72477893, downloaded March 24, 2017, http://dx.doi.org/10.2305/IUCN .UK.2015-4.RLTS.T5953A72477893.en.

5. D. Mudappa, K. Helgen, and R. Nandini, *Viverra civettina*, The IUCN Red List of Threatened Species 2016: e.T23036A45202281, downloaded March 24, 2017, http://dx.doi.org/10.2305/IUCN.UK.2016-1.RLTS.T23036A45202281.en.

6. A. Kumar, M. Singh, and S. Molur, *Macaca silenus*, The IUCN Red List of Threatened Species 2008: e.T12559A3358033, downloaded March 24, 2017, http://dx.doi .org/10.2305/IUCN.UK.2008.RLTS.T12559A3358033.en.

7. BirdLife International, "Species Factsheet: *Anthus nilghiriensis*," accessed April 11, 2016, http://datazone.birdlife.org.

8. BirdLife International, "Species Factsheet: *Haliastur indus*," accessed April 11, 2016, http://datazone.birdlife.org; BirdLife International, "Species Factsheet: *Psittacula columboides*," accessed April 11, 2016, http://datazone.birdlife.org.

9. M. M. Trak et al., "Creeping Environmental Problems in the Pamir Mountains: Landscape Conditions, Climate Change, Wise Use and Threats," in *Climate Change Impacts on High-Altitude Ecosystems*, ed. Münir Öztürk et al. (Cham, Switzerland: Springer International, 2015), 665–95.

10. World Heritage Convention, United Nations Education, Scientific and Cultural Organization, "Ngorongoro Conservation Area," accessed October 11, 2016, http://whc.unesco.org/en/list/39/.

11. Pedro Rosabal and José Pedro de Oliveira Costa, "Report of UNESCO-IUCN Monitoring Mission to Canaima National Park, Venezuela," UNESCO 23rd session, Paris, May 16–19, 1999, http://whc.unesco.org/document/134048.

12. Florida Museum of Natural History, "About the Everglades," accessed October 11, 2016, https://www.flmnh.ufl.edu/southflorida/regions/everglades.

13. International Union for Conservation of Nature, "The IUCN Red List of Threatened Species," accessed March 11, 2016, https://www.iucn.org/theme/species/our -work/iucn-red-list-threatened-species.

14. WWF, *Living Planet Report 2014: People and Places, Species and Spaces* (Gland, Switzerland: WWF International, 2014).

15. WWF, *Living Planet Report 2016: Risk and Resilience in a New Era* (Gland, Switzerland: WWF International, 2016).

16. Intergovernmental Panel on Climate Change, *Climate Change 2014: Synthesis Report.* Contribution of Working Groups I, II and III to the Fifth Assessment Report of the Intergovernmental Panel on Climate Change [Core Writing Team, R.K.

Pachauri and L.A. Meyer (eds.)] (Geneva, Switzerland: IPCC, 2014), http://www.ipcc.ch/report/ar5/syr/.

17. *Before the Flood*, directed by Fisher Stevens, RatPac Documentary Films, Appian Way, 2016, film.

18. J. E. Lovelock and L. Margulis, "Atmospheric Homeostasis by and for the Biosphere: The Gaia Hypothesis." *Tellus* 26, no. 1/2 (1974): 2–10.

19. I. Angus, *Facing the Anthropocene: Fossil Capitalism and the Crisis of the Earth System* (New York: Monthly Review Press, 2016).

20. International Geosphere-Biosphere Programme, "Earth System Definitions," accessed February 27, 2017, http://www.igbp.net/globalchange/earthsystemdefinitions.4.d8b4c3c12bf3be638a80001040.html.

21. Sybil P. Seitzinger et al., "International Geosphere–Biosphere Programme and Earth System Science: Three Decades of Co-evolution," *Anthropocene* 12 (December 2015): 3–16, http://dx.doi.org/10.1016/j.ancene.2016.01.001.

22. Johan Rockström and Mattias Klum, *Big World, Small Planet* (Stockholm: Max Strom, 2015), 32.

23. P. Magalhães et al., eds., *The Safe Operating Space Treaty: A New Approach to Managing Our Use of the Earth System* (Cambridge: Cambridge Scholars, 2016).

24. Rockström and Klum, *Big World, Small Planet*, 32.

25. W. Steffan et al., *Global Change and the Earth System: A Planet under Pressure* (Berlin: Springer, 2004).

26. W. Steffen et al., *Global Change and the Earth System*, Global Change—The IGBP Series (Berlin: Springer, 2004); W. Steffen et al., "The Trajectory of the Anthropocene: The Great Acceleration," *Anthropocene Review* 2, no. 1 (2015), 81.

27. United Nations, Department of Economic and Social Affairs—Population Division, *World Population Prospects: The 2015 Revision, Key Findings and Advance Tables*, Working Paper No. ESA/P/WP.241, 2015.

28. D. H. Meadows and Club of Rome, *The Limits to Growth: A Report for the Club of Rome's Project on the Predicament of Mankind* (New York: Universe Books, 1972); D. H. Meadows, J. Randers, and D. L. Meadows, *The Limits to Growth: The 30-Year Update* (White River Junction, VT: Chelsea Green, 2004).

29. P. R. Ehrlich and J. P. Holdren, 1972. "Critique: One Dimensional Ecology," *Bulletin of the Atomic Scientists* 28, no. 5 (1972): 16, 18–27; B. Commoner, *The Environmental Cost of Economic Growth in Population, Resources and the Environment* (Washington, DC: Government Printing Office, 1972), 339–63; J. D. Sachs, *Commonwealth: Economics for a Crowded Planet* (New York: Penguin, 2008); Rockström and Klum, *Big World Small Planet*.

30. Earth Overshoot Day, accessed January 23, 2017, http://www.overshootday.org.

31. UN Food and Agriculture Organisation, "Towards a New Green Revolution," accessed January 20, 2017, http://www.fao.org/docrep/x0262e/x0262e06.htm.

32. "Planetary Boundaries—An Update," Stockholm Resilience Centre, January 16, 2015, http://www.stockholmresilience.org/research/research-news/2015-01-15 -planetary-boundaries---an-update.html.

33. Arctic Council, *Arctic Resilience Report*, ed. M. Carson and G. Peterson (Stockholm: Stockholm Environment Institute and Stockholm Resilience Centre, 2016), http:// www.arctic-council.org/arr.

34. Arctic Council, *Arctic Resilience Report*.

35. Intergovernmental Panel on Climate Change, *Climate Change 2014*.

36. J. Tanzer et al., eds., *Living Blue Planet Report: Species, Habitats and Human Well-Being* (Gland, Switzerland: WWF International, 2015).

37. C. Wilkinson, *Status of Coral Reefs of the World: 2008* (Townsville, Australia: Global Coral Reef Monitoring Network and Reef and Rainforest Research Centre, 2008).

38. Great Barrier Reef Marine Park Authority, "Record-Breaking Sea Surface Temperatures," accessed October 11, 2016, http://www.gbrmpa.gov.au/media-room/coral -bleaching/record-breaking-sea-surface-temperatures.

39. J. Xu et al., "The Melting Himalayas: Cascading Effects of Climate Change on Water, Biodiversity, and Livelihoods," *Conservation Biology* 23, no. 3 (2009): 520–30.

40. J. Forrest et al., "Conservation and Climate Change: Assessing the Vulnerability of Snow Leopard Habitat to Treeline Shift in the Himalaya," *Biological Conservation* 150, no. 1 (2012): 129–35.

41. W. Wang et al., "Rapid Expansion of Glacial Lakes Caused by Climate and Glacier Retreat in the Central Himalayas," *Hydrological Processes* 29, no. 6 (2015): 859–74; K. Manish et al., "Modelling the Impacts of Future Climate Change on Plant Communities in the Himalaya: A Case Study from Eastern Himalaya, India," *Modeling Earth Systems and Environment* 2, no. 2 (2016): 1–12; A. Hoy et al., "Climatic Changes and Their Impact on Socio-economic Sectors in the Bhutan Himalayas: An Implementation Strategy," *Regional Environmental Change* 16, no. 5 (2016): 1401–15.

42. United Nations Framework Convention on Climate Change, "Paris Agreement— Status of Ratification," accessed January 31, 2017, http://unfccc.int/paris_agreement/items/9444.php.

43. United Nations Secretary-General, "Statement by the Secretary-General on the Paris Agreement on Climate Change," October 5, 2016, https://www.un.org/sg /en/content/sg/statement/2016-10-05/statement-secretary-general-paris-agreement -climate-change.

44. S. J. Armitage, C. S. Bristow, and N. A. Drake, "West African Monsoon Dynamics Inferred from Abrupt Fluctuations of Lake Mega-Chad," *Proceedings of the National Academy of Sciences* 112, no. 28 (2015): 8543–48.

45. Ellen Gray, "NASA Satellite Reveals How Much Saharan Dust Feeds Amazon's Plants," February 22, 2015, https://www.nasa.gov/content/goddard/nasa-satellite -reveals-how-much-saharan-dust-feeds-amazon-s-plants.

CHAPTER 3

The Energy Crisis:
From Fossil Fuel Abundance to
Renewable Energy Constraints

Richard Heinberg

T HE TERM *ENERGY CRISIS* was on nearly everyone's lips in the 1970s;
today it is not. However, the challenges now facing the world's energy systems are arguably far greater than those of the 1970s, and most available evidence suggests that they are about to get more daunting still.

An energy crisis can threaten nearly all we care about because energy
enables us to accomplish everything we are doing: growing food, transporting
people and goods, warming or cooling our homes and offices, manufacturing
products, constructing roads and buildings, disposing of wastes, and so on.
During the twentieth century, rapidly expanding energy supplies fueled economic expansion at a pace unprecedented in human history. An energy crisis
could reverse that pattern of growth and undermine the entire economy.

Today's scale of global energy use is staggering. Per capita usage has
increased more than 800 percent since the start of the Industrial Revolution;
in total terms (reflecting population growth), humans now use about twenty-
eight times as much energy as in 1800. That energy is used very unequally,
however: per capita usage in the United States is more than a hundred times

that in poor nations such as Ethiopia. Producing all this energy requires the extraction, processing, and delivery of 95 million barrels of oil each day worldwide, along with 3,500 billion cubic meters of natural gas and 7,900 million tons of coal annually.[1] These fossil fuels account for about 86 percent of global energy consumption; the other 14 percent requires the maintenance of thousands of hydroelectric dams, hundreds of nuclear reactors (which consume enriched fuel requiring more than 150 tons of natural uranium daily),[2] and almost 4 million tons oil equivalent of biomass each day, mostly in the forms of firewood and crops for biofuels.[3]

The vulnerabilities of our current energy system stem mostly from its reliance primarily on fossil fuels: nonrenewable, depleting resources that, when burned, release climate-changing greenhouse gases. In response to the threat of climate change, the world's nations have agreed to reduce their fossil fuel consumption (although actual rates have yet to be negotiated). To have a likely chance of limiting global warming to 2 degrees Celsius above the preindustrial average, greenhouse gas emissions would have to decline by at least 80 percent below 1990 levels by 2050, implying a rapid, dramatic shift in world energy sources.[4] It is difficult to adequately convey the enormity of the challenge implied in such a shift. Not only would it be unprecedented (previous energy transitions have simply seen new energy sources added to existing ones; this one would entail replacing most existing sources with new ones), but it would also require levels of investment measured in the tens of trillions of dollars.

Climate change is not the only challenge to our energy systems, however. Even if world leaders do nothing to respond to the climate threat, depletion will continue to eat away at the world's oil, gas, and coal reserves. Although very large fossil fuel resources remain, extraction has proceeded according to the low-hanging-fruit principle, whereby the fuels that are cheapest to produce and of highest quality are depleted first, leaving worse prospects for later. After more than 150 years of ever-increasing rates of extraction, the quality of fossil fuel resources being produced now is in many cases much poorer than was the case just decades ago, and it is rapidly declining.

This trend is clearest in the case of oil, where most new production projects—including the mining of bitumen sands in Canada, the extraction of tight

oil using horizontal drilling and hydrofracturing ("fracking"), and the production of oil offshore in waters more than a mile in depth—are categorized
as "unconventional" and are far more capital intensive than the conventional
crude oil drilling that fueled the world during the twentieth century. Further,
petroleum production is dogged by a steady decline in thermodynamic efficiency as measured in terms of energy returned on energy invested (EROEI,
or EROI).[5] Because the purpose of oil production is to provide useful energy
to society, steep increases in the energy cost of producing an average unit of
refined petroleum product (such as gasoline or diesel fuel) imply serious trouble for the petroleum industry and for the societal systems that depend on oil
(including transport and agriculture). The vast majority of oil resources still
in place will never be produced simply because their low net energy yield will
not justify the level of financial investment required (figure 3-1). The global oil
industry is already in turmoil, and its prospects for the future are grim.[6] The

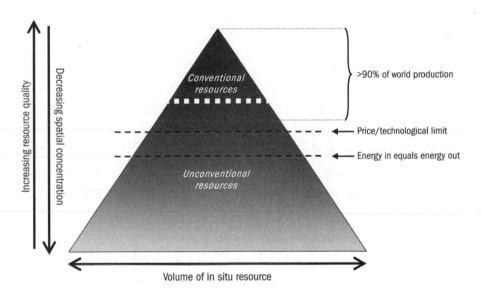

Figure 3-1. The pyramid of fossil fuel resource volume versus resource quality.
This illustration shows the relationship of in situ resource volumes to the distribution of
conventional and unconventional accumulations and the generally declining net energy and
increasing difficulty of extraction as volumes increase lower in the pyramid.
Source: J. David Hughes, *Drill, Baby, Drill: Can Unconventional Fuels Usher in a New Era of
Energy Abundance?* (Santa Rosa, CA: Post Carbon Institute, 2013), 44, http://www.postcar
bon.org/publications/drill-baby-drill/.

same trends of increasing capital requirements and declining thermodynamic efficiency are occurring in the natural gas and coal industries, although they have not proceeded as far as in the case of oil.

These two challenges—climate change and the effects of depletion—will require action if we are to avoid economic and environmental calamity. Such action would entail the replacement not only of energy production infrastructure, but also of much of our energy usage infrastructure, which was designed to take advantage of the specific capabilities of fossil fuels. Market forces will not be sufficient to drive investment at sufficient rates to enable a nondisruptive energy transition. Currently, however, there is little sign of the political will that would be required to adequately support the transition with public policy.

In short, it is indeed a crisis, if still a relatively quiet one, although it probably will not remain quiet for long. Let us explore it in more detail, examining the status of each of our current primary energy sources.

Current Energy

Oil is the world's top energy source, delivering about 33 percent of total energy used. Global oil production rates, having grown steadily for the last 150 years, appear now to be leveling off and are likely on the verge of drifting downward as a result of declining rates of investment in new projects.[7] Although oil prices are no lower than their historic inflation-adjusted average, they are not high enough to justify many of the more expensive "unconventional" production projects, and as already noted, most remaining oil resources fall into that category. World oil discoveries have shrunk dramatically in recent years, and oil companies are seeing falling profits.[8]

Petroleum accounts for about 95 percent of current transport energy, and the entire economy depends on motorized transportation. Thus, any problems with maintaining the oil industry would have system-wide impacts until full-scale replacements for oil and its services are ready.

Coal provides 29 percent of total world energy (17 percent of US energy),[9] with 39 percent of world electricity deriving from coal combustion (38 percent in the United States).[10] It is the most carbon-intensive of fossil fuels and is responsible for higher levels of lung disease in nations that rely on it heavily. Large coal resources remain, scattered in many nations, but several key nations (including the United States, China, the United Kingdom, and Germany) have already mined their best resources, and economically minable amounts may be much smaller than many often-quoted estimates suggest.[11] China's coal consumption, which increased dramatically during the first decade of the twenty-first century, has now begun to decline; indeed, although consumption is still increasing in India and a few other nations, global coal consumption may be peaking.

Natural gas provides 24 percent of world energy and 22 percent of primary energy for world electricity generation (in the United States, the percentages are 31 of total and 24 of electricity generation). Natural gas is also used for space heating and for the production of nitrogen fertilizer for agriculture. Extraction rates for natural gas are rising globally, although extraction in the United States—recently greatly supplemented by shale gas produced through fracking—is now on the decline.[12] Some resource assessments suggest that world gas extraction is likely to peak around the middle of the 2020s.[13]

When burned, natural gas produces less carbon dioxide than coal does per unit of energy. Recent assessments of the extent and impacts of methane leakage from production operations suggest that, overall, natural gas may be as harmful to the climate as coal, however.[14]

Nuclear power produces electricity via 447 commercial reactors currently operating worldwide (99 in the United States); collectively, they produce about 4 percent of world energy and 12 percent of world electricity (8 percent of all energy consumed in the United States and 19 percent of US electricity). Uranium, the fuel for the nuclear cycle, is a depleting nonrenewable resource, and the peak of world uranium production may well occur by 2030, according to some estimates.[15] The average grade of mined uranium has declined substantially in recent years because the best reserves are already depleted. Recycling of fuel and the employment of alternative nuclear fuels are possible, but the needed technology has not been adequately developed.[16] Further, nuclear power plants are so costly to build that unsubsidized nuclear plants are not economically competitive with coal, natural gas, or renewable energy sources. Although

Russia, China, and India are constructing new reactors, other countries are decommissioning them at an increasing pace.[17] New nuclear technologies will require decades of development and very high levels of investment.

The full nuclear energy lifecycle emits much less carbon dioxide than the burning of coal to produce an equivalent amount of energy, although uranium mining and enrichment and plant construction entail considerable carbon emissions. Storage of radioactive waste is highly problematic, and efforts to find a long-term storage solution (using reinforced canisters buried deep underground at a geologically stable site) have failed miserably.

Wind, which supplies around 1.5 percent of total world energy and 2 percent of electricity (2 percent of energy and 3 percent of electricity in the United States), is now the cheapest new source of electricity in many places, although integration with existing power grids is problematic in cases in which wind's share of total electricity generation is high. Wind power's intermittency requires redundant generation capacity, energy storage, or demand management. Wind power is a renewable source of energy, and there is very large potential for growth in generation: it has been estimated that developing just 20 percent of the world's wind potential would produce at least eight times the current world electricity demand.[18] Installed capacity is currently growing at more than 25 percent per year; in 2015, nearly $110 billion was invested in the industry.[19]

Environmental impacts from wind energy occur mostly in the production and installation of turbines, which require concrete, steel, and rare earth minerals.

Hydropower supplies 17 percent of all electrical energy worldwide (with 15 percent coming from large dams) and 6 percent of all electrical energy in the United States. This supply represents 7 percent of total energy worldwide and 2.5 percent in the United States. Unlike fossil energy sources, with hydropower most energy and financial investment occurs during project construction, with very little required for maintenance and operations. Therefore, electricity from hydro is generally cheap.

Energy analysts and environmentalists are divided on the environmental impacts of hydropower. Proponents see it as a clean, renewable source of energy; detractors see it as having environmental impacts from reservoir creation, dam construction, water quality changes, and destruction of native habitat as large as, or larger than, those of some conventional fossil fuels.

Solar photovoltaics (PV) systems currently supply 0.2 percent of world energy and 0.3 percent of electricity (0.4 percent of energy and 0.5 percent of electricity in the United States). The cost of new PV systems has plummeted in recent years as most manufacturing has moved to China and as new processes have been adopted. Because an enormous amount of energy is transmitted to Earth's surface in the form of solar radiation, tapping this source has great potential. Even a very small fraction of this energy flow would be enough to satisfy current world electricity demand. Solar shares with wind the problems of intermittency; hence, source redundancy, storage, and demand management are all necessary. Costs of new PV systems are unlikely to continue falling at the same pace they have in recent years, due to the relatively fixed cost of installation, inverters, brackets, and other equipment needed (PV panels alone already represent a minor part of final cost). Worldwide investment in solar PV grew 12 percent in 2015 over the previous year, to $161 billion.[20]

As with wind, solar power's environmental impacts occur mostly in the production and installation stages, particularly with utility-scale solar farms built in fragile desert ecosystems. Most panels require aluminum, glass, and silicon in a highly purified form.

Biomass, including *biofuels*, accounts for approximately 10 percent of the world's total energy usage.[21] Traditional biofuels (wood and animal dung) are used by up to three billion people for cooking and heating. Newer forms of biomass usage involve converting wood, crops, manures, or agricultural waste products into liquid or gaseous fuel, using it to generate electricity, or using it to cogenerate heat and electricity. World electric power generation from biomass and waste was about 445 terawatt hours (TWh) in 2014, 2 percent of the world total. In 2010, 2.7 percent of the world's liquid fuels consisted of biofuels such as ethanol from corn or sugarcane, or biodiesel produced from soybeans and palm oil.[22]

Biomass power plants are typically regionally supplied and therefore limited in size—studies have found that transporting the biomass from to source to furnace more than about 50 miles requires more energy that it produces[23]—but they provide reliable baseload power. Biogas can be used like natural gas and burned as fuel in anything from a small cookstove to an electric power plant. Biogas can be produced on an industrial scale from waste materials, but it is difficult to find estimates of the possible size of this resource. Burning biomass and biogas is considered to be carbon neutral because, unlike fossil fuels, they operate within the biosphere's carbon cycle: they release carbon dioxide when burned, but absorb carbon dioxide while growing. Moreover, biomass would ordinarily release carbon dioxide naturally to the atmosphere by decomposition or burning. Using waste sources of biogas like cow manure or landfill gas can also reduce emissions of methane, a more powerful greenhouse gas.

Biomass is a renewable resource, although it is not a particularly expandable one. Although biofuels have been touted as a substitute for liquid fuels in transport systems, most biofuels show poor thermodynamic efficiency (a lot of energy is required to produce them per unit of energy delivered).

Geothermal power and *tidal power* currently provide only a small share of world energy (geothermal is by far the larger of these two sources, accounting for 0.1 percent of world energy, 0.9 percent of electricity). Both produce electricity, although geothermal is also used to provide heat directly; both also depend on favorable geography. Currently, the only places being exploited for geothermal electrical power are ones where natural hydrothermal resources exist in the form of hot water or steam reservoirs.

Globally, there are about 500 megawatts of installed capacity of tidal power; given the relatively low capacity factors of tidal power, it provides a negligible contribution to total world energy. Once a tidal generating system is in place, it has low operating costs and produces reliable, although not constant, carbon-free power. Sites for large installations are limited to a few channels and tidal basins around the world, however.

Transition Challenges

If a shift away from our current reliance on oil, coal, and natural gas is necessary and inevitable, what alternatives could be most quickly and cheaply ramped up to fill the gap? A survey of options for replacement sources suggests solar and wind as the most likely candidates. How could the transition from fossil fuels to renewable energy be accomplished? What would the result look like?

I recently collaborated with David Fridley, staff scientist at Lawrence Berkeley National Laboratories, to assess the opportunities and roadblocks implied by a shift to an all-renewable (mostly solar and wind) global energy system.[24] Although other researchers have focused primarily on the questions of how many wind turbines and solar panels would be required and how to deal with the problem of supply intermittency, we aimed to engage in a more wide-ranging inquiry.

As other analysts before us have noted, a shift to solar and wind for electricity generation implies an efficiency opportunity: thermal generation (using coal, natural gas, biomass, or uranium as a heat source) is inherently inefficient, with most of the initial energy wasted.[25] Wind and solar produce electricity directly, implying a steep reduction in wasted energy. Regarding the critical issue of transportation, internal combustion engines (powered by fossil fuels) are inherently highly inefficient at turning fuel energy into mechanical motion, whereas electric motors are highly efficient. Therefore, an economy running on renewable electricity is likely to require less energy in total than one running on nonrenewable electricity. Some inefficiencies will nevertheless be added to the energy system, including losses from energy storage and long-distance transmission, to the extent that these strategies are used to balance supply intermittency. Overall, the transition will represent a trade-off between costs involved in making a renewable energy system act essentially like the current one and the costs implied in adapting our energy usage patterns to the inherent qualities and characteristics of renewable resources.[26]

Currently, only about 20 percent of final energy globally is used in the form of electricity. Thus, a transition to mostly wind and solar electricity would require that many technologies that use energy be electrified (such as by substituting battery-electric vehicles for gasoline or diesel-burning vehicles) or powered with renewables some other way (such as by using renewable electricity to make liquid or gaseous fuels out of water and carbon dioxide from industrial sources). Some substitutions will be relatively easy, such as trading natural gas space heaters for electric air-source heat pumps. Some will be difficult, such as finding ways to fuel aviation and shipping with renewable power. Making concrete will be a hefty challenge, as will maintaining the consumer electronics industry, which relies greatly on the use of petrochemicals and long-distance transportation.

The solar and wind energy industries are growing fast. As noted earlier, however, to avoid globally catastrophic climate change and to break our dependence on fossil fuels before depletion makes them damagingly expensive, we need to transition the bulk of the global energy system to renewables within just the next few decades. If we are to achieve that goal, the pace of investment and build-out both in energy supply technologies (solar panels and wind turbines) and new energy usage technologies (electric vehicles, heat pumps, etc.) will need to increase at least tenfold.[27] Very large research and development investments will be required for the replacement of industrial technologies that currently rely on fossil fuels. The scale and pace of the effort that is required have been compared to the US armament effort during World War II, when the entire automobile industry was shifted toward the building of tanks, jeeps, and other military equipment. In the current instance, as in that historic example, only concerted government policy is likely capable of pushing the effort forward fast enough to succeed.

In the early stages of the transition, we will be using fossil fuels to build, transport, and install solar panels, wind turbines, public transit, and other infrastructure needed to reduce our consumption of fossil fuels. Thus, to avert a short-term spike in carbon emissions, we will need to prioritize fossil fuels, especially oil, for transition purposes, which means ramping down other uses (e.g., in commercial aviation) very quickly indeed. As fossil fuels grow costlier to extract, governments may be tempted to use available energy and capital merely to maintain existing consumption patterns. That would eventually lead to climate chaos, a gutted economy, and no continuing wherewithal to build a bridge to a renewable energy future.

How much energy will be available to society at the end of the transition? There are too many variables (including rates of investment and the capabilities of renewable energy technologies to power their own manufacture as the transition proceeds) to permit accurate estimates. Taking the most readily evident constraints and opportunities into account, however, Fridley and I conclude that available energy amounts are likely to be much smaller than official agencies have been forecasting based on past energy demand trends. Further, a more modest overall energy system would be more affordable to construct—and the measures needed to manage supply intermittency would be easier and cheaper—than would be the case if the current system were simply expanded year after year to meet forecast demand. That is because, in a smaller system, a larger proportion of energy could come from user-controlled renewable energy sources such as hydro, biomass, and geothermal, which offer less potential for expansion than solar or wind.

When thinking about future energy demand, it may also be helpful to keep ecological footprint analysis in mind. The Global Footprint Network annually calculates the footprint of nations based on the amount of land and water area (natural capital) required to provide the goods and services consumed in that nation.[28] The current per capita footprint in the United States is four times what is sustainable globally. Therefore, asking whether renewable energy could enable Americans to maintain their current levels of consumption is equivalent to asking whether renewable energy can keep them living unsustainably. One way or another, consumption of energy and materials in wealthy nations must eventually decline.

An all-renewable economy may be very different from the economy we know today. It will likely be slower and more local than today's, and it will be a conserver economy rather than a consumer economy.

The energy transition will represent an enormous societal shift; historically, during past shifts, there were winners and losers. If we do not pay attention to equity issues, it is possible that only the rich will have access to affordable energy.

At the end of the transition, we will achieve savings in the energy expenditures needed for each increment of economic production (thanks to increased efficiency), and we will be rewarded with a quality of life that is perhaps preferable over our current one (although for most Americans, material consumption will be scaled back). We will have a more stable climate and greatly reduced health and environmental impacts from energy production. Still, the transition will entail costs in investment, regulation, and the requirement to change behavior and expectations.

Conclusion

The energy crisis grows in severity with each year that it remains unrecognized and unaddressed. Although we may be encouraged to know that solar and wind electricity generation capacity is expanding quickly, current build-out rates are still far too low, and issues like falling energy returned on energy invested and the need for the prioritized usage of fossil fuels for transition purposes are not being discussed by policy makers. There seems to be little willingness among planners and politicians to find ways to substantially reduce overall energy demand.

What is actually required is nothing less than a near complete redesign of industrial systems and a substantial downsizing of energy usage in industrialized nations. If policies and leadership to accomplish these goals are not forthcoming, the eventual result will be dire. Nations will simply burn whatever fossil fuels can be extracted affordably, wrecking the global climate while their economies collapse (probably in stages) due both to declining thermodynamic efficiency and to snowballing environmental impacts. If we do not spend effort now in transitioning agriculture to renewable fuels, the result will be falling output and, eventually, mass global hunger. If we do not design and build renewable energy transport systems now, trade and travel will eventually grind to a near standstill. If we do not find substitutes for fossil fuels in industrial processes soon, those processes will gradually cease to produce the streams of goods that people depend on. The energy dilemma could hardly be more critical to our future, but there is as yet little evidence that it is being taken seriously.

Notes

1. "BP Statistical Review of World Energy 2016," accessed March 27, 2017, https://www.bp.com/content/dam/bp/pdf/energy-economics/statistical-review-2016/bp-statistical-review-of-world-energy-2016-full-report.pdf. The figure for oil includes crude oil, condensate, natural gas liquids, shale oil, and tar sands; it excludes biofuels.

2. World Nuclear Association, "Uranium Production Figures, 2004–2014," July 2015, http://www.world-nuclear.org/information-library/facts-and-figures/uranium-pro duction-figures.aspx. The number used here is for traded quantities of natural uranium metal prior to enrichment.

3. International Energy Agency, "World Energy Outlook" (Paris: International Energy Agency, 2014), 257.

4. See http://grist.org/climate-energy/yes-the-u-s-can-reduce-emissions-80-by-2050 -in-six-graphs/.

5. Charles A. S. Hall, "The History, Future, and Implications of EROI for Society," in *Energy Return on Investment: A Unifying Principle for Biology, Economics, and Sustainability* (Cham, Switzerland: Springer International, 2017).

6. Lauren Gensler, "Profits Are Still Tumbling at America's Big Oil Companies," *Forbes*, October 28, 2016, http://www.forbes.com/sites/laurengensler/2016/10/28 /exxonmobil-chevron-earnings-oil-prices-2.

7. Richard Heinberg, "The Peak Oil President?," Post Carbon Institute, January 11, 2017, http://www.postcarbon.org/the-peak-oil-president/; Wood Mackenzie, "Global Upstream Investment Slashed by US$1 Trillion," June 15, 2016, https:// www.woodmac.com/analysis/global-upstream-investment-slashed-by-US1-trillion.

8. Charles Kennedy, "The Worst Oil Crisis Ever? IEA Sees Unprecedented Decline in Investment," Oilprice.com, September 14, 2016, http://oilprice.com/Energy/Ener gy-General/The-Worst-Oil-Crisis-Ever-IEA-Sees-Unprecedented-Decline-In-Invest ment.html; International Energy Agency, "World Energy Investment 2016."

9. "BP Statistical Review of World Energy 2016."

10. "Breakdown of Electricity Generation by Energy Source," The Shift Project Data Portal, accessed March 27, 2017, http://www.tsp-data-portal.org/Break down-of-Electricity-Generation-by-Energy-Source#tspQvChart.

11. David Rutledge, "Estimating Long-Term World Coal Production with Logit and Probit Transforms," *International Journal of Coal Geology* 85, no. 1 (2011): 23–33.

12. US shale gas production rose dramatically after 2008 and has since been the subject of much enthusiasm, but the geological realities of shale plays are such that significant continued production growth is unlikely. See J. David Hughes, *2016 Shale Gas Reality Check: Revisiting the U.S. Department of Energy Play-by-Play Forecasts through 2040 from Annual Energy Outlook 2016* (Santa Rosa, CA: Post Carbon Institute, 2016), http://www.postcarbon.org/publications/2016-shale-gas-reality -check/.

13. Werner Zittel, Jan Zerhusen, and Martin Zerta, *Fossil and Nuclear Fuels—The Supply Outlook* (Berlin: Energy Watch Group, 2013), 91.

14. Robert Howarth, Renee Santoro, and Anthony Ingraffea, "Methane and the Greenhouse-Gas Footprint of Natural Gas from Shale Formations," *Climatic Change* 106, no. 4 (2011): 679–90.

15. Michael Dittmar, "The End of Cheap Uranium," *Science of the Total Environment* 461/462 (2013): 792–98.

16. Estimates of time to commercialization for new nuclear technologies such as fission or thorium-based reactors have been consistently twenty to thirty years away since at least the 1960s. The economics of nuclear remain profoundly unfavorable; see Trevor Findlay, "The Future of Nuclear Energy to 2030 and Its Implications for Safety, Security and Nonproliferation" (Waterloo, ON: Centre for International Governance Innovation, 2010), 85.

17. Jon Samseth et al., "Closing and Decommissioning Nuclear Power Reactors," in *UNEP Year Book 2012* (Nairobi, Kenya: United Nations Environment Programme, 2012), 35–49.

18. Xi Lu, Michael B. McElroy, and Juha Kiviluoma, "Global Potential for Wind-Generated Electricity," *Proceedings of the National Academy of Sciences* 106, no. 27 (2009): 10933–38.

19. Tom Swanson, "Wind Energy Investment Increases Worldwide," Pew Charitable Trusts, June 14, 2016, http://www.pewtrusts.org/en/research-and-analysis/analysis/2016/06/14/wind-energy-investment-increases-worldwide.

20. Frankfurt School–UNEP Centre/BNEF, "Global Trends in Renewable Energy Investment 2016" (Frankfurt, Germany: Frankfurt School of Finance and Management, 2016), 15.

21. International Energy Agency, "World Energy Outlook," 257.

22. REN21, "Renewables 2011 Global Status Report" (Paris: REN21 Secretariat, 2011).

23. IRENA, "Biomass for Power Generation," in *Renewable Energy Technologies: Cost Analysis Series* (Bonn, Germany: International Renewable Energy Agency, 2012), 27; International Energy Agency, "World Energy Outlook," 257.

24. Richard Heinberg and David Fridley, *Our Renewable Future: Laying the Path for One Hundred Percent Clean Energy* (Washington, DC: Island Press, 2016).

25. For examples of the thermal efficiency of heat cycles, see University of Washington, "Improving IC Engine Efficiency," http://courses.washington.edu/me341/oct22v2.htm.

26. Heinberg and Fridley, *Our Renewable Future.*

27. Heinberg and Fridley, *Our Renewable Future.*

28. For more information, see http://www.footprintnetwork.org/.

CHAPTER 4

The Economic Crisis: The Limits of Twentieth-Century Economics and Growth

Joshua Farley

ECONOMIC GROWTH IS A RECENT PHENOMENON in human history, becoming noticeable within a single lifetime only since the eighteenth century (i.e., since the dawn of the Industrial Revolution, the development of the modern market economy, and the transition to fossil fuels).[1] Just prior to the Industrial Revolution, it took the English economy more than 400 years to double in size.[2] Growth rates steadily increased thereafter, with a great acceleration in economic growth, resource depletion, waste emissions, and ecological degradation beginning around 1950.[3] The global economy grew ninefold in the twentieth century even as population quadrupled.[4] According to World Bank data, the global economy's most recent doubling in size (as measured by gross domestic product) took just more than a decade, from 2003 to 2014.[5]

Economic growth as a whole has unquestionably brought incredible (albeit highly unequal) benefits to humanity, but it cannot be sustained on a finite planet. From physics, we know that it is impossible to create something from nothing, to create nothing from something, or to do work without energy. With current technologies, the only "something" available for economic production is the raw material provided by our finite planet. If we increased raw material consumption by just 3 percent per year, it would grow from 1 kilogram to the mass of the planet in well under two thousand years. Actual ecological constraints, however, are far more binding on economic growth than such geophysical constraints. In their natural state, many of the raw materials converted into economic products serve as the structural building blocks of global ecosystems. When we transform these building blocks into economic products faster than they can renew, we not only deplete our resource stocks, we threaten to fundamentally alter ecosystem processes upon which humans and most other life forms depend.[6]

Energy poses yet another constraint on economic growth. Renewable energy sources like solar, wind, and hydro are inexhaustible relative to human time scales and are abundant in the sense that there is no competition for use across geographical locations. They are only available at a given rate over time and are difficult to capture and store, however. Fossil fuels and fissionable elements, in contrast, are available as finite, energy-dense stocks that can be consumed as fast as we can extract them. One person's use of such nonrenewable resources unavoidably leaves less for others, forcing competition for access.[7] Fossil fuels currently account for nearly 82 percent of primary energy use and must eventually run out,[8] but again, ecological constraints are far more binding than geophysical ones. The rate of emissions of waste products from fossil fuel extraction and combustion, ranging from oil spills to greenhouse gases, far exceeds the rate at which ecosystems can absorb them, and these emissions accumulate as harmful stocks that further threaten essential ecosystem processes.[9]

Even if we transitioned entirely to "clean" renewable energy, the ecological costs of ongoing economic growth would continue to threaten catastrophic changes to the global ecosystem—ranging from mass extinctions to runaway climate change—that could ultimately prove incompatible with human civilization.[10] In addition, the marginal costs (the cost of the next unit of something) of economic growth borne by the global ecosystem are increasing. The first 100 parts per million (ppm) increase in atmospheric carbon dioxide from preindustrial levels threatens agricultural production, weather-related disasters, and coastal flooding; the next 100 ppm increase will have dramatically worse effects.[11] Marginal benefits of growth remain very high for the global poor, but fall rapidly once basic needs are met. Incremental wealth flows increasingly to the rich,[12] who benefit the least. When the marginal costs of economic growth exceed the marginal benefits, additional growth becomes uneconomic and makes us worse off than before. Unfortunately, whereas the benefits of growth are easily privatized, the costs are borne by society as a whole, so self-interested individuals have an incentive to produce more at society's expense.[13] Complicating matters even further is that the greatest known threats to the global ecosystem include agricultural production and fossil fuel use;[14] rapidly reducing either could have catastrophic impacts on human welfare, especially on the poor.

Thus, we face a global economic crisis. The current system is dependent on two things that cannot continue—constant economic growth and unbridled consumption of fossil fuels—but there are no easy ways to quickly adapt this system to the planet's very real ecological constraints without risking the well-being of billions of people. A decisive change—a transformation to a different kind of system—is both necessary and inevitable.

The challenge we face is to build an economic system that does not exceed planetary boundaries yet remains capable of satisfying basic human needs for all. The ecological-economic system is complex and adaptive, composed of innumerable interacting feedback loops and characterized by unpredictable surprises that can have major impacts on system functions. It is therefore impossible to identify the precise nature of the economic system we require, let alone a path to achieving it. It is possible, however, to identify some of the major challenges we face and aim to overcome them based on what is biophysically and behaviorally possible, with clear goals concerning what is socially and ethically desirable. As we strive to move toward our desired economic system, we will gain more knowledge of what works and what does not, and we can adjust our path accordingly.

Complex Systems, Resilience, and Antifragility

Ecosystems and economies are both complex systems. Complex systems are characterized by highly nonlinear behavior, emergent properties (properties arising in a system because of the interactions between its components), time lags, and unpredictable surprises; they function at multiple, interconnected scales of space, time, and organization.[15] Complex systems also self-regulate: they keep their behavior within certain bounds so that the system as a whole continues functioning as in the past. These bounds are really *thresholds* because once they are crossed, the system's regular structure and function change, sometimes irrevocably. One function of a system's resilience is to keep the system from crossing these thresholds.

System thresholds can be crossed by sudden disruptions as well as by smooth and continuous changes in stressors. Common ecological stressors associated with economic activities include overharvesting of renewable resources, pollution, habitat loss, and the dispersion of invasive species through international trade.[16] We rarely know precisely where thresholds lie, but crossing them can induce a sudden shift to a very different system,[17] with potentially catastrophic results. Furthermore, there may be significant time lags between an economic activity and its ultimate ecological impact. For example, we have been emitting greenhouse gases by burning fossil fuels for over 150 years, but even if all emissions stopped tomorrow, the global climate would continue to warm for decades; if positive feedback loops kick in, those decades become millennia.[18] We are almost certainly near many such thresholds and may have irreversibly exceeded some already.[19]

Socioeconomic thresholds are crossed when a smooth change in the quantity of an essential good or service leads to profound impacts on individual humans or the whole economy. For example, food consumption below some critical level leads to death for the individual; at a societal scale, it can lead to social turmoil, violence, and political and economic collapse.[20] Sudden reductions in fossil fuel consumption trigger economic recessions, and it is quite likely that more dramatic reductions would trigger economic collapse.[21]

Beneficial thresholds may also exist in the form of major technological breakthroughs that either shift the economy into a fundamentally new and favorable dynamic or prevent it from crossing a looming economic or ecological threshold. Scientists have long warned about the human population surpassing Earth's carrying capacity, resulting in a population crash;[22] technological breakthroughs ranging from crop rotation and plant breeding to nitrogen fixation have held off this outcome, although there is no guarantee they can continue to do so. Technological breakthroughs can also have unintended negative consequences, such as the impact of chlorofluorocarbons on the ozone layer[23] or of DDT on birds.[24] Truly novel ecological and technological changes are impossible to predict.[25] Highly improbable ones with enormous impacts on society are known as "black swans"; although any individual black swan may be impossible to predict, they are recurrent phenomena that account for many of the most dramatic changes to the human system.[26]

Given the complexities of multiple system thresholds and unpredictable black swan events, a system can absorb only so much disturbance while performing the same functions. Resilience is "the capacity of a system to absorb disturbance and reorganize so as to retain essentially the same function, structure and feedbacks—to have the same identity."[27] Macroeconomists have developed tools that helped maintain the structure and function of our growth-dependent economy, but only at the expense of the structure and functions of the global ecological system on which the economy depends. Long-term resilience of the economy requires a reduction in resource use and waste emissions to levels compatible with a healthy and resilient global ecosystem. Within the current economic regime, however, economic contraction imposes unacceptable human costs. The economy therefore requires transformation into a new regime that prioritizes the supply and equitable distribution of essential resources, including food, water, energy, and ecosystem services. Unfortunately, we have already exceeded critical ecological boundaries[28] and will likely face a growing number of black swan–type crises.

Meeting basic human needs and repairing the damage to global ecosystems while confronting black swans requires an economic system that is not just resilient but "antifragile," that is, strengthened by perturbations. Redundancy, preserving options, and small size can all help build antifragile systems.[29] As we will see in the next section, building an antifragile economy requires insights into the economic characteristics of essential resources and essential processes as well as the "prisoner's dilemmas" surrounding their continued provision. It also requires careful assessment of the existing system's capacity to allocate essential resources and the potential for new economic institutions to do so.

See chapters 7 through 9 on systems literacy, sustainability science, and resilience science for a full discussion of the concepts in this section.

Essential Resources, Essential Processes, and Prisoner's Dilemmas

Scaling back the economy's resource use and waste emissions to levels that no longer threaten global ecosystems will be exceptionally difficult. To avoid unacceptable human suffering and accompanying instability, the economic system must prioritize the provision of basic needs—specifically, essential resources like food, energy, and water, and essential ecological processes like the water cycle, the nutrient cycle, and the maintenance of a habitable climate. In short, an economic system's failing to meet people's basic needs is a symptom of low overall resilience, and the system will soon cross a threshold (likely accompanied by social instability) into a different, possibly less-desirable reality.[30]

Essential resources have unique economic characteristics. In a market economy, demand is a function of price: when price goes up, consumer demand goes down. The demand for essential resources, however, shows comparatively little response to changes in price; for example, in the United States, a 1 percent increase in the price of food reduces demand by only about 0.08 percent.[31] In economic jargon, these resources have a low elasticity of demand. Elasticity of demand is also a function of income. In the United States, people spend only 6.6 percent of their income on food for home consumption.[32] In many poor countries, however, people spend well over half of their income on food. In Tanzania, for example, a 1 percent increase in price reduces food demand by approximately 0.65 percent.[33] Such drastic cuts in food consumption can cause significant malnutrition and misery, which can then lead to the breakdown of social and political stability.[34] The underlying problem is structural: markets systematically allocate essential resources to those who need them least.

Essential ecological processes also have unique economic characteristics that can be best understood by thinking of them in terms of a game theory scenario: the prisoner's dilemma. In a prisoner's dilemma, each participant can cooperate with others or can defect; universal cooperation leads to the optimal outcome for society, but defection leads to the best outcome for the individual, regardless of what others do.[35] For example, people can cooperate to protect the essential processes of the global climate by incurring the costs of reducing their greenhouse gas emissions, but if one individual nevertheless chooses to continue producing emissions, that person gains all the benefits of that choice while sharing the costs of climate change with everyone. Similarly, if nobody chooses to reduce their emissions, an individual would gain no benefit by doing so on their own. The situation is similar for investments in technologies that reduce ecological impacts: the more people who adopt them, the better, and adoption is maximized when the underlying information is freely available to all.[36] If everyone contributes to their development, green technologies are likely to improve rapidly. An individual who refuses to contribute pays no costs and can free-ride on the contribution of others, however.

Again, the underlying problem is structural. Market economies reward (and indeed, assume) self-interest, and in a prisoner's dilemma, a purely self-interested individual will always defect. To achieve optimal social outcomes, though, cooperation is essential.[37]

The Current Market System

Market economies are poorly suited for building resilience, allocating essential resources, or solving prisoner's dilemmas. One of the main problems arises from mainstream economic theory, which maintains that free markets are self-regulating systems that guarantee a resilient equilibrium balancing supply and demand of all goods, services, and factors of production. If a resource becomes scarce, its price increases, spurring consumers to reduce demand and producers to increase supply or to develop substitutes through technological innovation. In fact, free markets are not sufficiently self-regulating to either cope with the realities of the planet's ecological constraints or meet the long-term basic needs of humanity because of four main issues: (1) externalities, (2) inequity of purchasing power, (3) the need for cooperation, and (4) the special role of technology. Each is described below.

Economic activities have unintended impacts on others that are not captured by prices; they are called *externalities*. For example, the social and environmental costs of climate change are rarely reflected in the prices for fossil fuels and are hence external to market decisions. In theory, if these costs are internalized into market prices—for example, by taxing activities with negative impacts (e.g., carbon emissions), subsidizing activities with positive impacts (e.g., green technology development), or creating private property rights to incentivize stewardship (e.g., to oceanic fisheries or to the ecosystem's capacity to sequester greenhouse gases)—prices will shift to again ensure equilibrium and drive technological solutions to resource scarcity. In other words, mainstream economic theory holds that the single feedback loop of market prices is sufficient to guarantee a resilient and optimal equilibrium for an ever-growing economy.[38] In reality, however, no complex system can be driven to equilibrium by a single feedback loop, and recurring bubbles and busts are empirical proof that market economies are not the kinds of systems that stay in equilibrium.[39] Furthermore, it is impossible to assign property rights to climate stability and other essential ecosystem services or to accurately internalize into market prices the costs of degrading these services.

Concerning the allocation of essential resources, market demand is determined by preferences weighted by *purchasing power*. During the 2007–2008 food crisis, the price of staple grains doubled. Consumers in rich countries, where food accounts for only a small share of income and more than 30 percent of food is thrown into the garbage, scarcely noticed the price increases; in poor countries, however, malnutrition increased by forty million people. Markets systematically allocate essential resources to those willing to pay the most; they are generally the richest individuals, who objectively receive the lowest utility from additional consumption. Where purchasing power is equitable, markets are more likely to allocate essential resources to those who need them most, but there is considerable evidence that unregulated capitalist economies systematically concentrate wealth in the hands of the few.[40]

As discussed earlier, the special economic characteristics of essential ecological processes means that their management is best approached as a kind of prisoner's dilemma. Solving prisoner's dilemmas requires *cooperation*, however, market economies are driven by competition and can make people less cooperative. Indeed, a common method our current economic system uses for countering selfishness—providing monetary payments for contributing to the public good (i.e., paying people to do something instead of relying on people to act voluntarily)—can actually undermine people's intrinsic motivation to cooperate, in essence making them more selfish.[41] Moreover, research has found that simply priming people to think about wealth or money makes them more selfish: they become less social, less likely to ask for or offer help, less empathic, less honest, less moral, and interestingly, more favorable to free market economics and more likely to justify inequality.[42]

Finally, we now live in an information economy, and like essential resources and essential processes, *information* has unique economic characteristics. For example, the information embodied in a green technology is not a scarce resource that is depleted through use, but rather is improved. When someone switches to a green technology, everyone benefits. Furthermore, there can be extremely high one-time costs to develop a new technology, whereas the cost of disseminating the underlying knowledge is (in the age of the internet) negligible. The cost per adopter of developing the technology therefore decreases with the number of adopters. Resources with these characteristics are known as "natural monopolies" because a single producer minimizes costs and because competition unnecessarily replicates high fixed costs. In contrast, a patent on a green technology creates a legal monopoly that discourages others from using or improving upon the technology; adoption of the green technology is reduced, and everyone is worse off (except perhaps the patent holder).[43] Clearly, markets are not a promising solution to our most serious problems.

Toward an Economics of Cooperation

Although mainstream economic theory is populated by purely self-interested, perfectly rational, and insatiable consumer and producers,[44] actual humans are clearly capable of cooperative and even altruistic behavior. In the context of evolutionary biology, true altruism is defined as one individual's sacrifice of evolutionary fitness to enhance that of another unrelated individual.[45] Some evolutionists claim that such fitness-reducing behavior simply cannot survive the process of natural selection,[46] but there is compelling evidence to the contrary. Although more selfish individuals can increase their relative fitness by taking advantage of more altruistic ones, groups with more altruistic individuals are more likely to survive and reproduce than those with more selfish individuals. In humans and a few other species, selection at the group level favors altruism, even as within-group selection favors selfishness. The result is a species capable of both self-interested and cooperative, altruistic behavior.[47]

This behavioral flexibility is important in the modern world because different economic challenges favor different types of behavior and different institutions can be designed to stimulate appropriate behaviors. For example, the use of fossil fuels by one person leaves less for others (making competition inevitable), and it is easy to assign property rights to fossil fuels. Market competition is thus well suited to allocating fossil fuels and other resources that can be privately owned and are depleted through use. In contrast, there is no competition for solar energy in the sense that capture at one physical location does not leave less available for capture elsewhere (although if we capture too much, it would compete with ecological demands). To better capture and store a diffuse and intermittent flow of photons requires new technologies, which improve when freely shared with others. Free, open-access knowledge would speed both the rapid development and the widespread adoption of solar energy and green technologies in general.[48] Efficient provision of solar energy is just one example of a prisoner's dilemma that would benefit from a cooperative economy.

To build its resilience, an economy must therefore build behaviors and institutions that promote cooperation and altruism at the scale necessary to manage the myriad prisoner's dilemmas it faces. Punishing defectors in prisoner's dilemmas encourages cooperation by making defection a losing strategy. Although both punishment and reward improve cooperation, punishment appears to be more effective than cooperation, and both together appear to be most effective.[49] Punishments can range from social ostracism of free riders to imprisonment of tax cheats; rewards can range from public funding for open-access green technology innovations to social admiration for philanthropists and other altruists. Such behaviors and institutions already exist but remain inadequate, undermined by a market ideology that assumes greed, minimal government, and private property rights drive efficient outcomes.

Two other mechanisms for promoting cooperation are reciprocity and group formation.[50] People have a powerful tendency to reciprocate, helping others who help them or members of their group.[51] The strategy of first cooperating in a prisoner's dilemma and then doing whatever the other player does ("tit-for-tat") is a winning strategy in modeled prisoner's dilemma games.[52] Importantly, we evolved to cooperate within groups but not necessarily between them. In small group settings, it is possible to keep track of cooperators and defectors, both directly by remembering past interactions and indirectly by learning of their reputation from others. Simply identifying as a group stimulates both within-group cooperation and between-group competition or even hostility,[53] but who we consider a member of our group is culturally defined.[54] Our challenge is to develop groups that correspond to the scale of the prisoner's dilemmas we face, which range from local watersheds to the planet as a whole.

Climate change and other ecological crises have already set in motion major disruptions to the production of food and other essential resources. The downside of failing to provide essential resources is so severe that an antifragile economy must prioritize their redundant provision over market efficiency. This could be achieved, for example, by a network of largely autonomous community economies. The asymmetries characterizing the benefits of essential resources favor cooperation. If one community or individual with an excess of essential resources helps another with a deficit, the cost to the former is negligible, whereas the benefit to the latter is immeasurable. In a conventional market transaction, the deficit community or individual pays the surplus one for additional resources, and then the economic relationship is over. In contrast, when a surplus is freely shared, the recipient incurs a moral obligation to reciprocate. If in the future the roles are reversed and the former deficit community donates its surplus to its neighbor, both communities have received far more benefits from the other than they have sacrificed. Although a market exchange ends economic relationships, cooperative exchanges strengthen them.[55] Diversity increases the likelihood that at least some communities can adapt to unpredictable disruptions. Poorly adapted communities will fail, but can then reorganize by adopting technologies and institutions from more robust communities. This evolutionary selection is an antifragile process in which stressors weed out failures and increase the average fitness of those who survive. Furthermore, when production is local, both producers and consumers are directly affected by the ecological and social impacts of their consumption, which automatically internalizes externalities.

Conclusion

The economy is a complex, adaptive system in a state of continual evolution. The rate of economic change is increasing, making the future increasingly unpredictable. Under these circumstances, it is not enough to build a resilient economy. Instead, we must focus on maintaining the resilience of the global ecosystem that sustains the economy. The economy itself must dramatically reduce its current level of resource extraction, energy use, and waste emissions. It must also reorganize into a system capable of meeting basic needs without perpetual growth while being buffeted by unpredictable perturbations and stressors. If civilization is to survive this transition, it must develop economic institutions capable of managing prisoner's dilemmas, which will require unprecedented levels of global cooperation. This chapter suggests some possible first steps toward achieving a cooperative economy not only capable of addressing our immediate challenges, but also of growing stronger in the process, building our capacity to address unpredictable but inevitable challenges in the future.

Notes

1. R. Heilbroner, *Visions of the Future: The Distant Past, Yesterday, Today, Tomorrow* (New York: Oxford University Press, 1995).
2. S. Broadberry et al., *British Economic Growth, 1270–1870* (Cambridge: Cambridge University Press, 2015).
3. W. Steffen et al., "The Anthropocene: Conceptual and Historical Perspectives," *Philosophical Transactions of the Royal Society A: Mathematical, Physical and Engineering Sciences* 369, no. 1938 (2011): 842–67.
4. J. B. Delong, *Macroeconomics* (Burr Ridge, IL: McGraw-Hill, 2002).
5. "World Bank Open Data," accessed February 8, 2017, http://data.worldbank.org/.

6. E. P. Odum, *Ecology and Our Endangered Life-Support Systems* (Sunderland, MA: Sinauer, 1989); N. Georgescu-Roegen, *The Entropy Law and the Economic Process* (Cambridge, MA: Harvard University Press, 1971).

7. N. Georgescu-Roegen, "Energy and Economic Myths," *Southern Economic Journal* 41, no. 3 (1975): 347–81; H. Daly, "Steady-State Economics versus Growthmania: A Critique of the Orthodox Conceptions of Growth, Wants, Scarcity, and Efficiency," *Policy Sciences* 5, no. 2 (1974): 149–67.

8. International Energy Agency, *2014 Key World Energy Statistics* (Paris: International Energy Agency, 2014).

9. Intergovernmental Panel on Climate Change, *Climate Change 2014: Synthesis Report*, Contribution of Working Groups I, II, and III to the Fifth Assessment Report of the Intergovernmental Panel on Climate Change, Core Writing Team, R. K. Pachauri and L.A. Meyer, eds. (Geneva, Switzerland: IPCC, 2014), http://www.ipcc.ch/report/ar5/syr/.

10. J. Rockström et al., "A Safe Operating Space for Humanity," *Nature* 461, no. 7263 (2009): 472–75; W. R. Catton, *Overshoot: The Ecological Basis of Revolutionary Change* (Champaign: University of Illinois Press, 1982).

11. Intergovernmental Panel on Climate Change, *Climate Change 2014*; T. P. Hughes et al., "Multiscale Regime Shifts and Planetary Boundaries," *Trends in Ecology and Evolution* 28, no. 7 (2013): 389–95.

12. T. Piketty, *Capital in the 21st Century* (Cambridge, MA: Harvard University Press, 2014); Organisation for Economic Co-operation and Development, *Divided We Stand: Why Inequality Keeps Rising* (Paris: OEDC, 2011); Oxfam International, *An Economy for the 1%: How Privilege and Power in the Economy Drive Extreme Inequality and How This Can Be Stopped*, 210 Oxfam Briefing Paper (Oxford: Oxfam International, 2016).

13. H. E. Daly, "Ecological Economics and Sustainable Development, Selected Essays of Herman Daly Advances," in *Ecological Economics*, ed. J. C. J. M. van den Bergh (Northampton, MA: Edward Elgar, 2007).

14. H. C. J. Godfray, "Food and Biodiversity," *Science* 333, no. 6047 (2011): 1231–32; J. A. Foley et al., "Solutions for a Cultivated Planet," *Nature* 478, no. 7369 (2011): 337–42; W. Steffen et al., "Planetary Boundaries: Guiding Human Development on a Changing Planet," *Science* 347, no. 6223 (2015).

15. D. Meadows, *Thinking in Systems: A Primer* (White River Junction. VT: Chelsea Green, 2008).

16. R. Muradian, "Ecological Thresholds: A Survey," *Ecological Economics* 38, no. 1 (2001): 7–24.

17. M. Scheffer et al., "Early-Warning Signals for Critical Transitions," *Nature* 461, no. 7260 (2009): 53–59.

18. T. M. Lenton et al., "Tipping Elements in the Earth's Climate System," *Proceedings of the National Academy of Sciences* 105, no. 6 (2008): 1786–93; F. Pearce, *With Speed and Violence: Why Scientists Fear Tipping Points in Climate Change* (Boston: Beacon Press, 2007).

19. Rockström et al., *A Safe Operating Space*; W. Steffen, J. Rockström, and R. Costanza, "How Defining Planetary Boundaries Can Transform Our Approach to Growth," *Solutions* 2, no. 3 (2001): 59–65.

20. I. Perez and ClimateWire, "Climate Change and Rising Food Prices Heightened Arab Spring," *Scientific American*, March 4, 2013, http://www.scientificamerican .com/article/climate-change-and-rising-food-prices-heightened-arab-spring/;J.Berazneva and D. R. Lee, "Explaining the African Food Riots of 2007–2008: An Empirical Analysis," *Food Policy* 39 (2013): 28–39.

21. R. Heinberg, *The Party's Over: Oil, War and the Fate of Industrial Societies* (Gabriola Island, BC: New Society, 2003); C. A. S. Hall and J. W. Day Jr., "Revisiting the Limits to Growth after Peak Oil," *American Scientist* 97 (2009): 230–37.

22. T. R. Malthus, *An essay on the principle of population, as it affects the future improvement of Society; with remarks on the speculations of W. Godwin, M. Condorcet and other writers,* (London: J. Johnson, 1798); P. Ehrlich, *The Population Bomb* (New York: Ballantine, 1968); W. Catton, *Overshoot: The Ecological Basis of Revolutionary Change* (Urbana: University of Illinois Press, 1980).

23. M. J. Molina and F. S. Rowland, "Stratospheric Sink for Chlorofluoromethanes: Chlorine Atomic-catalysed Destruction of Ozone," *Nature* 249, no. 5460 (1974): 810–12.

24. R. Carson, *Silent Spring* (Boston: Houghton Mifflin, 1962).

25. M. M. Faber, J. L. Proops, and R. Amstetten, *Evolution, Time, Production and the Environment* (New York: Springer-Verlag, 1998).

26. N. Taleb, *The Black Swan: The Impact of the Highly Improbable,* 2nd ed. (New York: Random House, 2010).

27. Brian Walker and David Salt, *Resilience Practice: Building Capacity to Absorb Disturbance and Maintain Function* (Washington, DC: Island Press, 2012), 3.

28. Steffen et al., *Planetary Boundaries.*

29. N. N. Taleb, *Antifragile: Things That Gain from Disorder* (New York: Random House, 2014).

30. J. Farley et al., "Extending Market Allocation to Ecosystem Services: Moral and Practical Implications on a Full and Unequal Planet," *Ecological Economics* 117 (2015): 244–52.

31. J. Seale Jr., A. Regmi, and J. Bernstein, "International Evidence on Food Consumption Patterns," Electronic Report from the Economic Research Service, Technical Bulletin No. 1904, US Department of Agriculture, October 2003.

32. US Department of Agriculture, *Percent of Consumer Expenditures Spent on Food, Alcoholic Beverages, and Tobacco That Were Consumed at Home, by Selected Countries, 2014* (Washington, DC: Economic Research Service, USDA, 2016).

33. Seale, Regmi, and J. Bernstein, "International Evidence."

34. Berazneva and Lee, "Explaining the African Food Riots."

35. A. Rapoport and A. M. Chammah, *Prisoner's Dilemma* (Ann Arbor: University of Michigan Press, 1965).

36. The main input into any new technology is information, and making it free will reduce the cost of developing even better technologies. See J. Farley and S. Perkins, "Economics of Information in a Green Economy," in *Building a Green Economy*, ed. R. Robertson (East Lansing: Michigan State University Press, 2013), 83–100.

37. R. M. Axelrod, *The Evolution of Cooperation* (New York: Basic Books, 1984); M. Nowak and R. Highfield, *SuperCooperators: Altruism, Evolution, and Why We Need Each Other to Succeed* (New York: Free Press, 2011).

38. J. Gowdy, *Microeconomic Theory Old and New: A Student's Guide* (Stanford, CA: Stanford University Press, 2009).

39. J. Farley et al., "Monetary and Fiscal Policies for a Finite Planet," *Sustainability* 5, no. 6 (2013): 2802–26; M. Hudson, *The Bubble and Beyond* (Dresden, Germany: Islet, 2012).

40. Piketty, *Capital in the 21st Century*.

41. B. S. Frey, "Pricing and Regulating Affect Environmental Ethics," *Environmental and Resource Economics* 2, no. 4 (1992): 399–414; B. S. Frey and R. Jegen, "Motivation Crowding Theory," *Journal of Economic Surveys* 15, no. 5 (2001): 589–611; A. F. Reeson and J. G. Tisdell, "Institutions, Motivations and Public Goods: An Experimental Test of Motivational Crowding," *Journal of Economic Behavior and Organization* 68, no. 1 (2008): 273–81; S. Bowles, "Policies Designed for Self-Interested Citizens May Undermine 'The Moral Sentiments': Evidence from Economic Experiments," *Science* 320 no. 5883 (2008): 1605–9.

42. K. D. Vohs, N. L. Mead, and M. R. Goode, "The Psychological Consequences of Money," *Science* 314, no. 5802 (2006): 1154–56; K. D. Vohs, N. L. Mead, and M. R. Goode, "Merely Activating the Concept of Money Changes Personal and Interpersonal Behavior," *Current Directions in Psychological Science* 17, no. 3 (2008): 208–12; E. M. Caruso et al., "Mere Exposure to Money Increases Endorsement of Free-Market Systems and Social Inequality," *Journal of Experimental Psychology: General* 142, no. 2 (2013): 301–6; P. K. Piff et al., "Higher Social Class Predicts Increased Unethical Behavior," *Proceedings of the National Academy of Sciences* 109, no. 11 (2012): 4086–91.

43. The main input into any new technology is information, and making it free will reduce the cost of developing even better technologies. See J. Farley and S. Perkins,

Economics of Information; I. Kubiszewski, J. Farley, and R. Costanza, "The Production and Allocation of Information as a Good That Is Enhanced with Increased Use," *Ecological Economics* 69, no. 6 (2010): 1344–54.

44. R. H. Thaler, *Misbehaving: The Making of Behavioral Economics* (New York: Norton, 2015).

45. E. Sober and D. S. Wilson, *Unto Others: The Evolution and Psychology of Unselfish Behavior* (Cambridge, MA: Harvard University Press, 1998).

46. R. Dawkins, *The Selfish Gene*, 2nd ed. (New York: Oxford University Press, 1990).

47. M. A. Nowak, "Five Rules for the Evolution of Cooperation," *Science* 314, no. 5805 (2006): 1560–63; D. S. Wilson, *Evolution for Everyone: How Darwin's Theory Can Change the Way We Think about Our Lives* (New York: Delacorte, 2007); E. O. Wilson, *The Social Conquest of Earth* (New York: Liveright, 2012); C. Darwin, *The Descent of Man* (London: Penguin Classics, 2004).

48. Farley and Perkins, *Economics of Information*.

49. J. J. Wu et al., "The Role of Institutional Incentives and the Exemplar in Promoting Cooperation," *Scientific Reports* 4 (2014): 6421.

50. Nowak, *Five Rules*.

51. Nowak, *Five Rules*; S. Bowles and H. Gintis, "The Evolution of Strong Reciprocity: Cooperation in Heterogeneous Populations," *Theoretical Population Biology* 65, no. 1 (2004): 17–28.

52. Axelrod, *The Evolution of Cooperation*.

53. C. Haney, W. C. Banks, and P. G. Zimbardo, "Interpersonal Dynamics in a Simulated Prison," *International Journal of Criminology and Penology* 1 (1973): 69–97; M. Sherif, *In Common Predicament: Social Psychology of Intergroup Conflict and Cooperation* (Boston: Houghton Mifflin, 1966).

54. Sober and Wilson, *Unto Others*; Wilson, *Social Conquest of Earth*.

55. S. Gimbel, *Redefining Reality: The Intellectual Implications of Modern Science*, Course No. 4140, The Great Courses, 2015, http://www.thegreatcourses.com /courses/redefining-reality-the-intellectual-implications-of-modern-science.html.

CHAPTER 5

The Equity Crisis: The True Costs of Extractive Capitalism

Sarah Byrnes and Chuck Collins

INEQUALITY IS A PROBLEM as old as the hills. As long as people have competed for resources and status, there have always been some who acquired more at the expense of others, whether through luck, skill, guile, or violence. With the Industrial Revolution in the nineteenth century came a new set of economic systems that served to benefit those with wealth and extract from those without. Among them was modern capitalism, the system adopted by most of the western world. In the United States in particular, capitalism was combined with a political system that compensated for only some of its inherited and created inequities (and that generally has done so unequally along racial lines).

This model came to dominate the global economy by the end of the twentieth century, but soon began to show signs of instability. People in the most developed countries faced chronic unemployment as yet more factories moved abroad to cheaper labor markets, leading to the biggest resurgence of nationalist politics since World War II. People in developing countries saw many lifted out of poverty, but many were also left behind while elites got richer and while pollution, corruption, and violence often worsened. Add in the Middle East refugee crisis, the splintering of the European Union, and the election of an unapologetically disruptive economic protectionist as president of the United States in 2016, and it is clear that the equity challenges of the past decades have become a global equity crisis.

Extractive Capitalism

The term *extractive capitalism* captures the way in which our current political-economic system has created this crisis, extracting wealth from Earth, workers, and communities without fair payment or regard for the problems that ensue. Indeed, it is not so much the functions of capitalism itself but the extractivist mind-set behind it that is the driver of the inequity, both historically and today. "Extractivism," as Naomi Klein explained, "is a nonreciprocal, dominance-based relationship with Earth, one of purely taking. It is the opposite of stewardship, which involves taking but also taking care that regeneration and future life continue."[1] Extractivism creates what are called sacrifice zones, areas that, as journalist Chris Hedges described, "have been offered up for exploitation in the name of profit, progress, and technological advancement."[2] Underlying this process is the hierarchical belief that some people are "less than fully human, which [makes] their poisoning in the name of progress somewhat acceptable."[3] It is a hierarchical mind-set, and it operates throughout our global economy.

Hierarchy has likely existed as long as there have been humans. The past five hundred years have seen it egregiously manifested in the slave trade and colonialism. In North America, European colonists often confronted indigenous people and cultures that embodied the principle of stewardship and then exterminated them and ruthlessly exploited the freshly appropriated ecosystems. Today, again, we often see these two behaviors linked. Disregard for Earth often corresponds with disregard for people, workers, and communities.

Fortunately, the hierarchical mind-set that values some people above others has never had a complete monopoly on human thinking or ways of life. In the United States, New Deal policies enacted after 1932 were perhaps the most notable political effort to put a brake on domestic exploitation and protect people from the raw forces of concentrated extractive power. There are shadow sides to this story, however. For one, New Deal and post–World War II policies deliberately excluded people of color, furthering the legacy of racism and setting the stage for today's racial wealth gap and racial caste system.[4] In combination with the unfettered use of then-abundant fossil fuels, such policies created a large—and largely white—American middle class that expanded until the late 1970s. Since then, though, the hierarchical mind-set has again been on the rise—now in the form of powerful extractive multinational corporations—and the middle class has been shrinking.

Economic Inequality

Today, we face historic levels of economic inequality both within and among nations. In the United States, we have witnessed an acceleration of income and wealth inequalities and a growing and pernicious racial wealth divide. Since 1979, real wages for the bottom 70 percent of US workers have remained stagnant, requiring people to work more hours and take on debt to maintain their standards of living.

Private wealth ownership, which is a significant indicator of generational inequality, has become concentrated in fewer and fewer hands. Most of the gains in assets and income since 2008 have flowed disproportionately to the top 0.1 percent of households. This top one-tenth of 1 percent (an estimated 115,000 households with net worth that starts at $20 million) now own more than 20 percent of all US household wealth, up from 7 percent in the 1970s. This subgroup is the true American elite class, and they now own as much as the bottom 90 percent of US households combined.[5]

The higher up the income ladder, the more concentrated the wealth is among a small number of people. The members of the Forbes 400 list of wealthiest Americans alone now own about as much as the bottom 62 percent of the population, roughly equal to the wealth of the entire African-American population plus a third of the Latino population. The twenty richest people in the United States—a group that could fit comfortably in one single Gulfstream G650 luxury jet—now own more wealth than the bottom half of the American population.[6] These statistics likely underestimate current levels of wealth con-centration because a huge percentage of assets owned by the wealthy are hidden through the growing use of offshore tax havens and complicated legal trusts.[7]

The persistent racial wealth divide in the United States has been com-pounded by overall inequality trends. The median wealth of white households is thirteen times greater than black households and ten times greater than Latino households. Modest gains over the last three decades in black and Latino wealth barely close the gap. If average black wealth grows at the same rate that it has over the last three decades, it will be 228 years before it equals the amount of wealth possessed by white households today. That is only 17 years shorter than the institution of slavery in the United States, which lasted 245 years. For Lati-nos, it will take 84 years to reach average white wealth today.[8] All these trends put us on track for a future characterized by hereditary aristocracy and racial economic apartheid.

Power and Inequality

Economic inequality does not blossom in a vacuum. A concentration of wealth breeds a concentration of political power and vice versa. One of the dynamics of inequality is that the beneficiaries of the political-economic system turn their greater wealth into political clout, tilting the playing field further toward finan-cial benefit. Today, this role is played by the global corporate elite—the benefi-ciaries of corporate extractivism—which has used its clout to privatize public resources, slash public spending on social programs, and eliminate worker and environmental protections.

One result of this ever-tilting playing field is that sacrifice zones have expanded; they now include once-unaffected communities and populations. In fact, the decline of the American middle class can be understood as part of this larger trend away from shared prosperity for the majority toward extreme wealth for only some (and sacrifice for others). Beyond a lack of wealth and lower real income, more and more people (both in the United States and abroad) are being impacted by problems such as food and water shortages, energy price spikes, financial instability, massive storms, unemployment and underemployment, droughts, new diseases, and sea-level rise. In each case, the elites remain invulnerable (for now), while the sacrifice zones of heightened vulnerability expand.

Multiple Crises

For generations, people in the developing world have been living without sufficient access to energy, economic opportunity, or a clean environment. These challenges are not new, and they have certainly been crises at local and national levels in different parts of the world. The equity crisis we speak of today reflects that these problems are now so acute, so globally pervasive, and so intertwined with other issues that a decisive change is both necessary and inevitable. In this way, we can see how the global environmental (chapter 2), energy (chapter 3), and economic (chapter 4) crises simultaneously create and are caused by a global equity crisis (all together, the E^4 crises).

Climate change provides the most obvious illustration. The most developed countries in the world historically account for most of the carbon emissions (almost 70 percent) that are now causing climate change.[9] Through a mixture of geographic luck, military power, and preexisting wealth and technology, they were able to access, extract, and consume fossil fuel resources earlier than other countries, setting the stage for greater inequality. They grew wealthier in the process, but over time, their ever-growing consumption of fossil fuels exacerbated environmental destruction, global economic inequality, and (nonrenewable) energy resource depletion.

Today, it is clear that the benefits of this setup have disproportionately flowed to the richest countries while the poorest countries have disproportionately suffered the negative effects, including in the form of climate change impacts. Consider landlocked Bolivia, which relies for its drinking water on mountaintop glaciers that are running dry in warming weather. Look at island nations like the Maldives, Kiribati, and Fiji, which are literally losing their land to the rising seas. What about low-lying Bangladesh, which produces just 0.3 percent of world emissions and has seen massive displacement due to sea-level rise (by 2050, as many as 50 million Bangladeshis may be displaced)? A *New*

York Times article from 2014 gave a face to this terrifying new environmen-tal-economic-energy-equity reality:

> When a powerful storm destroyed her riverside home in 2009, Jah-anara Khatun lost more than the modest roof over her head. In the aftermath, her husband died and she became so destitute that she sold her son and daughter into bonded servitude. And she may lose yet more.
>
> Ms. Khatun now lives in a bamboo shack that sits below sea level about 50 yards from a sagging berm. She spends her days collecting cow dung for fuel and struggling to grow vegetables in soil poisoned by salt water. Climate scientists predict that this area will be inun-dated as sea levels rise and storm surges increase, and a cyclone or another disaster could easily wipe away her rebuilt life. But Ms. Kha-tun is trying to hold out at least for a while—one of millions living on borrowed time in this vast landscape of river islands, bamboo huts, heartbreaking choices and impossible hopes.[10]

The impacts of climate change are now clearly being felt in the United States. Superstorm Sandy in 2012—which devastated oceanside communities in New Jersey and New York and flooded parts of lower Manhattan—was a nationwide wake-up call. Massive blizzards, multiyear droughts, and enormous wildfires are the new normal in many parts of the country. The Atlantic hurri-cane season is now longer.

For most upper-middle class and wealthier Americans—including the elites, the top tenth of the richest 1 percent—climate change is a real but man-ageable problem: they have the financial resources to prepare (or move) their households for extreme weather, energy disruptions, pricier food, and scarcer water. Some of the world's wealthiest even plan to retreat to enclaves to escape climate chaos, buying mountain fortresses in the Rocky Mountains and "get away" farms in New Zealand with airplane landing strips.[11] As the global sac-rifice zones expand and the disruptions of climate change are more broadly felt, however, no corner of the planet will be exempt. Island paradises will be swamped from rising seas, and mountain redoubts will be choked with the smoke of burning forests.

The deeply systemic ecological catastrophe we are facing will wipe out our natural ecosystems, the foundations of all private wealth. There is no wealth on a degraded Earth, without clean water and healthy oceans. As scientist Johan Rockström of the Stockholm Resilience Centre writes, "We're still blind, despite all the science, to the fact that wealth in the world depends on the health of the planet."[12] All humanity—billionaire hedge fund managers, suburban soccer moms, and Bangladeshi farmers—is now wound together, our fate linked to our ability to respond to a planetary challenge bigger than anything we have faced before.[13]

Searching for Solutions

Throughout history, when those in power cannot or will not address problems that the populace cares about, the powerful have often resorted to scapegoating minority groups as a distraction. As the E[4] crises—and our leaders' failure to adequately resolve them—have become more apparent in recent years, such scapegoating (generally targeting people of color and immigrants) has become a dominant voice in national politics. With it has come a call to return to a past era when America was "great," presumably the period of growing middle-class wealth immediately after World War II (and before the civil rights movement) discussed above.

This hearkening back to a mythical golden age of the United States obviously ignores historical reality in a number of ways, including pervasive discrimination and violence against people of color and women as well as unchecked environmental destruction. Especially important with regard to today's inequities (economic, social, and political) is that it ignores the exclusion of people of color—particularly African Americans, the largest US minority group—from the post–World War II polices that created the middle class. As economics journalist Bryce Covert noted:

> Perhaps no program was as important in creating the middle class
> of the 1950s and '60s as the G.I. Bill. The government spent more

than $95 billion on it between 1944 and 1971, and millions of people used its benefits to buy homes, go to college, start businesses and find jobs.... Black veterans' applications for business assistance were routinely denied. Those seeking a college education were crowded into limited slots in segregated institutions.... The G.I. Bill did create a more middle-class society, but almost exclusively for whites.[14]

Other programs of the period similarly made it hard for people of color (and particularly African Americans) to enter the middle class. The federal home mortgage tax deduction spurred suburbanization, but racist bank lending policies and real estate practices meant that people of color largely did not benefit. The Social Security program, enacted just before World War II, did not originally apply to agricultural and domestic workers, sectors in which 60 percent of black workers and 85 percent of black women, respectively, were employed when the program started. When we ignore this part of the picture, we unintentionally set the stage for the kind of whitewashed nostalgia that has played a dominant role in US politics since the 2016 election cycle.

This nostalgia (among other factors) won the 2016 election, and the consequences for equity issues were readily apparent. Public spending on health care and public tax collection were both targeted for cuts, a strategy commonly labeled "austerity" when applied to other countries. Racist views that had once been universally denounced were met with silence and tacit acceptance and were allowed to spread. This combination of elite-driven austerity and white-nationalist populism—especially against a background of job loss due to globalization and mechanization—makes for an incredibly toxic political space. In such a situation, it is nearly impossible to use official political processes to address any of the crises we face.

As such, we will not see policies capable of addressing the E[4] crises until there is a radical shift in political power. No quick technical fixes could truly address these crises anyway; to do that, we must also end the hierarchical mind-set that values some humans over others and humans above the rest of nature. We must replace this mind-set with a new narrative and moral framework that assesses our decisions by their effects on people, places, and Earth, not by the potential profits to be made. Otherwise, we will continue to lack the moral and analytical tools needed to stop harmful practices.

The Impacts of Exploitation

Exploitation abounds in our current system. Consider farms in Florida and California where workers spend fifteen-hour days in fields full of pesticides picking strawberries and tomatoes for the global market. Consider sweatshops in Asia, or mines in Africa. This picture reveals that it is not only elites who occupy a privileged place in the global hierarchy: it is the middle classes as well. (In fact, Americans earning the median income or higher are among the top 2% of global earners.)

Our use of fossil fuels provides some of the starkest examples of how extractivism requires exploitation. In a manifestation of our energy crisis (see chapter 3)—and the lobbying power of fossil fuel companies—natural gas fracking rigs dot backyards from Pennsylvania to Texas; trains carry dusty, toxic coal through vulnerable ecosystems; and oil refineries expose neighboring communities to carcinogenic pollution. The process of extracting, transporting, and refining fossil fuels is without a doubt destructive, and that is long before they are burned and their emissions cause further damage.

The communities exploited by fossil fuel extractivism are almost always those most affected by poverty and racial discrimination. There are more than 150 oil refineries in the United States, and although they are known to emit toxins and carcinogens, regulators and industry claim that these emissions are kept to safe levels. According to the environmental law organization Earthjustice, however, seven million Americans living near oil refineries—half of whom are people of color—"have an increased cancer risk from the release of more than 20,000 tons of toxic air pollutants like mercury, arsenic and lead each year."[15] In the United States, people of color are much more likely than whites to live in the "sacrifice zones" near oil refineries and other toxic facilities such as waste transfer stations, landfills, and chemical plants. Beneath this exploitation lies the apparent belief that the victims are somehow unimportant. "Poisoning in the name of progress" becomes an acceptable cost of extractive capitalism.[16] A national environmental justice movement has been fighting this environmental racism for decades, with mixed success.

Poor whites have also suffered from fossil fuel extractivism, perhaps most dramatically in the Appalachian region where coal—which still provides half of the electricity in the United States—has been mined since the 1800s. Today, coal is extracted through a process called mountaintop removal mining, which has destroyed entire communities and buried vibrant ecosystems under toxic slurry. Like earlier methods of coal mining, it directly exploits and endangers workers. The mining unavoidably kicks up a lot of coal dust; miners inhale the dust, which then sits in their lungs and can neither be removed nor destroyed by the body. Eventually, the buildup causes coal worker's pneumoconiosis, commonly known as black lung disease. It has killed tens of thousands of people over the years, including as many as ten thousand people as recently as 1995–2005.[17] Black lung disease leaves miners' lungs scarred, shriveled, and black. Edward Petsonk, a West Virginia doctor, described black lung disease as being "like a screw being slowly tightened across your throat. Day and night towards the end, the miner struggles to get enough oxygen. It is really almost a diabolical torture."[18] Coal companies have knowingly subjected their workers to this diabolical torture for decades. When coal mining is the only way to feed a family, many miners will do it, even if they suspect that they are endangering their lungs. Workers have been known to collude in coal companies' tactics to get around safety regulations, for example, by moving dust monitors around to better-ventilated areas.[19]

It is possible to imagine having both a healthy environment and good paying jobs, although the political-economic system of American extractive capitalism makes that exceedingly difficult. In this context, it should come as no surprise that we have been unable to stop climate change despite the existential threat it poses to our species. The relentless drive for profit simply outmuscles any attempt to rein in emissions. So we are caught in a vicious cycle: to extract fossil fuels, sacrifice zones are needed, and more of these zones are created as we burn ever more fossil fuels. Sacrifice zones produce carbon emissions, and carbon emissions produce sacrifice zones.

It is also possible to imagine the discovery of fossil fuels as a sort of test for humanity. We first harnessed this extraordinary form of energy at significant scale in the nineteenth century, and we quickly learned that harvesting this resource came at a cost to those who extract and refine it. We might have extracted small, healthy amounts slowly over the course of hundreds of years, protecting the health and safety of the workers in the meantime. Or, we might just have left it all in the ground. If either had been our path, we would not be facing a climate crisis today.

We took a different path, though. We consumed huge amounts of fossil fuels to build a standard of living that has had undeniable benefits in terms of life expectancy, health, and mobility while ignoring its adverse impacts. We are now in a situation in which we must leave all that remains in the ground, not only to avoid even worse climate change, but also because we have been unable to devise a nonexploitative way of extracting, producing, and consuming fossil fuels. It will not be possible to do so until we stop turning a blind eye to the suffering that the extractive mind-set has caused.

A Just Transition

Extractivism is not an inevitable aspect of human nature, as countless indigenous cultures embodying an ethic of stewardship attest. Indeed, there are now many proposed models for a nonextractivist economics suitable for the modern industrial world (the New Economy Coalition is a hub for such ideas).[20] What, though, will it look like to put a nonextractivist model into practice?

The answer might come from the Just Transition movement, which advocates for ensuring that the transition to a post-carbon economy does not unjustly leave workers or communities behind. It integrates the interests of both the labor movement and the environmental movement, demanding that we end fossil fuel dependence for the sake of the climate while also taking care of the communities that rely on the fossil fuel industry for their livelihoods.[21]

Environmental organizing efforts in the United States have often failed to address the underlying concerns of workers and communities. In comparison, the German labor movement has embraced a rapid transition to decentralized renewable energy and away from fossil fuels and nuclear power. Because there are strong social safety nets in most European countries, labor unions and workers are full partners in the energy transition. As Joe Uehlein of the Labor Network for Sustainability noted:

> German workers have less to fear. They already have a just transition in the form of a social safety net. [They] are not afraid that they will lose their health care, pension, paid vacation, and affordable education for [their] kids.... What [environmentalists] need to understand is the centrality of work in people's lives—and that in a society with deep social insecurity, your job is everything. One's livelihood, retirement, hopes and dreams. We have everything to fear from an environmental movement that is silent about workers.[22]

Activists who come out of the labor movement, like Uehlein, believe that the environmental movement must be champions of a just transition program for workers, especially when the results of their advocacy would eliminate jobs. It would include the creation of a just transition fund for workers and communities adversely affected by the shift away from fossil fuels. Another component of a just transition plan is to create resilience and decent-paying jobs through massive investment in green infrastructure, including renewable energy generating facilities and retrofits to existing infrastructure.

As communities self-organize to start their own projects and campaigns, alternatives and resistance to the extractivist system are emerging across the United States. One example of such work is the Jamaica Plain New Economy Transition (JP NET) in Boston. Founded in 2010 by a group of neighbors in this diverse Boston neighborhood and inspired in part by the global Transition Towns movement, JP NET has sparked a wide range of activities to strengthen community resilience in food systems, energy, and livelihoods. The group's projects have included the Jamaica Plain Time Exchange bartering network, the "Cancer Free Economy" effort to help businesses find alternatives to toxic chemicals, the Boston Food Forest Coalition, the JP Local First business association, and the Egleston Farmers Market. Through JP NET, neighbors have convened educational events and work days and have brought people together across differences in race, class, language, and subneighborhood. They also resisted the construction of a new gas pipeline being built through Boston neighborhoods, with vigils, rallies, and blockades; hundreds were ultimately arrested in protest.

Despite the hope embodied by such actions and movements, it may be difficult to imagine overcoming the extractive, colonial mind-set that has dominated the West for centuries, especially in the time frame allowed us by the physics of climate change. It is worth considering this quote from civil rights activist Anne Braden, however:

> In every age, no matter how cruel the oppression carried on by those in power, there have been those who struggled for a different world. I believe this is the genius of humankind, the thing that makes us half divine: the fact that some human beings can envision a world that has never existed.[23]

We must envision a world that has never existed as we set about righting the one we have now. We must envision a world in which profits are never more important than people's bodies. We must envision a human community that lives in harmony with Earth's limits rather than in a constant attempt to dominate and exploit. This project is essentially one of reconnection: reconnecting people with one another and with our planetary home. Although challenging, the work of reconnecting can actually be liberating and joyful. We have an opportunity to reconceive of the good life in a way that is truly inclusive and sustainable. It is uncharted but exciting territory, yet it is territory that we must explore together if we are to survive the crises we face.

Notes

1. Naomi Klein, *This Changes Everything: Capitalism versus the Climate* (New York: Simon and Schuster, 2014), 181. Readers are strongly encouraged to read this seminal book.
2. Chris Hedges and Joe Sacco, *Days of Destruction, Days of Revolt* (New York: Nation Books, 2012), 1.
3. Klein, *This Changes Everything*, 310.

4. See Michelle Alexander, *The New Jim Crow: Mass Incarceration in the Age of Color-blindness* (New York: New Press, 2010) and Chuck Collins et al., *The Ever-Growing Gap: Without Change, African-American and Latino Families Won't Match White Wealth for Centuries* (Washington, DC: CFED and Institute for Policy Studies, 2016), http://www.ips-dc.org/report-ever-growing-gap/.

5. Emanuel Saez and Gabriel Zucman, "Wealth Inequality in the United States since 1913: Evidence from Capitalized Income Tax Data," *Quarterly Journal of Economics*, October 2015, http://gabriel-zucman.eu/uswealth/.

6. Chuck Collins and Josh Hoxie, "Billionaire Bonanza: The Forbes 400 and the Rest of Us," Institute for Policy Studies, December 5, 2015, www.ips-dc.org/billionaire-bonanza/.

7. See Chuck Collins, "The Panama Papers Expose the Hidden Wealth of the World's Super-Rich," *Nation*, April 5, 2016. See also Robert S. McIntyre, Richard Phillips, and Phineas Baxandall, "Offshore Shell Games 2015: The Use of Offshore Tax Havens by U.S. Multinational Companies," Citizens for Tax Justice and US PIRG, October 5, 2015, http://ctj.org/ctjreports/2015/10/offshore_shell_games_2015.php#.VpEOgBFl3kE; and Gabriel Zucman, *The Hidden Wealth of Nations: The Scourge of Tax Havens* (Chicago and London: University of Chicago Press, 2015).

8. Collins et al., "Ever-Growing Gap."

9. Klein, *This Changes Everything*, 409. The United States, 5 percent of the world's population, is responsible for about 14 percent of all emissions.

10. Gardiner Harris, "Borrowed Time on Disappearing Land: Facing Rising Seas, Bangladesh Confronts the Consequences of Climate Change," *New York Times*, March 28, 2014, http://www.nytimes.com/2014/03/29/world/asia/facing-rising-seas-bangladesh-confronts-the-consequences-of-climate-change.html.

11. Chuck Collins, "To Billionaire Doomsday Preppers: Your Wealth Won't Save You," *Yes! Magazine*, February 21, 2017, http://www.yesmagazine.org/new-economy/to-billionaire-doomsday-preppers-your-wealth-wont-save-you-20170221.

12. Johan Rockström and Mattias Klum, *Big World, Small Planet* (Stockholm: Max Strom, 2015), 8.

13. See the discussion of the wealthy's stake in great inequality in Chuck Collins, *Born on Third Base: A One Percenter Makes the Case for Tackling Inequality, Bringing Wealth Home, and Committing to the Common Good* (White River Junction, VT: Chelsea Green, 2016).

14. Bryce Covert, "Make America Great Again for the People It Was Great for Already," *New York Times*, May 16, 2016, https://www.nytimes.com/2016/05/16/opinion/campaign-stops/make-america-great-again-for-the-people-it-was-great-for-already.html.

15. Lisa Garcia, "Communities Near Oil Refineries Must Demand Cleaner Air," Earth-justice, August 21, 2014, http://earthjustice.org/blog/2014-august/communities-near-oil-refineries-must-demand-cleaner-air.

16. Klein, *This Changes Everything*, 310.

17. Dave Jamieson, "Black Lung Disease Rates Skyrocket to Highest Levels since 1970s," *Huffington Post*, September 15, 2014, http://www.huffingtonpost.com/2014/09/15/black-lung-disease-levels-letter_n_5824470.html.

18. Chris Hamby, "The New Face of Black Lung," *Mother Jones*, July 9, 2012, http://www.motherjones.com/environment/2012/07/coal-mining-black-lung-return.

19. Hamby, "The New Face of Black Lung."

20. For more information, see http://ncweconomy.net/.

21. A good example of just transition efforts in the Kentucky coal fields is profiled in Sheryl Gay Stolberg, "Beyond Coal: Imagining Appalachia's Future," *New York Times*, August 18, 2016, http://www.nytimes.com/2016/08/18/us/beyond-coal-imagining-appalachias-future.html?_r=2.

22. Chuck Collins, "Can We Earn a Living on a Living Planet?," *American Prospect*, October 13, 2014, http://prospect.org/article/must-environmentalists-and-labor-activists-find-themselves-odds-each-other.

23. Anne Braden, "Finding the Other America," *Fellowship* 72, no. 1/2 (2006), text online at http://november.org/BottomsUp/reading/america.html.

CHAPTER 6

The Roots of Our Crises: Does Human Nature Drive Us toward Collapse?

William Rees

> Nothing in biology—including human affairs—makes sense except in the light of evolution.
> —adapted from Theodosius Dobzhansky, "Biology, Molecular and Organismic"[1]

IT HAS BECOME THE STUFF of daily headlines: the world is in overshoot, with humans wrecking the environment, destroying their own habitat, and undermining the functional integrity of the very biophysical systems upon which they are dependent. Strident warnings of ecological crisis and runaway climate change have gone virtually unheeded for decades. Indeed, the human ecological footprint[2] has expanded exponentially with population and consumption since the early nineteenth century. Brief remissions in recent years are attributable not to deliberate policy correctives but rather to temporary economic setbacks.[3]

Because such self-destructive behavior seems irrational, *Homo sapiens* has sometimes been called a "rogue species." That description is not correct.

111

Humanity's growing ecological burden actually stems mostly from people acting entirely naturally. In fact, *H. sapiens'* ecological behavior differs from that of non-human species in only one important respect: humanity's natural but ultimately self-destructive expansionist tendencies are being *amplified* by purely cultural factors. Nature and nurture combined give crushing weight to the problem.

These realities have grave implications; accelerating ecological degradation on a finite planet can terminate only in systems failure. Humanity's high intelligence—the capacity to reason from the evidence and plan ahead—should be sufficient to avoid this fate. How, then, can we explain our collective paralysis? Why has the "official world" failed to do anything truly effective to mitigate the ecological crisis? Is it just possible that because some of the basic causal behaviors are "natural," there is little we *can* do to avoid ignominious collapse? These are, or should be, the framing questions for policies and initiatives at any scale in the twenty-first century.

Global "Patch Disturbance"

Despite self-proclaimed exceptionalism, *H. sapiens* is a product of evolution. Natural selection has endowed humans with traits and behaviors that enhance prospects for survival in competitive environments, including the universal capacity for exponential growth and a corresponding appetite for essential resources. Like bacteria on a petri dish or any invasive species introduced to a new habitat, human populations will expand, occupying all accessible habitat(s) and consuming available resources, until constrained by negative feedback (e.g., disease, competition, resource shortages, self-pollution).

Consider, too, that humans are large warm-blooded mammals with correspondingly large per capita energy and material demands and that we live in extended social groups. It follows that even hunter-gatherers would have a substantial impact on the energy dynamics and physical structure of their eco-systems. Indeed, *H. sapiens* is an archetypal patch-disturbance species, which is defined as any organism that, usually by central-place foraging, degrades a small "central place" greatly and disturbs a much larger area away from the central core to a lesser extent.[4] The process is as natural as it is inevitable.[5]

Of course, humans have a leg up over other species in the evolutionary competition. Creative intelligence and technology enable us to adapt to virtually every ecosystem/habitat type on the planet (or, more correctly, we adapt virtually every ecosystem to serve human purposes). This capacity has enabled *H. sapiens* to invade every significant "patch" of potentially habitable environment on Earth, competitively displacing other species with similar demands.[6] Humans now boast the widest geographic range of any terrestrial vertebrate species. Meanwhile, technological progress continuously redefines what constitutes an "available resource." Today, we can economically mine metal ores with such low concentrations of desirable metals and minerals that they were considered worthless rock just a few decades ago. Material constraints on growth seem to dissolve with each new advance.

As if *natural* expansionism were not enough, by the 1950s, all the world's major governments and international agencies began to actively promote economic growth as the solution to many of society's problems.[7] The effect of this progrowth alliance between our natural tendencies and our cultural inclinations is unprecedented. It had taken all of human history for the population to reach 2.5 billion in 1950, but it took just thirty-seven years to double to 5 billion. Indeed, during the twentieth century, the human population ballooned almost fourfold to 6 billion,[8] and world gross domestic product expanded nineteenfold in real terms. By one account, "the total amount of goods and services produced in the twentieth century is estimated to have exceeded the cumulative total output over the preceding recorded human history."[9] Ironically, whereas people today think of rapid growth as the norm, the past century and a half is the single most *anomalous* period in human history. Only the most recent seven or eight generations—of roughly ten thousand since the emergence of *H. sapiens*—have experienced sufficient growth and technological change in their lifetimes to notice!

Given this accelerating momentum, it should be no surprise that human demands on nature dwarf those of ecologically similar species by a hundredfold or more.[10] *H. sapiens* has become, directly or indirectly, the dominant macroconsumer in all major terrestrial and accessible marine ecosystems on Earth; we are likely the most voraciously successful predatory and herbivorous vertebrate ever to walk this finite planet. Wild nature is, of course, proportionately diminished. By 2000, the biomass of humans and their domestic livestock made up more that 97 percent of the total biomass of terrestrial mammals.[11] Earth is humanity's petri dish; the entire planet has become the (much-disturbed) human patch.

The Struggle Within: *H. sapiens* as a Conflicted Species

There are indeed potions in our own bodies and brains capable of
forcing on us behaviors that we may or may not be able to suppress
by strong resolution.
—António Damásio, *Descartes' Error*[12]

H. sapiens is an inherently conflicted species. Although people are routinely rational in many situations, there will be contexts in which the same individuals act out of rage, hatred, love, or other powerful emotions in ways that are utterly untainted by reason.

On one level, the explanation is simple. The human brain evolved in stages with each new neural component becoming integrated with preexisting structures. The cerebral cortex—the seat of reason, self-awareness, analytic prowess, language, and voluntary movement in humans—is the most recent major add-on. It makes up the bulk of the cerebral hemispheres in humans but was essentially layered over the evolutionarily older limbic system (complex emotions, motivation, and relationships) and the truly ancient (reptilian) brain stem (basic emotions, autonomic functions, and survival instincts, including lying and cheating). Although each of these "subbrains" and related components is structurally distinct, the brain functions as an integrated whole; expressed human behavior generally reflects a complex interplay of rational, emotional, and instinctive impulses.[13]

This can be a problem. Blind emotion and instinct might dominate a person's behavior in particular circumstances, but because the corresponding brain centers operate *beneath* consciousness, our conscious selves cannot, by definition, be aware of their influence.[14] Some people think that they are acting reasonably even on occasions when others view them as ill-tempered wing nuts.

The point is that most expressed human behavior, from routine one-on-one interaction to international political posturing, is shaped, in part, by innate, subconscious mental processes and their associated chemical/hormonal agents.[15] Indeed, everyone will eventually encounter circumstances in which conscious intelligence founders absolutely. Defensive emotions might combine with sheer survival instinct to override reason in responding to perceived threats to one's hard-won social status or political/economic power. Passion often trumps reason.

In the long-term evolutionary scheme of things, this strategy has apparently paid off. (Persistence and universality are good evidence that a trait has survival value.) Indeed, selection pressures might have limited the circumstances in which logic and reason prevail over seemingly "primitive" but more tried-and-true impulses. That said, behaviors that worked well for the *individual* at earlier stages in human evolution (e.g., defending one's personal status) might be fatal to the common good today. Climate change, ecological degradation, and nuclear weapons proliferation, for example, are complex, inherently *collective* problems that demand well-reasoned, collective solutions. They can be addressed only through international cooperation in the development of long-term policies and plans based on solid biophysical evidence.

It is therefore disturbing that so much political discourse today is tainted by misinformation, magical thinking, and appeals to the basest of human instincts. We seem to be entering a twenty-first century "endarkenment," "a period in which truth ceased to matter very much, and dogma and irrationality became once more respectable."[16] In 2016, the Oxford Dictionaries declared "post-truth" to be the word of the year, defining it as "relating to or denoting circumstances in which objective facts are less influential in shaping public opinion than appeals to emotion and personal belief."[17] (Lies frequently trump facts.)

It is tempting to speculate that the cerebral cortex—that youngest and least "experienced" of major brain components—remains very much a work in progress. Perhaps *H. sapiens'* reasoning powers are not yet sufficiently sophisticated or masterful to be trusted with control over human destiny. Although we might question the potential efficacy of collective intelligence, however, we can be certain that denial, racism, scapegoating, and like motivations have become tragically maladaptive in an era of global climate chaos, incipient resource scarcity, and increasing geopolitical tension.

The Social Construction of (Un)reality

> If we are unable to identify reality and therefore unable to act...,
> then we are not simply childish but have reduced ourselves to figures
> of fun—ridiculous figures of our unconscious.
> —John Ralston Saul, *The Unconscious Civilization*[18]

Another "natural" human quality that confounds sustainability is that we pretty much make things up as we go along. Religious doctrines, political ideologies, cultural myths, and even academic paradigms and scientific theories are all complex "social constructs." Each such set of beliefs and assumptions, values, and norms is a product of the human mind, some of which may be elevated to the status of "received wisdom" by custom or formal agreement.[19]

Some social constructs are *entirely* made up; there is nothing in the nonhuman world that corresponds to "democracy" or "gay rights," for example. Other mental fabrications describe actual biophysical phenomena such as "gravity" or "the hydrologic cycle" that exist quite independently of whether or how humans conceive of them. Still other constructs lie somewhere between. We can probably all agree that an "economy" comprises that set of activities pertaining to the production, distribution, and consumption of goods and services and that such activities occur in all societies, but there are many competing economic paradigms, and some peoples might have no formal concept of the economy at all.

Three points central to (un)sustainability emerge. First, all knowledge—everything we take to be "true,"—is to some degree socially constructed. Second, whether or not they correspond to anything in the real world, social constructs can be extremely powerful. Religious doctrines, political ideologies, and much less formal beliefs can all masquerade as "reality" in our consciousness. Once firmly entrenched, they serve as perceptual filters through which we interpret new information and effectively determine how each of us acts in the real world. Third, as Neil Postman observed, "You may say, if you wish, that all reality is a social construction, but you cannot deny that some constructions are 'truer' than others."[20] It follows that some strongly held common beliefs might be little more than shared illusions.[21]

Which brings us back to the economy—specifically, to "economics," the socially constructed systems that effectively determine how society interacts with the ecosphere.

The world's dominant economic construct is neoliberal market economics, and that immediately presents a problem: the assumptions of the foundational model make no reference to biophysical reality. The starting point for mainstream analysis, "the circular flow of exchange value," sees the economy as a mechanically reciprocating exchange of goods and services between households and firms measured solely in abstract monetary units.[22] As ecological economist Herman Daly argued, however, describing the economic process as a circular flow while ignoring one-way irreversible energy and material throughput is akin to describing a living body as a circulatory system with no reference to the digestive track.[23] Even prominent mainstream economist Ronald Coase agreed that "existing economics is a theoretical system which floats in the air and which bears little relation to what happens in the real world."[24]

In effect, economists perceive the economy and the environment as separate systems. Economic analysis is thus uninformed by feedback from the complex spatial and temporal dynamics—the lags, thresholds, and other nonlinear phenomena—that characterize the ecosystems with which the economy interacts in the real world. Economists also assume that technological efficiency can compensate for resource depletion or, if necessary, that human ingenuity will find substitutes for any failing natural resource or life-support function. Just two constructed assumptions—that the economy and the ecosphere are separate systems and that technology can replace nature—free the human enterprise conceptually from biophysical constraints. Could there be a more supportive— and dangerously illusory—match for humanity's natural expansionist tendencies? With neoliberal economics, we are piloting Spaceship Earth guided by the intellectual equivalent of a 1955 Volkswagen Beetle owner's manual.

Why You Cannot Teach an Old Dog New Tricks

> The masses have never thirsted after truth. They turn aside from evidence that is not to their taste, preferring to deify error.
> —Gustave le Bon, *The Crowd: A Study of the Popular Mind*[25]

What if an illusory model entrenches itself and effectively blocks evidence that something is awry? Indeed, people *do* get stuck in familiar patterns of thinking and in comfortable behavioral grooves. Again, it is "human nature."

Cognitive neuroscience reveals that in the course of normal development and maturation, repeated experiences and sociocultural inputs influence the architecture of the brain's synaptic circuitry. In effect, socially constructed beliefs, values, and norms acquire a *physical presence*, a synaptic model of the repeated stimuli. Subsequently, people tend to think in terms of their preformed circuitry and are attracted to compatible people and similar experiences. At some point, too, the relationship between external stimuli and internal structures is inverted: instead of the environment creating new synapses, people behave in ways that protect *established* mental structures from hostile inputs. That is to say, "when faced with information that does not agree with their [existing] internal structures, they deny, discredit, reinterpret or forget that information."[26]

It is easy to understand how such culturally determined neural imprinting might arise through natural selection. Humans are highly social; we live in groups of mutually interdependent individuals. It could therefore be advantageous to passively acquire quasi-permanent neurological blueprints of tribal social and behavioral norms simply through repeated early exposure. Adaptive beliefs and values would enhance individual reproductive success and group survival in competitive environments or during periods of short-term resource scarcity; any concomitant behavior rigidity would not be penalized because, early in human evolutionary history, changes in cultural context and the natural environment would have generally been imperceptibly slow.

That was then, however. Today, both cultural and ecological changes are rapid and accelerating so that synaptic metaphors and entrenched thought-frames can become maladaptive. Rapid climate change and plunging biodiversity, for example, utterly confound the central myth of neoliberal economics that there is no inherent conflict between economic growth and the environment. No matter! If hostile facts do not fit our preconstructed frames, we tend to keep the frames and discard the facts.[27] Such denial often has a neurocognitive component and, whether explicit or implicit, enables people to carry on their comfortable lives untroubled by encroaching reality.[28] Economic growth thus remains every government's unchallenged solution for everything that ails us, from chronic poverty to (ironically) environmental degradation.

Scale and the Limits of Mind

A defining mark of human "progress" is the increasing scale and integration of just about everything. Tribal bartering evolved through village, regional, and national economies, and with globalization and world trade, we are currently witnessing the economic integration of the entire planet. The scope of effective governance itself has not quite kept pace with economic integration, but it has transcended rural villages and regional fiefdoms to embrace fewer and larger twentieth century nation-states. Today, we hear the call for global governance structures to match the reach of modern economic entities (e.g., transnational corporations) and their environmental impacts.

The entire process is problematic. It may be natural for people to want more and better and bigger, and technology facilitates continuous scaling up. In the process, however, humans are interfering with mind-bogglingly complex natural systems and creating massively complex systems of their own with no heed to the limited capacity of the human mind/brain to understand and control the behavior of either. A system of ten major elements has just 45 potential first-order interactions (direct interactions between any two major components); a system just twice the size has 190, or more than four times as many.[29] Thus, a village economy might have a dozen major players and a manageable number of interactions, but a global economy has thousands of significant elements and millions of unknowable-before-the-fact potentially unmanageable relationships. (There should be no surprise that economists are dismally poor at predicting major trends and events; the 2008 financial crisis comes to mind.)

The same arithmetic applies to political systems: how many pundits had egg on their faces for failing to understand the complex, divisive dynamics of the 2016 Trump electoral victory, for example? Consider the multiple layers of interacting human and natural systems whose intricacy surely calls into question the potential effectiveness of global governance and systems management. High systemic complexity implies that managers will be incapable of predicting, let alone understanding, many emergent behaviors of human-made hybrid socioecological systems.

What we are ultimately up against has been captured in what is known as the first law of cybernetics.[30] In its simplest form, this law states that if a management/control system is to succeed, it must be as complex as the system being managed; that is, it must be able to identify and respond effectively to all relevant behaviors of that system. As noted, that is impossible for large interacting systems with multiple major components, thousands of possible interactions, and unknown numbers and kinds of inherently unpredictable emergent effects. Certainly top-down centralized control is doomed to failure (again, that technically straightforward manual for our Volkswagen Beetle is useless for the complex and multiscalar dynamics of Spaceship Earth). Even single-purpose instruments such as regional or global trade treaties (e.g., the North American Free Trade Agreement and the World Trade Organization) produce myriad unintended consequences, including accelerating climate change and resource depletion.

This all suggests that sustainability might reside, in part, in decentralized forms of governance. A loose federation of regional governments, each with effective management control over "local" economies and essential ecosystems, is one possible model. Imagine a networked system of quasi-independent regions, each scaled to minimize surprise and enhance manageability. No regional subsystem would be allowed to become "too big to fail," but should one collapse, it would not be able to take down the whole network. This model is exactly opposite of post–World War II global trends.

Panarchy and the Collapse of Civilizations

> What is perhaps most intriguing in the evolution of human societies
> is the regularity with which the pattern of increasing complexity is
> interrupted by collapse.
> —Joseph Tainter, "Sustainability of Complex Societies"[31]

Another challenge to human agency is that natural systems seem to repeat cyclical development patterns that unfold in distinctive phases: rapid growth, consolidation/conservation, release (or "collapse"), and reorganization. We observe this pattern in the histories of living things, from cells to entire ecosystems, over periods ranging from hours to epochs. Resilience thinkers refer to the repeating patterns as adaptive cycles (because each iteration provides an opportunity for the system to adapt to changing conditions) and use the term *panarchy* (literally, "ruling over everything") to describe the nested hierarchy of living systems.[32]

Consider an adaptive cycle at the ecosystem level. The initial *growth*-oriented phase is an open pioneering phase that provides opportunities for innovation and adaptation. New species might invade and force others to adjust in various natural recombination "experiments"; the system as a whole is resilient and best able to adapt to larger-scale external changes (e.g., climate evolution). The subsequent *consolidation* phase sees a shift in systems structure as opportunistic pioneer species are gradually displaced by more efficient specialists. Thus, diversity and resilience decline and growth slows while internal connectedness and interdependence increase; resources (e.g., ecosystems' wealth in the form of nutrients and biomass energy) accumulate in a shrinking number of dominant species now competing for ever-scarcer external supplies. The system becomes more rigidly homogenous, conservative, and structurally brittle, which increases its vulnerability to unexpected shock. When such a shock occurs (e.g., severe drought or a forest fire), the mature ecosystem *collapses*, dissipating its accumulated nutrients and resetting for subsequent *reorganization* with initiation of a new cycle. If we can understand the internal dynamics of these natural cycles, "it seems possible to evaluate their contribution to sustainability and to identify the points at which a system is capable of accepting positive change."[33]

Where does the human system come in? It turns out that there is more than a passing resemblance between ecologists' adaptive cycles and the disturbingly regular cycles of collapse that plague human societies. Indeed, for all our high intelligence and confidence in our own exceptionalism, human societies have historically been alarmingly true to the rules of panarchy.

Anthropologist Joseph Tainter views human societies as problem-solving entities.[34] From this perspective, any growing "pioneering" society will eventually be challenged by some significant problem that forces it to search for innovative solutions, that is, to adapt. At first, this strategy succeeds and the system thrives, better prepared for the next challenge. The problem is that each major adaptation generates greater complexity, which implies higher levels of social, institutional, and technological organization. The larger, more complex society also demands greater energy and material inputs to maintain its structural and functional integrity, which means further complexification to ensure reliable supplies.[35]

As decades and centuries pass, established institutions and bureaucracies become more rigidly unresponsive to citizens' needs. Institutional incompetence is chronic, and there may be evident corruption at the top (as in the consolidation phase discussed above). Investment in systems maintenance and in addressing new problems yields declining marginal returns; public infrastructure crumbles, and innovation and resilience decline. Naturally, people feel overtaxed relative to perceived benefits and become disenchanted with their economic and ruling elites.

As tensions, adversity, and dissatisfaction build up, society becomes increasingly ill-prepared to cope with the next big challenge, whether political, economic, or ecological. Societal collapse—either slow decline or rapid implosion—is inevitable.[36] Significantly, the progressive cultural rigidity, policy intransigence, and social discontent characterizing the consolidation and collapse phases are entirely consistent with (and perhaps even predictable from) our understanding of socially constructed "reality," quasi-permanent cognitive imprinting, and *H. sapiens'* limited capacity to cope with complexity.

Epilogue: The Failure of Intelligence

This chapter argues that *H. sapiens* is not primarily a rational species. To begin, humans are driven by the universal tendency of living organisms to occupy all accessible habitats and use up all available resources with little heed for the future.[37] Uncontrolled, this instinct alone is a recipe for resource depletion and conflict. It is certainly a root cause of climate change, energy shortages, fisheries collapses, landscape degradation, and associated geopolitical tensions. Is *H. sapiens* unsustainable by nature?

Theoretically, of course, *H. sapiens* has the reasoning power and foresight to avoid ecological and consequent geopolitical catastrophe, but high intelligence is frequently overridden by defensive emotion and instincts. This problem may be particularly intractable if society continues to operate from ideological constructs (like neoliberal economics) with only tenuous links to biophysical reality (and worse still if those constructs become etched in people's behavioral neurocircuitry). Consider, for example, that many people now bolster their belief in infinite material growth on the *additional* mythic grounds that the economy is "decoupling" from nature. This illusion is fatally stunning for a species that has become the most significant consumer organism in every major accessible ecosystem on Earth and the greatest geological force changing the face of the planet.

Allegiance to magical thinking is an ancient problem for human societies. Historian Barbara Tuchman noted that, even in ordinary situations, "woodenheadedness, the source of self-deception ... plays a remarkably large role in government. It consists in assessing a situation in terms of preconceived fixed notions while ignoring or rejecting any contrary signs. It is acting according to wish while not allowing one's self to be deflected by the facts," with frequent dire consequences.[38]

What, then, can we expect in extraordinary circumstances? Global techno-industrial capitalist society currently confronts several macrochallenges, including faltering economies, the rise of oligarchies, rampant corruption, widening income gaps, popular disenchantment, accelerating climate change, and ecological decline. To top it off, the world "system" is vastly too complex to fully comprehend, let alone manage.

Our very existence is proof that primitive emotion and survival instincts have historically served us well. Crude instincts, however, have become dangerously maladaptive in the complex geopolitical environment they have helped create. The world is at a tipping point and needs a reality check. The time has come to acknowledge the subliminal drivers and constructed myths that have brought us to crisis and strive consciously to hold them in check. Let governments admit that conventional models of the economy and human economic behavior are dangerously laughable caricatures, that unlimited material growth on a finite planet is an impossibility theorem, that the (un)sustainability crisis is a collective problem that demands collective solutions, and that cooperation is essential for mutual survival. In short, the world community must rewrite its sociocultural narratives and create economic and social models that are truer to reality. The future of humanity resides in the ascendance of humanity's higher intellectual powers in dealing with the complexity of our times. A livable future resides in people rising above simplistic visceral responses in the exercise of true agency. The global community must deliberately *choose* to design an adaptive survival strategy that reflects contemporary reality.

This whole chapter has been dedicated to showing why such a reasonable, consistent-with-the-evidence strategy is unlikely to be realized. But perhaps things are changing; this may be the new age of unreason, though there are also signs of awakening. Many citizens have come to realize that for the first time in human (evolutionary) history, collective reason *must* prevail over subliminal drivers (e.g., short-term narrow self-interest) if civilization is to survive. If enough people so awaken, it would constitute a conscious cultural adaptation to a truly unprecedented predicament. It may also well be the only thing that can ensure that there will be additional generations of *H. sapiens*.

Notes

1. T. Dobzhansky, "Biology, Molecular and Organismic," *American Zoologist* 4, no. 4 (1964): 449.
2. M. Wackernagel and W. E. Rees, *Our Ecological Footprint—Reducing Human Impact on the Earth* (Gabriola Island, BC: New Society Publishers, 1996); W. E.

Rees, "Ecological Footprint, Concept of," in *Encyclopedia of Biodiversity*, 2nd ed., ed. S. A. Levin (New York: Elsevier, 2013).

3. WWF, *Living Planet Report 2016* (Gland, Switzerland: WWF International, 2016).

4. Revised from J. Logan, *Patch Disturbance and the Human Niche*, accessed November 3, 2016, http://dieoff.com/page78.htm; and J. Logan, email exchanges with the author.

5. See R. J. Naiman, "Animal Influences on Ecosystem Dynamics," *BioScience* 38 (1988): 750–52. In 1988, *Bioscience* published "How Animals Shape Their Ecosystems," a special issue (vol. 38, no. 11) of the journal. Predictably, with the exception of a passing reference to modern humans as "primary agents of environmental change," *Homo sapiens*—that greatest of all patch disturbers—was not included.

6. W. E. Rees, "Patch Disturbance, Eco-Footprints, and Biological Integrity: Revisiting the Limits to Growth," in *Ecological Integrity: Integrating Environment, Conservation and Health*, ed. D. Pimentel, L. Westra, and R. Noss (Washington, DC: Island Press, 2000), 139–56.

7. P. A. Victor, *Managing without Growth: Slower by Design, Not Disaster* (Cheltenham, UK: Edward Elgar, 2008).

8. It will top 7.5 billion in 2017.

9. International Monetary Fund, *World Economic Outlook: Asset Prices and the Business Cycle*, May 2000, 150–51, http://www.imf.org/external/pubs/ft/weo/2000/01/pdf/chapter5.pdf.

10. C. W. Fowler and L. Hobbs, "Is Humanity Sustainable?," *Proceedings of the Royal Society of London, Series B: Biological Sciences* 270 (2003): 2579–83.

11. V. Smil, "Harvesting the Biosphere: The Human Impact," *Population and Development Review* 37, no. 4 (2011): 613–36, http://www.vaclavsmil.com/wp-content/uploads/PDR37-4.Smil_.pgs613-636.pdf.

12. A. Damasio, *Descartes' Error: Emotion, Reason and the Human Brain* (New York: Avon, 1994), 121.

13. For an early exploration of "the triune brain," see P. MacLean, *The Triune Brain in Evolution: Role in Paleocerebral Functions* (New York: Plenum Press, 1990).

14. See M. Buchanan, "What Made You Read This?," *NewScientist* 195, no. 2611 (2007): 36–39.

15. See Damasio, *Descartes' Error*, 121.

16. See D. Colquhoun, "The Age of Endarkenment," *Guardian*, August 15, 2007, https://www.theguardian.com/science/2007/aug/15/endarkenment.

17. A. Flood, "'Post-Truth' Named Word of the Year by Oxford Dictionaries," *Guardian*, November 15, 2016, https://www.theguardian.com/books/2016/nov/15/post-truth-named-word-of-the-year-by-oxford-dictionaries.

18. J. R. Saul, *The Unconscious Civilization* (Concord, ON: House of Anansi Press, 1955), 21–22.

19. See Peter Berger and Thomas Luckmann, *The Social Construction of Reality* (New York: Random House, 1966).

20. Neil Postman, *Building a Bridge to the Enlightenment: How the Past Can Improve Our Future* (New York: Knopf, 1999), 76.

21. The scientific method, particularly experimentation, is designed specifically to avoid this problem. It is the only way of knowing that explicitly tests its constructs (hypotheses) against reality so that, once accepted, formal theories are the "truest" possible representations of reality.

22. Firms pay households in exchange for labor and investment (national income); households spend an equivalent amount on goods and services provided by firms (national product).

23. Herman Daly, *Steady-State Economics*, 2nd ed. (Washington, DC: Island Press, 1991).

24. R. Coase, "Interview with Ronald Coase," Inaugural Conference, International Society for New Institutional Economics, St. Louis, MO, September 17, 1997, http://www.coase.org/coaseinterview.htm.

25. G. le Bon, *The Crowd: A Study of the Popular Mind* (1896; repr., Kitchener, ON: Batoche Books, 2001), 64.

26. B. Wexler, *Brain and Culture* (Cambridge, MA: MIT Press, 2006), 180.

27. G. Lakoff, *Don't Think of an Elephant! Know Your Values and Frame the Debate* (White River Junction, VT: Chelsea Green, 2008).

28. K. M. Norgaard, *Living in Denial: Climate Change, Emotions, and Everyday Life* (Cambridge MA: MIT Press, 2011).

29. The number of possible first-order interactions in a system increases approximately as one-half the square of the number of components.

30. Control systems science.

31. Joseph A. Tainter, "Sustainability of Complex Societies," *Futures* 27, no. 4 (1995): 397–407.

32. L. H. Gunderson and C. S. Holling, eds., *Panarchy: Understanding Transformations in Human and Natural Systems* (Washington, DC: Island Press, 2002).

33. C. S. Holling, "Understanding the Complexity of Economic, Social and Ecological Systems," *Ecosystems* 4 (2001): 390–405.

34. Joseph Tainter, *The Collapse of Complex Societies* (Cambridge: Cambridge University Press, 1988).

35. For example, it is likely that chronic food shortages stimulated the "discovery" of agriculture. The resultant food surpluses, in turn, enabled the complexification of society: population growth; division of labor, including the emergence of priesthoods, a bureaucracy, and armies; the flowering of arts and crafts (technology); the development of cities; and so forth. Soil depletion (a new challenge) required further complexification in the form of engineered irrigation or territorial conquest.

36. For multiple examples, see Tainter, *The Collapse of Complex Societies*; and J. Diamond, *Collapse: How Societies Choose to Fail or Succeed* (New York: Viking/Allen Lane, 2005).

37. Economists have formalized humanity's innate short-sightedness (preference for the here and now) with the concept of "social discounting."

38. B. W. Tuchman, *The March of Folly: From Troy to Vietnam* (New York: Knopf, 1984), 7. See also D. Westen, *The Political Brain: The Role of Emotion in Deciding the Fate of the Nation* (New York: Perseus, 2007).

PART II

Gathering the Needed Tools

CHAPTER 7

Systems Literacy:
A Toolkit for Purposeful Change

Howard Silverman

L IFE IS FULL OF UNKNOWNS and rich with complexities. Two people experiencing a situation might interpret it differently. Even familiar situations might take unpredictable turns.[1]

Systems thinking is a way of seeing patterns amid the messiness of life. Patterns give coherence to one's experience. A systems toolkit of methods, models, concepts, and metaphors can be used both to interpret such patterns and to inform one's actions. For today's challenges—for creating a post-carbon world—familiarity with this toolkit represents a basic and essential literacy.[2]

A core concept in this systems toolkit is *feedback*: the circularity of influence. This circular pattern is instantly familiar. We have all personally experienced vicious circles, like when you cannot sleep because you are thinking about the next day's work, and the more you think about it, the more your insomnia is reinforced; or an online video that goes viral when it reverberates through social media, with initial support building more support in a bandwagon effect. These are examples of *reinforcing* or *positive feedback*. The complementary pattern is *regulatory* or *negative feedback*. My body, for example, regulates its own temperature; similarly, a thermostat monitors and adjusts the room temperature, according to the preference that one sets (figure 7-1).[3]

Patterns like these can be found across systems that are ecological as well as social, biological as well as material. A key systems method for learning about a situation is to compare and contrast a similar one, taking the second as a lens or model for looking back at the first.[4] We can learn about one organization by viewing it against others, learn about practices for purposeful change by examining what has worked (or not) elsewhere, and ultimately learn what it is to be human by seeing our lives reflected and refracted both in other species and in digital worlds of our own making.

Through such analogies and distinctions, the pioneers of systems theory

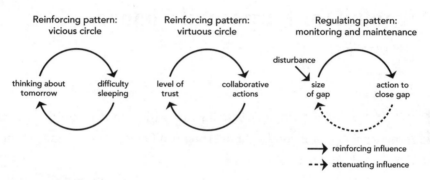

Figure 7-1. Feedback dynamics.
Two familiar examples of reinforcing feedback patterns, vicious circles and virtuous circles, are shown here. The example on the left reads: An increase in thinking about tomorrow leads to an increase in difficulty sleeping, which leads to an increase in thinking about tomorrow. The middle example reads: An increase in the level of trust leads to an increase in collaborative actions, which leads to an increase in the level of trust. A third, regulating pattern, is shown on the right. Applied to the example of a thermostat, it reads: An increase in the size of the gap (between monitored and desired temperatures) leads to an increase in action to close the gap (which then leads to a decrease in action to close the gap, which leads again to an increase in the gap, based on the differential with the outside temperatures). Each of these diagrams should be understood as a generalized model, representing what happened at one time, or what tends to happen *ceteris paribus*, "with all other things being equal."
    The use of visual imagery—including works of art, maps, graphs, and doodles as well as the types of diagrams shown here—is an important method in one's systems toolkit. During facilitations and conversations, visual imagery can support collective and comparative sensemaking among participants. Through such sensemaking, we reflect on our experiences, negotiate meanings, and imagine or enact new stories.
Illustration: Crystal Rome and Howard Silverman

sought to get beyond the constraints of academic disciplines, "beyond reductionism," and to develop a "science of synthesis."[5] This approach put them at odds with academic traditions and was one way in which systems critiques challenged basic assumptions of the Western intellectual tradition. Then, as now, the stakes could hardly be higher. "The major problems of the world," declared anthropologist Gregory Bateson, "are the result of the difference between how nature works and the way people think."[6]

Examining how nature works, environmental philosopher John Muir famously wrote, "When we try to pick out anything by itself, we find it hitched to everything else in the universe."[7] Muir's words, intuitive and enchanting, can also be misleading. Although it is true that nothing can be picked out by itself, it is also true that some hitches are tighter than others. "Everything is not connected to everything," clarified philosopher of science Donna Haraway, "everything is connected to something."[8] In those connections—loose or tight, sometimes reinforcing, sometimes regulating—are life's patterns.

Purposeful Behavior

Although the word *feedback* is relatively recent, dating to the 1800s or early 1900s, feedback processes are themselves both timeless and unavoidable.[9] Farmers on marginal lands long ago learned at their peril that as soil quality degrades, the land becomes more vulnerable to further erosion. Against this unwinding, rice farmers across Asia, for example, built terraces on steep slopes so as to retain water and maintain soils.[10]

The earliest recorded feedback control device is a water clock from ancient Alexandria. This ingenious mechanism used a float valve to self-regulate a steady drip of water into a holding tank, enabling one to read the time by examining the water level in the tank. A twelfth-century Chinese text tells of a similarly inventive tool: a bamboo drinking straw with a weighted stopper inserted into the tube. When sucking either too quickly or too slowly, the stopper would seal the valve, thereby regulating an equitable flow of liquid to each person drinking. In the eighteenth century, James Watt built a steam engine that self-regulated its velocity with a centrifugal flyball device called a governor. All these early regulatory mechanisms were constructed through experimentation, with little analytical theorizing. That began to change in 1868 with James Clerk Maxwell's paper "On Governors" and then in the twentieth century with technological breakthroughs in areas such as radar, acoustics, targeting, and navigation. Systems understandings that had been around for millennia began to be analyzed, formalized, and reinterpreted.[11]

"All purposeful behavior may be considered to require negative feed-back," wrote Arturo Rosenblueth, Norbert Wiener, and Julian Bigelow.[12] Wiener, a mathematician, and Bigelow, an engineer, were engaged in the World War II challenge of trying to develop an antiaircraft missile launcher that could calculate an airplane's trajectory, anticipate its forward motion, and shoot it down. Writing with Rosenblueth, a physiologist, they generalized their experiences and inquiries to biological and social systems. In a 1948 book, Wiener called this new field of practice and study *cybernetics*.[13]

The word *cybernetics* comes from the ancient Greek for "steersman." The person steering a boat must purposefully and iteratively sense the boat's trajectory, compare the current course with an overall goal, and adjust accordingly. That is the basic regulatory (negative feedback) pattern that occurs throughout our lives. As I walk down the street or hallway, I sense and adjust so as to avoid others in my path; as I talk with my friends, I watch their eyes and their body language, to see how my words are being received. Then, in the course of these activities, I might have a reflexive, gut-check moment, when I feel the need to re-examine my purposes or goals, or perhaps merely the effectiveness of my approach. Sensing that the winds and waves are unfavorable, the steersman may turn course to head back. Talking with my friends, I may sense that I am not connecting and decide to drop the subject until another day.[14] Figure 7-2 illustrates this pattern.[15]

This gut-check accounting for purpose matters more in some areas of research and practice than others.[16] The activities of the physicist, for example, will never influence the physical dynamics of planetary motion. Likewise, my prediction, "It looks like a sunny day," has no effect on the day's weather. In social situations, however, my decisions and actions do have an influence. If I decide to join Twitter, Instagram, or the latest social media platform, I thereby

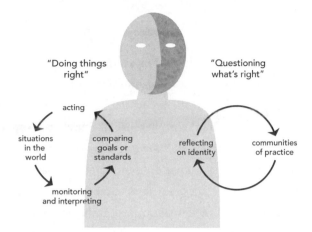

Figure 7-2. Purposeful behavior.
We are always engaging in situations in the world. In a systems view of routine engagements, one acts and seeks to monitor and interpret the effects of one's actions, given
other potential influences on the situation. One then compares the monitored effects with
relevant goals or standards, and perhaps one initiates a follow-up action. In such routine
engagements, one is concerned with "doing things right." Then, one might have a gut-check
moment. One might feel the need to "check one's moral compass" and reexamine the goals
or standards according to which one engages in the world. To what extent do these goals or
standards reflect one's values, one's sense of identity? Unsatisfied with merely "doing things
right," one asks, how am I sensing or deciding what's right? Perhaps one seeks affirmation,
maybe unconsciously, by observing behaviors or imagining conversations with those in
the communities one looks to for experience, values, or judgment. Broadening the scope
of one's observations may bring fresh perspectives. These feedback loops ("doing things
right" and "questioning what's right") are sometimes referred to as first- and second-order
cybernetics or single- and double-loop learning.
Illustration: Crystal Rome and Howard Silverman

reinforce the platform's network effect: the more people who participate,
the more value it provides, and the higher its likelihood of success. "When
you cut your hair short," argued economist Thomas Schelling, "you change,
ever so slightly, other people's impressions of how long people are wearing
their hair."[17]

Given today's challenges, our purposes matter greatly. We all participate
in systems that we rely on for our food, water, energy, housing, transportation, education, health care, and so on, but such systems may not be achieving
one's goals or reflecting one's values. When that is the case, systems literacy can
inform one's efforts toward purposeful change.

Identity

We shape the world, and the world shapes us; that is a systems perspective on the human experience. An infant develops in relationship with those who rear her. We each become attached to the types of music we enjoy. In politics, my vote for a particular party strengthens my sense of myself as a supporter of this party. We are creatures of habit. One's *identity* develops in affiliation with the social systems—groups, norms, and so on—in which one participates.[18]

In ecological terms, the shape-and-be-shaped pattern of a system with its environment is sometimes called structural coupling or niche construction theory. Each cell and each organism must obtain energetic inputs from its environment, and with each consumption of food and each release of waste, it thereby modifies its environment, perhaps to its own detriment.[19] "Organisms do not experience environments," wrote geneticist Richard Lewontin. "They create them."[20]

In biology, consider symbiotic relationships. Looking back in time, all plant and animal life can be traced to the evolution of eukaryotic (i.e., nucleated) cells. It is now widely accepted that eukaryotes evolved through symbiosis: the living together of different organisms or, specifically, the integration of genetic material across organisms.[21] Looking inward, half or more of the cells in my body are bacterial, and this microbiome is critical to my own health.[22] "We have never been individuals," maintained developmental biologist Scott Gilbert and colleagues.[23] "We are walking communities," insisted evolutionary theorist Lynn Margulis.[24]

Be it socially, ecologically, or biologically, life is interconnected in complex ways, and these interconnections challenge individualistic understandings of human identity.

Emergent Social Patterns

"You can't truly want anything," taunted physicist Sean Carroll. "You're just a collection of atoms, and atoms don't have wants."[25] Carroll's quip illustrates the folly of reductionism—of trying to reduce all life's complexities to physical phenomena.

Although I am but atoms, such atoms hardly describe the whole of me. Likewise, the experience of water's wetness is not to be found in its hydrogen and oxygen molecules, and the experience of conversation emerges in and among those who speak and listen. *Emergence* is the phenomenon that a system exhibits behaviors or properties that arise from interactions among its structures or participants. More is different. The whole is more than the sum of the parts.[26]

As a result and in our social lives, events can take us by surprise: new industries are created, energy prices spike, and political waves come and go. Even so and beneath the flux, there are *patterns*: feedback-driven recurrences. Many such patterns are familiar in one form or another; the internet has helped to make them more visible. I have touched on ones like virtuous and vicious circles, bandwagon effects, and network effects. Here are two more types.

One emergent pattern is the power-law distribution, also known as the success-to-the-successful model or the 80/20 rule. The pattern is that, in general terms, a minority of the participants account for a majority of the activity (i.e., "20" percent account for "80" percent, although actual figures vary). Today, for example, Google, Facebook, and a few other websites and apps account for most internet use. Similarly, a few of the world's languages account for most of the speakers, and a minority of scientific papers account for a majority of citations from other papers. Another instance of this pattern is the recurring tendency of the rich to get richer. If I have a lot of resources—financial assets, social privilege, education, and so on—these resources enable me to gain more.[27]

Other patterns are based on the viral popularity or bandwagon effect described above. There might be a threshold of collective behavior in which the situation tips one way or another. For example, one's decision to leave a party or to vote for a particular candidate can be influenced by one's observations of what others are doing. Then the party might suddenly empty out or an unexpected candidate might emerge on top. Furthermore, collective outcomes may not be consistent with individual desires. Neighborhoods can become segregated, even when some people in the city prefer more diversity. Similarly, social media platforms can turn into echo chambers or filter bubbles in which opposing views are rarely encountered, despite individual preferences to the contrary.[28]

Counteracting such recurring tendencies is a question of design. Take the rich-get-richer pattern. One mechanism for regulating this tendency is a progressive income tax. Another is a protocol for periodic debt forgiveness, like the "jubilee" custom described in the Bible. Other policy designs might alleviate systemic inequities. One is a universal basic income for all citizens; another is a national fund of shared, common assets, the sale or rental of which provides dividends to all citizens.[29]

New policies or regulations will lead to newly emergent and possibly unanticipated systems behaviors. Thus, in policy and regulatory design, as in other fields of design, experimental, iterative, and adaptive are bywords of good practice.[30] "Social problems are never solved," cautioned design theorist Horst Rittel, writing in 1973 with urban designer Melvin Webber. "At best they are only re-solved—over and over again."[31]

Stability and Change

One commonality among all these systemic social patterns is simply time. History matters, and the order of events matters as well. As we live our lives, we each form, unconsciously or consciously, both our own identities and the identities of the systems in which we participate. Weighted with history, existing social systems develop a kind of stability or inertia. They reinforce or regulate existing behaviors, relationships, or biases. Powerful interests may seek to benefit from the status quo. We may feel stuck.[32]

"Creativity is a discontinuity," emphasized management theorist Russell Ackoff. "A creative act breaks with the chain that has come before it."[33] Based on the concept of a discontinuity or threshold, social innovation theorist Frances Westley and colleagues described three leverage points for systemic change in linked social-ecological systems: (1) destabilize undesirable systems, (2) strengthen alternatives, and (3) help individuals and organizations shift their affiliations from one to the next.

Consider the story of twentieth-century musical innovator Harry Partch, recounted in sociologist Howard Becker's "The Power of Inertia."[34] Partch created a nontraditional forty-three-tone musical scale and achieved some recognition, including Guggenheim grants and a concert at Carnegie Hall. He also encountered systemic difficulties. To stage a performance of his music, Partch had to devise a notation for his compositions, had to build his own instruments, and had to teach people to both read the new notation and play the new instruments. The notation, the instruments, and their practiced performance are each components of a social system, sometimes called a package or assemblage or, in the terminology of resilience and transition theory, a *regime*.[35] Notation, instruments, and practiced performance each reinforce the utility and value of the others, strengthening the stability of the regime as a whole. With his forty-three-tone alternative, Partch challenged the dominant regime of classical music composition, but the old regime proved more resilient.

Emphasizing the complexities in this story, Becker noted that whether Partch challenged the fundamental "identity" of classical music could not be conclusively stated one way or another. After all, his music was still composed by a composer, for an orchestra, to be performed in a concert hall. The music was packaged and sold in conventional ways. In sum, Partch was an innovator in some respects but not others.

This type of dilemma is quite common. Although a key strategy for escaping the stuckness of social systems is to strengthen their alternatives, what counts as alternative may be open to interpretation. Take electric cars, for example. If one is concerned about local air quality, electric cars are great because they emit no particulate pollution. If one is concerned about climate change, electric cars have a lot of potential, depending on sources of electricity. If, however, one is concerned about equity or urban sprawl, electric cars will seem less innovative. Their adoption does not directly challenge the transportation regime of private vehicle ownership and infrastructure, which is the dominant regime in most parts of the United States and many other countries. Electric cars are transformative in some respects but not others.

Faced with such complexities, farmer and essayist Wendell Berry advocated a design approach that he called "solving for pattern."[36] With each action or initiative, seek to simultaneously address as many of one's concerns as possible, without engendering new ones.

Practices for Purposeful Change

Systems views have significantly influenced contemporary understandings of the world. Looking back from 2016, science-fiction writer Bruce Sterling proclaimed, "Cybernetic feedback was Darwin-scale high concept."[37]

In this chapter, I have taken a broadly synthetic view of systems: from cybernetics, dynamics, and complexity to networks, resilience, and design.[38] I have woven a story of systems pioneers, systemic inquiries, and emergent patterns. Amid these narrative threads, there is also a story about *practices for purposeful change*. A systems perspective sheds light on such practices, the types of practices that can be used to develop capacities for change in personal, organizational, and social situations. In summary:

- Practices for change help in developing your capacity for action. To act with purpose is, as political theorist Hannah Arendt described, "to take an initiative" and "to set something into motion." Arendt distinguished such action from labor, "forced upon us by necessity," and from work, "prompted by utility."[39] This useful distinction invites the question, are there ways to align one's labor and work so as to support one's purposeful action?
- Practices for change help in becoming mindful of habitual entanglements. Pay attention to your own thinking. Develop gut-check sensibilities. Suspend assumptions, and question routines. It is not easy. "The great force of history," wrote novelist and social critic James Baldwin, "comes from the fact that we carry it within us, are unconsciously controlled by it in many ways."[40]
- Practices for change are practices of way-finding: making connections, developing potentialities, remaining adaptive, and finding one's flow. Systems scientist Donella Meadows once related, "My experience—having now many times created a vision and then brought it, in some form, into being—is that I never know, at the beginning, how to get there. But as I articulate the vision and share it with people, the path reveals itself."[41]
- Practices for change are appreciative. Look for signs of success. Some

people somewhere are working in ways that you would value as well. Community organizer John McKnight described beginning his engagements with the question, "What have people who live here done together to make things better?"[42] Philosopher C. West Churchman maintained, "The systems approach begins when first you see the world through the eyes of another."[43]

When existing systems have been destabilized, one might well feel a heightened sense of vulnerability. In such times, community support is essential. When existing systems have been destabilized is also when opportunities for systemic change arise. Another world is possible. Systems that are more equitable and more resilient to environmental change are ours to design and develop.

Notes

1. Note that key systems terms are used in various ways. The terms *complex* and *complexity*, for example, might refer to a tradition or field of systems study, a mathematical theory or approach, a descriptor of situations and systems in the world, or a descriptor of individual perceptions, as in "The complexity of a system is in the eye of the beholder," in C. S. Holling, "Perceiving and Managing the Complexity of Ecological Systems," in *The Science and Praxis of Complexity: Contributions to the Symposium Held at Montpellier, France, 9–11 May, 1984* (Tokyo: United Nations University, 1985), 217. For an introduction to the study of complexity, see Melanie Mitchell, *Complexity: A Guided Tour* (New York: Oxford University Press, 2009).

2. For the phrase *systems literacy*, I am indebted to Peter Tuddenham. Drawing on forty years of experience in systems education at the Open University, Ray Ison and Monica Shelley described systems literacy as a curriculum for helping students recover or foster a systemic sensibility and thereby develop systems thinking in practice. Ray Ison and Monica Shelley, "Governing in the Anthropocene: Contributions from Systems Thinking in Practice?," *Systems Research and Behavioral Science* 33 (2016): 589–94.

3. On feedback dynamics and diagrams, see Donella Meadows, *Thinking in Systems: A Primer* (White River Junction, VT: Chelsea Green, 2008); George P. Richardson, "Problems in Causal Loop Diagrams Revisited," *System Dynamics Review* 13 (1997): 247–52; and Peter M. Senge, *The Fifth Discipline: The Art and Practice of The Learning Organization* (New York: Currency / Doubleday, 1990).

4. General systems theory, in particular, has emphasized the study of isomorphisms or patterns. See, for example, Robert Rosen, "Old Trends and New Trends in General Systems Research," *International Journal of General Systems* 5 (1979): 173–84.

5. Arthur Koestler and J. R. Smithies, *Beyond Reductionism: New Perspectives in the Life Sciences* (New York: MacMillan, 1969); Debora Hammond, *The Science of Synthesis: Exploring the Social Implications of General Systems Theory* (Boulder: University Press of Colorado, 2003). For a contemporary example of a reductionism critique, see Joichi Ito and Jeff Howe, *Whiplash: How to Survive Our Faster Future* (New York: Grand Central, 2016).

6. Gregory Bateson, as quoted in his daughter Nora Bateson's film, *An Ecology of Mind* (Cologne, Germany: Mindjazz Pictures, 2011), http://www.anecologyofmind.com.

7. John Muir, *My First Summer in the Sierra, 1869* (Boston and New York: Houghton Mifflin, 1911), 243–44.

8. Donna Haraway, "Anthropocene, Capitalocene, Chthulucene: Staying with the Trouble," Aarhus University Research on the Anthropocene, May 9, 2014, https://vimeo.com/97663518.

9. *The Compact Oxford English Dictionary*, 2nd ed. (1991), dates the hyphenated word *feed-back* to 1920. Online etymological sources date the word, in hyphenated and two-word form, to 1909 and 1865, respectively. See https://en.wikipedia.org/wiki/User:Trevithj.

10. For a systems-based study of rice farming, see Stephen Lansing, *Perfect Order: Recognizing Complexity in Bali* (Princeton, NJ: Princeton University Press, 2006).

11. On the historical development of feedback control devices, see Otto Mayr, *The Origins of Feedback Control* (Cambridge, MA: MIT Press, 1970); David A. Mindell, *Between Human and Machine: Feedback, Control, and Computing before Cybernetics* (Baltimore, MD: Johns Hopkins University Press, 2002); and George Richardson, *Feedback Thought in Social Science and Systems Theory* (Waltham, MA: Pegasus Communications, 1991).

12. Arturo Rosenblueth, Norbert Wiener, and Julian Bigelow, "Behavior, Purpose and Teleology," *Philosophy of Science* 10 (1943): 19.

13. On Norbert Wiener and cybernetics, see Flo Conway and Jim Siegelman, *Dark Hero of the Information Age: In Search of Norbert Wiener—The Father of Cybernetics* (New York: Basic Books, 2005); Norbert Wiener, *Cybernetics or Control and Communication in the Animal and the Machine* (Cambridge, MA: MIT Press, 1948); and Jean-Pierre Dupuy, *The Mechanization of Mind: On the Origins of Cognitive Science*, trans. M. D. DeBevoise (Princeton, NJ: Princeton University Press, 2000).

14. For a contemporary perspective on cybernetics, see Paul Pangaro, accessed March 29, 2017, http://www.pangaro.com/definition-cybernetics.html.

15. The description of purposeful behavior in the caption of figure 7-2 draws on sources that include Chris Argyris, *On Organizational Learning*, 2nd ed. (Oxford: Blackwell,

1999); Daniel Kahneman, *Thinking, Fast and Slow* (New York: Farrar, Straus and Giroux, 2011); Ray Ison, *Systems Practice: How to Act in a Climate Change World* (London: Springer, 2010); Karl Weick, *Sensemaking in Organizations* (Thousand Oaks, CA: Sage Publications, 1995); and Etienne Wenger, *Communities of Practice: Learning, Meaning, and Identity* (Cambridge: Cambridge University Press, 1998).

16. On incorporating purpose, reflexivity, or complexity into scientific research and practice, see Hilary Bradbury, "Introduction: How to Situate and Define Action Research," in *The Sage Handbook of Action Research*, 3rd ed., ed. Hilary Bradbury (Thousand Oaks, CA: Sage, 2015); Karl H. Müller and Alexander Riegler, "Second-Order Science: A Vast and Largely Unexplored Science Frontier," *Constructivist Foundations* 10 (2015): 7–15; and Stuart A. Kauffman and Arran Gare, "Beyond Descartes and Newton: Recovering Life and Humanity," *Progress in Biophysics and Molecular Biology* 119 (2015): 219–44.

17. Thomas C. Schelling, *Micromotives and Macrobehavior* (New York: Norton, 1978), 28.

18. On identity, see Peter J. Burke and Jan E. Stets, *Identity Theory* (Oxford: Oxford University Press, 2009); Howard Silverman and Gregory M. Hill, "The Dynamics of Purposeful Change: A Model," *Ecology and Society* (in review); and Wenger, *Communities of Practice.*

19. On ecological theories of structural coupling and niche construction, see Fritjof Capra and Pier Luigi Luisi, *A Systems View of Life* (Cambridge: Cambridge University Press, 2014); John F. Odling-Smee, Kevin N. Laland, and Marcus W. Feldman, *Niche Construction: The Neglected Process in Evolution* (Princeton, NJ: Princeton University Press, 2003); and Thomas C. Scott-Phillips et al., "The Niche Construction Perspective: A Critical Appraisal," *Evolution* 68 (2014): 1231–43.

20. Richard C. Lewontin, *Biology as Ideology: The Doctrine of DNA* (New York: HarperCollins, 1991), 109.

21. This paragraph draws particularly on the work of Lynn Margulis. On Margulis's definitions of symbiosis and symbiogenesis, see Lynn Margulis and Dorion Sagan, *Acquiring Genomes* (New York: Basic Books, 2002); Lynn Margulis, "Lynn Margulis 2004 Rutgers Interview," uploaded April 12, 2010, https://www.youtube.com/watch?v=b8xqu_TlQPU; and Jan Sapp, "Too Fantastic for Polite Society: A Brief History of Symbiosis Theory," in *Lynn Margulis: The Life and Legacy of a Scientific Rebel*, ed. Dorian Sagan (White River Junction, VT: Chelsea Green, 2012). On the pre-Margulis origins of symbiosis theory, see Sapp, "Too Fantastic for Polite Society."

22. For a recent review of microbiological sciences, see Ed Yong, *I Contain Multitudes: The Microbes within Us and a Grander View of Life* (New York: HarperCollins, 2016).

23. Scott Gilbert, Jan Sapp, and Alfred I. Tauber, "A Symbiotic View of Life: We Have Never Been Individuals," *Quarterly Review of Biology* 87 (2012): 325.

24. Charles Mann, "Lynn Margulis: Science's Unruly Earth Mother," *Science* 252 (1991): 378.

25. Sean Carroll, *The Big Picture: On the Origins of Life, Meaning, and the Universe Itself* (New York: Dutton, 2016), 113.

26. On emergence, see P. W. Anderson, "More Is Different," *Science* 177 (1982): 393–96; and Steven Johnson, *Emergence: The Connected Lives of Ants, Brains, Cities, and Software* (New York: Scribner, 2001).

27. On the 80/20 or success-to-the-successful pattern, see Pierpaolo Andriani and Bill McKelvey, "From Gaussian to Paretian Thinking: Causes and Implications of Power Laws in Organizations," *Organization Science* 20 (2009): 1053–71; Albert-László Barabási, *Linked: How Everything Is Connected to Everything Else and What It Means for Business, Science, and Everyday Life* (New York: Plume 2003); David Clingingsmith, "Are the World's Languages Consolidating? The Dynamics and Distribution of Language Populations," *Economic Journal* 127 (2015): 143–76; Daniel H. Kim and Virginia Anderson, *System Archetype Basics: From Story to Structure* (Waltham, MA: Pegasus Communications, 1998); and Derek J. de Solla Price, "Networks of Scientific Papers," *Science* 149 (1965): 510–15.

28. On threshold models of collective behavior, see Mark Granovetter, "Threshold Models of Collective Behavior," *American Journal of Sociology* 83 (1978): 1420–43; Eli Pariser, *The Filter Bubble: How the New Personalized Web Is Changing What We Read and How We Think* (New York: Penguin Press, 2011); and Schelling, *Micromotives and Macrobehavior*.

29. For introductions to these policy designs, see https://en.wikipedia.org/wiki/Jubilee_(Christianity), https://en.wikipedia.org/wiki/Basic_income, and http://dividendsforall.net/.

30. On systems and design, see Howard Silverman, "Designerly Ways for Action Research," in *The Sage Handbook of Action Research*, 3rd ed., ed. Hilary Bradbury (Thousand Oaks, CA: Sage, 2015); and John Thackara, *How to Thrive in the Next Economy: Designing Tomorrow's World Today* (London: Thames and Hudson, 2015).

31. W. Horst, J. Rittel, and Melvin M. Webber, "Dilemmas in a General Theory of Planning," *Policy Sciences* 4 (1973): 160.

32. On time, stability, and inertia, see Scott E. Page, "Path Dependence," *Quarterly Journal of Political Science* 1 (2006): 87–115; and Ilya Prigogine and Isabelle Stengers, *Order Out of Chaos: Man's New Dialogue with Nature* (New York: Bantam, 1984).

33. Russell Ackoff, "If Russ Ackoff Had Given a TED Talk …," 1994, uploaded October 23, 2010, https://www.youtube.com/watch?v=OqEeIG8aPPk; Frances Westley et

al., "Tipping toward Sustainability: Emerging Pathways of Transformation," *Ambio* 40 (2011): 762–80.

34. Howard S. Becker, "The Power of Inertia," *Qualitative Sociology* 18 (1995): 301–9; Harry Partch, "Harry Partch—Music Studio," uploaded January 7, 2008, https://www.youtube.com/watch?v=P8NIpPhXpfQ.

35. On assemblage theory, see Manuel DeLanda, *Assemblage Theory* (Edinburgh: Edinburgh University Press, 2016). On transition theory, see Derk Loorbach, "To Transition! Governance Panarchy in the New Transformation," 2014, http://www.transitiefocus.com/wp-content/uploads/2014/11/To_Transition-Loorbach-2014.pdf. On resilience theory, see Brian Walker and David Salt, *Resilience Practice: Building Capacity to Absorb Disturbance and Maintain Function* (Washington DC: Island Press, 2012); and Westley et al., "Tipping toward Sustainability."

36. See chapter 9, "Solving for Pattern," in Wendell Berry, *The Gift of Good Land: Further Essays Cultural and Agricultural* (San Francisco: North Point, 1981).

37. Bruce Sterling, "How the Cyber Age Gave Peace a Chance," *New Scientist*, August 17, 2016, https://www.newscientist.com/article/mg23130874-700-how-the-cyber-age-gave-peace-a-chance/.

38. For synthetic views of systems traditions as belonging to a common field of study and practice, see Michael Jackson, *Systems Approaches to Management* (New York: Kluwer Academic, 2000); and Magnus Ramage and Karen Shipp, *Systems Thinkers* (London: Springer, 2009).

39. Hannah Arendt, *The Human Condition* (Chicago: University of Chicago Press, 1958), 177.

40. James Baldwin, "The White Man's Guilt," *Ebony* 20, no. 10 (August 1965): 47.

41. Donella Meadows, "The Power of Vision," International Society for Ecological Economics, 1994, uploaded July 9, 2010, http://vimeo.com/13213667.

42. John McKnight, "Asset Based Community Development," March 2, 2012, https://www.youtube.com/watch?v=pSwpQWAUQAc.

43. C. West Churchman, *The Systems Approach* (New York: Delacorte, 1968), 231. On appreciation, see also Geoffrey Vickers, *The Art of Judgment: A Study of Policy Making* (London: Chapman and Hall, 1965; Thousand Oaks, CA: Sage, 1995).

CHAPTER 8

A Crash Course in the Science
of Sustainability

Margaret Robertson

WHAT IS SUSTAINABILITY? Sustainability means enduring into the long-term future; it refers to systems and processes that are able to operate and persist on their own over long periods of time. The adjective *sustainable* means "able to continue without interruption" or "able to endure without failing." The word *sustainability* comes from the Latin verb *sustinēre*, "to maintain, sustain, support, endure," made from the roots *sub*, "up from below," and *tenēre*, "to hold." The German equivalent, *Nachhaltigkeit*, first appeared in the 1713 forestry book *Sylvicultura Oeconomica* written by Hans Carl von Carlowitz, a mining administrator in a region whose mining and metallurgy industry depended on timber and who realized that deforestation could cause the local economy to collapse. Carlowitz described how, through sustainable management of this renewable resource, forests could supply timber indefinitely.

We are part of linked systems of humans and nature, so the study of sustainability goes beyond environmentalism. A key attribute of the field is a recognition of three interrelated dimensions: ecological, economic, and social. The planet faces many problems that are connected, including poverty, impaired

147

health, overpopulation, resource depletion, food and water scarcity, political instability, and the destruction of the life support systems on which we all depend. Scholars debate about whether environmental destruction causes poverty or whether poverty causes environmental destruction out of sheer desperation, but it is agreed that they go together.[1] Because they are all connected, we cannot fix one problem in isolation.

The three dimensions of ecological sustainability, economic opportunity, and social inclusion are captured in the term *sustainable development*. The term was introduced in *World Conservation Strategy*, a 1980 report by the International Union for Conservation of Nature and the first international document to use the term.[2] It was made popular in the 1987 report *Our Common Future*, produced by the World Commission on Environment and Development and commonly known as the Brundtland report, which explicitly points at the connection between environment, economics, and equity. In the Brundtland report, sustainable development is defined as "development that meets the needs of the present without compromising the ability of future generations to meet their own needs."[3] (This wording has come to be the most commonly used definition of sustainability.) Sustainable development recognizes the rights of all people, including future generations, to grow and flourish.

These three dimensions—environment, economics, and equity—are sometimes called the "triple bottom line," a term introduced in 1997 by corporate responsibility expert John Elkington.[4] They are also known as the "three E's" and are sometimes referred to as the three pillars of sustainability or, in the business world, as "planet, people, and profit."[5]

Sustainability and Economics

We live on a rapidly changing planet that is fundamentally different than it was when any of us were children. Since the 1950s, population has more than doubled, global consumption of water has more than tripled, and the use of fossil fuels has quadrupled.[6] Synthetic pesticides and heavy metals are found in the tissues of every animal on Earth. The end of cheap fossil fuels is looming. The planet's sixth mass extinction is under way, with 50 percent of species alive today predicted to be gone by the year 2100.[7] Ninety percent of large fish have disappeared from many ocean fisheries, victims of overfishing. Where rivers empty into oceans, runoff laden with synthetic fertilizers has pulled oxygen out of coastal waters and left dead zones devoid of animal life. Coral reefs are dying and mollusk populations shrinking as carbon dioxide concentrations make ocean waters increasingly acidic. Mountain glaciers are melting, deserts are growing, sea level is rising, and waves of climate refugees are likely in the near future.

The driver of all this change is economic, in particular the economic growth model that has been at the core of human commercial activity since World War II. Ecological economists and other researchers say that continuation of the growth model is not just a bad idea; it is a physical impossibility.[8] The current economic system releases wastes into the environment faster than natural systems can process them and consumes renewable resources faster than they can be replenished. It consumes nonrenewable resources; once those are gone, they cannot be replenished.

Ecological economics is a branch of economics that developed in recent decades through the work of economists including E. F. Schumacher and Herman Daly and systems ecologist Robert Costanza. Conventional neoclassical economics sees nature as a supply depot and waste disposal service nested within the macroeconomy; Herman Daly referred to it as "empty world" economics because it developed during a time when humans were less numerous and it appeared that more forest, more prairie, and more ocean would always be available. In contrast, ecological economics sees the macroeconomy as a subsystem nested within the biosphere upon which it depends.[9] The field recognizes that, on a planet now filled with billions of humans, economics and ecosystems are interconnected in important ways and that it would be unrealistic to focus on either one to the exclusion of the other. Ecological economics can be thought of as "full world" economics.

Bringing together multiple disciplines can sometimes yield insights that were not previously known to either discipline by itself. Ecological economics is an example. Ecological economics joins together the fields of ecology and economics, applying natural laws—in particular the laws of thermodynamics—to the study of economics. A key idea is the recognition that growth cannot, in fact, go on forever, that nature has fundamental thresholds, and that there is no assurance that technological innovation can overcome problems caused by overshooting these limits. Instead of perpetual growth, ecological economics works toward optimization: a steady-state economy in dynamic equilibrium at an optimal scale. In this approach to economics without perpetual growth, equitable distribution will become important.[10]

To an ecological economist, growth is different from development. Growth is quantitative; it means an increase in size or an increase in production. Development is qualitative; it means an improvement in the quality of goods and services, with or without growth. Sustainable development involves an increase in quality without a quantitative growth in consumption or production. Sustainable growth is physically impossible because the biosphere is finite. In contrast, sustainable development—a qualitative change in which well-being does not decline and may improve—is indeed possible. Well-being includes both human quality of life and the health of all other parts of the biosphere. Sustainable development would keep natural capital intact, living off nature's income rather than consuming its capital.

Capital is the supply of resources; it is wealth used for the production of more wealth. *Human-made capital* includes things such as machinery, vehicles, tools, buildings, and money. *Natural capital* includes ecosystem services and physical natural resources.[11] Neoclassical economists generally believe that human-made capital can be substituted for natural capital as long as the total amount remains unchanged.[12] The idea is that scarcity of natural resources will raise market prices, reducing their demand, and that technological innovation will then find substitutes, an example of the notion that technology can solve any problem.[13] This concept was introduced in the 1970s, and by the 1990s, it had become known as *weak sustainability*.[14] In contrast, ecological economists believe that human capital and natural capital are not interchangeable and that natural capital is the limiting factor, an approach known as *strong sustainability*. The climate system and biodiversity are examples of critical natural stocks that cannot be replaced by human-made capital.[15]

Herman Daly offers an example from marine fisheries. The number of fish in the oceans constitutes natural capital. The total wealth derived from this capital—measured in quantity of catches—is limited by the number of fishing boats. When the number of fish declines, however, substituting more human-made capital in the form of more fishing boats and more nets will not restore the quantity of catches or maintain the original quantity of total wealth.[16] Strong sustainability has implications not only for economics but also for environmental ethics, the "rights of nature," and intergenerational equity (the rights of future generations).[17]

Governance and the Commons

In his 1968 article "The Tragedy of the Commons," biologist Garrett Hardin described a scenario in which herdsmen sharing a common pasture each reap a benefit from adding an animal to his herd. As a result, individuals are motivated to keep adding animals, even though the disadvantage of degradation from additional overgrazing is shared by all the herdsmen. The *tragedy of the commons* has been used as a metaphor for the problems of overuse and degradation of natural resources.[18] Hardin later clarified that what he described was actually a "tragedy of an unmanaged commons."[19]

Common pool resources (CPRs) are resources from which it is difficult to exclude or limit users and in which use of the resources by one person decreases the benefits for other users.[20] Examples include forests, fisheries, aquifers, and the atmosphere. A commons is not just a resource; it is a CPR, plus a community, plus a set of protocols (the rules and social practices for managing the resource).[21]

Understanding of commons governance was advanced by Elinor Ostrom, who was awarded the Nobel Prize in Economics in 2009 for her analysis of how local groups of users devise arrangements for managing common-pool resources. Ostrom's field studies of a diverse range of hundreds of enduring, self-governing CPRs found they all exhibit similar design principles: in each commons, there are clearly defined boundaries with respect to who has rights to appropriate the resource and the extent of the resource itself; users create rules based on local conditions; users participate in creating or influencing roles; there are methods of monitoring resource use; there is a system of graduated sanctions for "free riders" and users who violate the rules; there are mechanisms in place for resolving disputes; external governmental authorities do not prevent users from creating their own rules of use; and the commons are nested in multiple layers within larger systems of governance, a pattern she called polycentric governance.[22] These polycentric, overlapping systems featuring multiple governing authorities at differing scales illustrate that there is no one ideal approach. In some situations, self-organized community rules work best; in others, laws of larger government jurisdictions work best; and often, it is a combination of scales that works best.[23]

Commons are evolving social contracts for using shared resources, with rules finely tuned to local place that constantly adapt to changes. Commons are not the result of centralized direction or a single authority; they are self-organized groups of elements "whose rich patterns of interactions produce emergent properties that are not easy to predict by analyzing the separate parts of a system."[24] Such systems adapt by incrementally changing their rules, modifying the details but retaining coherence under changing conditions and thereby exhibiting the attributes of *resilience*. As with all resilient systems, diversity and the "emergence of complex larger-scale behavior" from interactions of smaller elements are key features.[25] Such systems often look messy but are, in fact, robust.

Systems Thinking and Sustainability

The study of sustainability is the study of systems. A *system* is a coherently organized set of interconnected elements that constitutes a whole,[26] where the identity of the whole is always more than the sum of its parts. The properties of the whole cannot be predicted by examining the parts; they are *emergent properties*, arising from the relationships and interactions of the parts. Systems are nested within other systems. A cell, an organ, and a human body are all systems, as are an ecosystem, an ocean, and an economy. Earth itself is a system, made of myriad other nested and interconnected systems; it is the focus of a field of study known as Earth system science. (For more on systems literacy, see chapter 7.)

Systems science became part of the public conversation in 1972 with the publication of the groundbreaking *Limits to Growth*, the result of a study by Massachusetts Institute of Technology systems scientists Donella Meadows, Dennis Meadows, and Jørgen Randers, commissioned by a think tank called the Club of Rome. The report included the first modern use of the word *sustainable*.[27] Using cutting-edge computer models, the researchers analyzed in detail how economic growth, consumption, and population growth would cause humans to exceed the limits of Earth's carrying capacity and lead to a condition of overshoot.

Carrying Capacity and Ecological Footprint

Carrying capacity is the maximum number of individuals a given environment can support indefinitely without degrading the ecosystem. For humans, some environments have a larger carrying capacity than others depending on the patterns of consumption of the human culture that lives there. Ultimately, the planet as a whole has a carrying capacity. If all humans on the planet had the same level of resource consumption as people in the United States and Canada, we would need 4.5 planet Earths even if the population did not grow at all. Given that the quantities of resources on the planet are more or less fixed, as population rises, the same resources must be divided among more people, so the per capita quantity that can be consumed sustainably shrinks.[28]

Even though most of humanity does not consume as much as Americans and Canadians do, collectively our consumption requires 140 percent of Earth's carrying capacity[29] and is on track to require 200 percent by the 2030s.[30] That is to say, we are already in *overshoot*: the condition in which human demands exceed the regenerative capacities of the biosphere by depleting its natural capital and overfilling its waste sinks. Herman Daly identified four conditions for avoiding overshoot: to live sustainably within Earth's carrying capacity, humans would need to (1) maintain the health of ecosystems (our life-support systems), (2) use renewable resources at a rate no faster than they can be regenerated, (3) use nonrenewable resources at a rate no faster than they can be replaced by the discovery of renewable substitutes, and (4) emit wastes and pollutants at a rate no faster than the rate at which they can be safely assimilated.[31]

Carrying capacity's inverse is the *ecological footprint*, a concept developed in the early 1990s by Mathis Wackernagel and William Rees. Ecological footprint analysis quantifies the amount of productive land and water area required to produce the resources we consume and to absorb the waste we generate (expressed as land area). Calculating ecological footprints allows human demand to be compared to the biosphere's carrying capacity. Ecological footprints are widely used and can be calculated at any scale, from an individual person to an entire nation. In 2010, the global carrying capacity of the planet was estimated to be 4.5 acres per person, whereas the global average ecological footprint was 6.7 acres per person,[32] which again indicates that humans have already overshot Earth's carrying capacity. (Meanwhile, the average ecological footprint in the United States was estimated in 2010 to be 19.8 acres per person.[33]) Footprint calculators are available through the Global Footprint Network website and elsewhere.

Ecological footprint analysis is a rigorous yet easily understandable tool for communicating impact, and it monitors the combined impact of a variety of indicators. It cannot, however, measure some kinds of impacts, such as water use, pollution, or ecosystem disturbance, nor can it measure ecosystem resilience or the economic and social dimensions of sustainability.[34] It documents lagging indicators, or what happened in the past, but it does not document leading indicators, numbers that change before results and thus predict future trends.

Renewable resources can support human activities indefinitely as long as we do not use them more rapidly than they can regenerate. It is analogous to living off the interest in a savings account and not spending the capital. We have the planetary equivalent of a savings account, but it is made of plants, animals, soil, water, and air.[35] This natural capital provides *ecosystem services*, the biological functions that support life, including provision of materials and food, assimilation of wastes, seed dispersal, pollination, nutrient recycling, purification of air and water, and climate regulation.

Living in the Anthropocene

Geologists divide time on Earth into segments based on physical characteristics of geology, climate, and life. The Holocene was the 10,000-year epoch spanning all written human history until now, a time between ice ages with a warm and unusually stable climate that allowed civilization to develop (see chapter 2, figure 2-1). These extraordinarily stable conditions made it possible for population to expand, agriculture to appear, and human cultures to arise and flourish.[36] Research indicates that without negative human impacts, the ideal conditions of the Holocene would probably have continued for several thousand years more.[37]

Now, however, we live at the beginning of a new geological epoch known as the Anthropocene, an unprecedented period in which human activity has become such a powerful force that it has major, planet-scale effects on climate and on every living system. The term *Anthropocene*, from the Greek words *anthropo*, "human," and *cene*, "new" or "recent," was proposed in 2000 by atmospheric chemist Paul Crutzen and biologist Eugene Stoermer. Each time period, such as an epoch, leaves behind a physical "stratigraphic signature" that will still be visible in the geological record millions of years from now.[38] Crutzen and Stoermer argued that observable changes in lake sediments, ice cores, atmospheric chemistry, and other indicators of humanity's planetary impact warranted recognition of the new epoch.

The International Commission on Stratigraphy (ICS) is the official body that formally establishes the geological time scale; the Anthropocene Working Group within the ICS is investigating whether a new epoch should be officially designated and, if so, what physical evidence should be used as its marker. The term is already used widely by scientists, the majority of whom agree that Earth has entered the Anthropocene.[39]

The Anthropocene epoch is generally understood to have begun around 1800 at the start of the Industrial Revolution.[40] Beginning in 1945, the Anthropocene entered a second stage researchers identify as the Great Acceleration, when multiple aspects of human impact—including population, resource use, and environmental deterioration—began expanding exponentially.[41] Graphs of each of these impacts reveal a similar curve, with a shape often compared to the blade of a hockey stick (see chapter 2, figures 2-2 and 2-3).

Humans have become a geological force on a planetary scale. One way to address the enormous challenges that confront us is to identify the global boundaries within which it is safe to operate for each of several interrelated systems.[42] In 2009, a group of scientists undertook a collaborative research effort to define the crucial processes and global boundary conditions that could ensure that the planet remains in a stable, Holocene-like state, a "safe operating space" within which human society could continue to develop.[43] They defined planetary boundaries for nine interdependent areas of the global commons—(1) climate change, (2) biodiversity loss, (3) excess nitrogen and phosphorus production, (4) stratospheric ozone depletion, (5) ocean acidification, (6) freshwater consumption, (7) land use change, (8) air pollution, and (9) chemical pollution—and mapped them onto a radial graph with one wedge for each area of concern and with boundaries denoted by concentric rings. The concept of planetary boundaries and their graphic illustration was a powerful way to communicate complex scientific issues to a broad lay audience (see chapter 2, figure 2-5).[44] The researchers found that humanity has already exceeded the safe boundaries for the first three: climate change, biodiversity loss, and nitrogen production.[45] As is typical of complex systems, the planetary boundaries are interconnected; so, crossing one boundary may shift the positions or critical thresholds of other boundaries.[46]

Sustainability and Resilience

Much sustainability work today focuses on the concept of resilience. Resilience science originated in the field of ecology and is based on the understanding that life is not static, that change is inevitable. Resilience is the capacity of a system to accommodate disturbance and still retain its basic function and structure;[47] it is the capacity to cope with change. A resilient system adapts to changes without losing its essential qualities. All systems that are resilient share common traits: they are self-organizing and feature diversity, redundancy, and connectivity. We understand that humans and nature are not separate, so, in sustainability work, the systems are known as social-ecological systems: linked systems of humans and nature.[48] (See chapter 9 for more on the science of resilience.)

Sustainability and resilience are not synonymous; rather, they are interrelated concepts. They provide complementary frameworks that are employed toward the same goal: to enable social-ecological systems to continue into the long-term future. A sustainability approach identifies long-term goals, examines strategies for achieving those goals, and systematically evaluates using indicators. A resilience approach emphasizes change as a normal condition, recognizes that a system may exist in multiple stable states, and focuses on building adaptive capacity to respond to unexpected shocks and disturbance. Sustainability scholar Charles Redman explained it this way: "Sustainability prioritizes outcomes; resilience prioritizes process."[49]

Conclusion

The Holocene has apparently come to an end, and humanity faces novel conditions that it has not encountered before. We face multiple, global-scale issues, including food scarcity, aquifer depletion, pollution, habitat destruction, extinction, depletion of renewable and nonrenewable resources, climate destabilization, social inequity, failing states, growing control by powerful corporate interests, and widening gaps between rich and poor. Many of these issues are what are known as *wicked problems*, problems that are difficult to solve because they are complex, interconnected, and continually evolving.[50] Behind them all lie two fundamental drivers: consumption, built on the economic growth model; and human population growth.

The question is not whether we will change; rather, the questions are how we will change and what form the transition will take. Navigating the shifting conditions will involve transformations in the sociocultural realm while we strive to avoid crossing planetary-scale thresholds into an undesirable state shift in the biospheric realm. It will also require that we find ways to live and work together like never before. We will need to shift rapidly away from fossil fuels, power our lives with renewable energy sources, and use energy—whatever the source—more efficiently than we do today. We will need to reduce per-capita resource consumption, provision ourselves from zero-waste circular economies, reduce population growth, and provide food to increasing numbers of people without converting new areas of land or destroying habitat. We will need to live within the planet's capacity to support us and our fellow creatures into the long-term future. We will need to define precisely what is meant by sustainability; use those definitions to measure and monitor trends so that we can assess when we are moving toward or away from sustainability; and develop evidence-based strategies with the potential for real, measurable progress.[51] We will need not just technological adaptations, but social and political ones as well. Sustainability will depend on having informed, ecologically literate citizens working toward healthy ecosystems, genuine social inclusion, and equitable distribution of resources. As we build the foundations for a thriving, sustainable human civilization and biosphere, we will need strong communities, networks of all kinds, and participatory governance at multiple scales.[52]

Humans have gone through several major transitions in their history: the discovery of fire, the development of language, the development of agriculture and civilization, and the Industrial Revolution. Today, we live on the threshold of what Richard Heinberg (chapter 3) has called the "fifth great turning,"[53] a turn away from a fossil fuel–powered, climate-destabilizing, growth-based industrial economy and toward a sustainable, regenerative society.

Portions of this chapter were adapted with permission from Margaret Robertson, Sustainability Principles and Practice, *2nd ed. (London: Routledge, 2017).*

Notes

1. Jeremy L. Caradonna, *Sustainability: A History* (New York: Oxford University Press, 2014).
2. Caradonna, *Sustainability*, 141.
3. World Commission on Environment and Development, *Our Common Future* (Oxford: Oxford University Press, 1987), 43.
4. John Elkington, *Cannibals with Forks: The Triple Bottom Line of 21st Century Business* (Gabriola Island, BC: New Society, 1998), 70.
5. Elkington, *Cannibals with Forks*, 55.
6. Jonathan Foley, "Boundaries for a Healthy Planet," *Scientific American*, April 2010, 54–57.
7. Edward O. Wilson, *The Future of Life* (London: Abacus, 2002), 102.
8. Herman Daly and Joshua Farley, *Ecological Economics: Principles and Applications* (Washington, DC: Island Press, 2003), 63.
9. Daly and Farley, *Ecological Economics*, 15.
10. Daly and Farley, *Ecological Economics*, 12.

11. Carl Folke, "Respecting Planetary Boundaries and Reconnecting to the Biosphere," in *State of the World 2013: Is Sustainability Still Possible?*, ed. Worldwatch Institute (Washington, DC: Island Press, 2013), 19.

12. Robert Costanza and Ida Kubiszewski, eds., *Creating a Sustainable and Desirable Future* (Singapore: World Scientific, 2014), 180.

13. Sustainable Scale Project, *Carrying Capacity*, 2003, http://www.sustainablescale.org/ConceptualFramework/UnderstandingScale/MeasuringScale/CarryingCapacity.aspx.

14. Herman E. Daly, "Economics in a Full World," *Scientific American* 293, no. 3 (September 2005): 103.

15. International Panel on Climate Change, *Climate Change 2014: Mitigation of Climate Change*, Contribution of Working Group III to the Fifth Assessment Report of the Intergovernmental Panel on Climate Change, ed. O. Edenhofer et al. (Cambridge: Cambridge University Press, 2014), 11.

16. Daly, "Economics in a Full World," 103.

17. Economist David Pearce, author of the 1989 best seller *Blueprint for a Green Economy*, illustrated the anthropocentric and ecocentric attributes of weak and strong sustainability along a "sustainability spectrum." David Pearce, *Blueprint 3: Measuring Sustainable Development* (London: Earthscan, 1993), 18–19.

18. Elinor Ostrom, *Coping with Tragedies of the Commons*, paper presented at the 1998 Annual Meeting of the Association for Politics and the Life Sciences, Boston, September 3–6, 1998, 1.

19. David Bollier, *Green Governance: Ecological Survival, Human Rights, and the Commons* (Cambridge: Cambridge University Press, 2013), 27.

20. Elinor Ostrom, *Governing the Commons: The Evolution of Institutions for Collective Action* (Cambridge: Cambridge University Press, 1990), 31.

21. Bollier, *Green Governance*, 141.

22. Ostrom, *Governing the Commons*, 88–101.

23. Elinor Ostrom, *The Future of the Commons: Beyond Market Failure and Government Regulation*. London: Institute of Economic Affairs, 2012), 70.

24. Ostrom, *Coping with Tragedies*, 21.

25. Ostrom, *Coping with Tragedies*, 21.

26. Donella Meadows, *Thinking in Systems: A Primer* (White River, VT: Chelsea Green, 2008), 188.

27. Caradonna, *Sustainability*, 138.

28. Robert Engelman, "Beyond Sustainababble," in *State of the World 2013: Is Sustainability Still Possible?*, ed. Worldwatch Institute (Washington, DC: Island Press, 2013), 9.

29. B. Ewing et al., *The Ecological Footprint Atlas 2010* (Oakland, CA: Global Footprint Network, 2010), 18.

30. Paul Gilding, *The Great Disruption* (New York: Bloomsbury, 2011), 52.

31. Herman E. Daly, *Steady-State Economics*, 2nd ed. (Washington, DC: Island Press, 1991).

32. Ewing et al., *Ecological Footprint Atlas 2010*, 18.

33. Ewing et al., *Ecological Footprint Atlas 2010*, 72.

34. Ewing et al., *Ecological Footprint Atlas 2010*, 90.

35. Paul Hawken, Amory B. Lovins, and L. Hunter Lovins, *Natural Capitalism: Creating the Next Industrial Revolution* (Boston: Back Bay Books, 2008).

36. Anders Wijkman and Johan Rockström, *Bankrupting Nature: Denying Our Planetary Boundaries* (London: Routledge, 2012), 38.

37. Wijkman and Rockström, *Bankrupting Nature*, 40.

38. Elizabeth Kolbert, *The Sixth Extinction: An Unnatural History* (New York: Picador, 2014), 109.

39. Working Group on the "Anthropocene," Subcommission on Quaternary Stratigraphy, International Commission on Stratigraphy, "What Is the 'Anthropocene'?—Current Definition and Status," last saved January 4, 2016, http://quaternary.stratigraphy.org/workinggroups/anthropocene/.

40. Paul J. Crutzen, "Geology of Mankind," *Nature* 415 (January 2002): 23.

41. Will Steffen, Paul J. Crutzen, and John R. McNeill, "The Anthropocene: Are Humans Now Overwhelming the Great Forces of Nature?," *Ambio* 36, no. 8 (December 2007): 617.

42. Folke, "Respecting Planetary Boundaries," 22.

43. Johan Rockström et al., "A Safe Operating Space for Humanity," *Nature* 461, 7263 (2009): 472–75; Anders Wijkman and Johan Rockström, *Bankrupting Nature: Denying Our Planetary Boundaries* (London: Routledge, 2012), 44.

44. Folke, "Respecting Planetary Boundaries," 29.

45. Rockström et al., "A Safe Operating Space"; Johan Rockström et al., "Planetary Boundaries: Exploring the Safe Operating Space for Humanity," *Ecology and Society* 14, no. 2 (2009): 1–3, www.ecologyandsociety.org/vol14/iss2/art32/.

46. Folke, "Respecting Planetary Boundaries," 26.

47. Brian Walker and David Salt, *Resilience Thinking: Sustaining Ecosystems and People in a Changing World* (Washington, DC: Island Press, 2006), xiii.

48. Brian Walker and David Salt, *Resilience Practice: Building Capacity to Absorb Disturbance and Maintain Function* (Washington, DC: Island Press, 2012), 1.

49. Charles L. Redman, "Should Sustainability and Resilience Be Combined or Remain Distinct Pursuits?" *Ecology and Society* 19, no. 2 (2014): 37, http://www.ecologyandsociety.org/vol19/iss2/art37/.

50. Will Steffen, "Connecting the Solution to the Problem," *Solutions* 5, no. 4 (July/August 2014): 1.

51. Engelman, "Beyond Sustainababble," 13.

52. Engelman, "Beyond Sustainababble," 17.
53. Richard Heinberg, *The End of Growth: Adapting to Our New Economic Reality* (Gabriola Island, BC: New Society Publishers, 2011), 284.

CHAPTER 9

A Crash Course in the Science of Resilience

Brian Walker and David Salt

W E LIVE IN UNCERTAIN TIMES. As the human population grows, the variety of life declines, ice caps shrink, and our Earth system behaves in ways its species have never experienced. The past no longer provides us with a guide to how the future will behave, and we search for solutions while moving into an increasingly uncertain space. In such a time, resilience science provides important insights to help communities engage with the complex set of challenges they need to navigate.

This book explores the many dimensions of community resilience. In this chapter, we introduce the building blocks of the science of resilience, often referred to as resilience thinking. (Resilience thinking is based in part on systems science and uses some of its terminology, so you may find it helpful to first read chapter 7 on systems literacy.)

Resilience thinking is a large and growing multidisciplinary field of investigation, and there is not enough space here to explore it in any depth. Rather, our aim is to outline some of the basics and share a few insights before explaining the building blocks of resilience thinking. First, it is helpful to provide a little context around the notion of resilience itself. It is a very popular word, and its widespread use has led to considerable confusion about what it is we are actually talking about.

The Idea of Resilience

The idea of resilience is appealing. It is invoked time and again in government policy, business rhetoric, and corporate mission statements. Why do so many of our leaders cite resilience as a goal of society or industry or any particular region?

One idea of resilience is the notion of "bouncing back." The word itself comes from the Latin *resiliens*, which is the act of rebounding. In this sense, resilience relates to the capacity of a system to recover after being hit by some disturbance. That is a fairly attractive concept to a leader, an executive, or a parent responsible for managing a government, a company, or a family because "having resilience" carries with it the connotation that the system is in good condition and is being managed well. "Having resilience" means that, come what may, our resilience will see us through and that we will bounce back to just how we were before. Although this notion of resilience is attractive, it does not reflect the essence of resilience thinking, namely, that resilience is an emergent property of a complex system (it arises out of the interaction of the parts of the system) and that it is not always a good thing.

Assessing or even describing resilience is not easy; "something to do with bouncing back" is hardly a precise definition. What is more, in popular usage there are many different notions of what you might consider in assessing how resilient something is. Some people associate resilience with a growing economy, others with high levels of education, and yet others with levels of trust and sharing in an open society.

Defining Resilience

Resilience scientists define resilience as the capacity of a system to absorb disturbance and reorganize so as to retain essentially the same function, structure, and feedbacks; that is, it is to have the same "identity." Put simply, resilience is the ability to cope with shocks and keep functioning in much the same kind of way as before.

There is no single measurement or number that captures resilience; rather, it is underpinned by a suite of attributes. The important point is that resilience thinking is a form of *systems thinking*. To understand, assess, and manage resilience requires a capacity to engage with the system. It requires the ability to—in one way or another—describe the identity of the system, how that identity might be changing over time, and what threatens that identity.

Systems are made up of many interacting parts, and the systems in which humans are most interested (families, communities, cities, catchments, regions, and nations, etc.) are *complex adaptive systems*, also known as *self-organizing systems*. The real value of resilience thinking is that it gives us a way to engage with this complexity.

Some people use the terms *complex* and *complicated* interchangeably, but they are actually quite different things, and the difference is significant. The parts (or components) that make up a simple system are connected to one another in a direct and unvarying way, like the cogs in a clock mechanism; an intricate clock mechanism is a complicated system, but it is not complex. The parts that make up a complex system are connected, but not in a direct, linear, or predictable way.

Self-organizing systems have three key characteristics: their parts can change in response to changes in the environment, new parts are often added to the system, and there is always some form of selection at work on parts of the system and their interactions. Resilience thinking is basically a set of ideas on how to engage with and understand the complexity that these interacting ingredients give rise to.

We live in a complex world. The consequences of this complexity become more understandable when we attempt to engage with the resilience of the systems around us, which brings us to our building blocks.

The Building Blocks of Resilience Thinking

The components of resilience thinking all relate in one way or another to how self-organizing systems behave. Here we summarize these building blocks (figure

9-1) under the headings that best describe them: thresholds and domains; spec-ified resilience, general resilience, and adaptive capacity; transformation and transformability; adaptive cycles; and connections across scales.

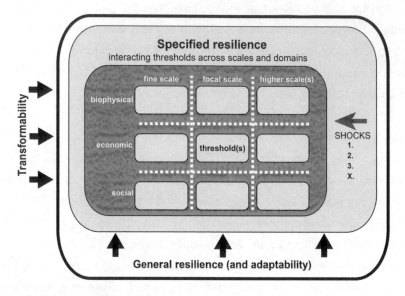

Figure 9-1. The building blocks of resilience thinking.
The building blocks include understanding thresholds, specified and general resilience, and transformability.
Source: Brian Walker and David Salt, *Resilience Practice: Building Capacity to Absorb Distur-bance and Maintain Function* (Washington, DC: Island Press, 2012).

Thresholds and Domains

An important feature of a complex system is that some of the significant changes that can occur in it do not happen smoothly. With such changes, part or even all of the system suddenly starts acting differently than it used to: we say that the behavior of the system has crossed a *threshold* from one *domain* to a different domain (figure 9-2). With this change of domain also comes a change in the system's identity (often with the loss of things we value in that system), and it is hard or sometimes impossible for the system to go back to the way it was.

Understanding thresholds and being alert for their presence are import-ant parts of resilience thinking. Thresholds are not everywhere, and where they do occur, the position of a threshold on the underlying variable can change

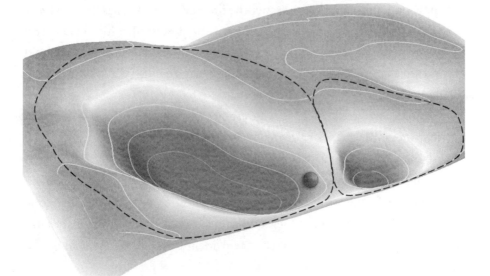

Figure 9-2. The system as a ball in a basin.
The ball is the state of the system. The basin in which it is moving is the system's domain; that is, it is the set of states that causes the ball to move toward equilibrium. The dotted line is a threshold separating alternate basins (or domains).
Source: Brian Walker and David Salt, *Resilience Thinking: Sustaining Ecosystems and People in a Changing World* (Washington, DC: Island Press, 2006).

(depending on other system variables). In other words, thresholds are not fixed. All that means that thresholds are very challenging to forecast and manage and are frequently not considered or even recognized.

In the definition of resilience, identity is a key word, and most people have their own idea about what constitutes the identity of the system in which they have a stake. For example, the identity of a farm might, according to the owner, be in the type of crop it produces and the owner's capacity to work with shifting markets and weather patterns. Of course, an identity is a multifaceted thing; it changes over time, and different people have different ideas of what a system's identity is (and what sustains that identity). Resilience practice is all about trying to bring those different ideas about identity together. It is about the *stakeholders* of a system sharing their mental models about how their system works.

Because resilience is the capacity of a complex system to cope with disturbance, what happens when a system is pushed too far? When the system does not come back to its original state after the pressure relents, it has lost its ability to reorganize and remain in the old domain; it has lost its identity and taken on a new one. That happens when an important system variable crosses a threshold beyond which a feedback mechanism changes, causing the system to then keep changing away from the domain it was in.

Around coral reefs, there is a threshold associated with the amount of nutrient present in the water. If the concentration goes above that level, algal growth outcompetes coral growth, and the reef then has a new, algal identity. A storm might damage the reef, but instead of coral reestablishing, you get algal-dominated reefs: the system has lost its resilience for remaining in the coral state. More than 80 percent of the Caribbean's coral reefs have been lost to this type of system shift. This new reef-system identity supports less fishing and attracts fewer tourists than before this shift.

On grassy rangelands, there is a threshold associated with the amount of grass. If the rangeland is overstocked and the amount of grass drops under a certain level, there is not enough grass to sustain regular fires, and the range-land then shifts to a woody shrub identity. Fire is the thing that structures these rangeland systems, and without regular fire, woody shrubs take over. The grass-dominated rangeland becomes a shrub-dominated rangeland with substantially less grazing potential than before.

For an example in the social domain, regional towns are sensitive to losing people. Thriving local economies can tip into stagnant backwaters when the population drops below a certain level, sometimes causing schools to close and house prices to plummet. Below some critical number of residents, the town changes from one of self-sustaining viability to one of shrinkage and loses its identity. Thresholds in the social domain are sometimes referred to as tipping points.

In all three examples (reefs, rangelands, and regional towns), the system does not look dramatically different as the threshold is crossed. Thus, people in it, or using it, are unlikely to know that a key feedback has changed and is now pulling in a different direction.

The domains on either side of a threshold can be defined by biophysical and social attributes of the system. An important part of resilience science is acknowledging that the social and biophysical attributes of a system are linked; indeed, the systems we work with are generally referred to as *social-ecological systems*. Of course, resilience science is hardly alone in highlighting these linkages. The hallmark of most sustainability science in recent decades has been the acknowledgment that environmental issues and social (including economic) issues are interconnected (e.g., triple-bottom-line accounting). An important insight provided by resilience science, however, is that linkages across domains are often connected to the nonlinear (i.e., complex) behavior associated with thresholds. In other words, if a system crosses a threshold separating two domains, it could trigger the crossing of another threshold elsewhere in the system.

For example, a rancher (or pastoralist) can carry a certain amount of debt. Beyond some critical level, however, the burden of debt might require the farmer to engage in imprudent management decisions, such as overstocking, to service that debt. Crossing this debt threshold in the economic domain might cause a threshold to be crossed in the biophysical domain with grass levels being reduced beyond a threshold at which woody shrubs dominate (and productivity plummets). It might also be the reverse: overstocking leads to the biophysical threshold being crossed, woody shrubs dominate, and grazing productivity falls, requiring unsustainable levels of debt to be taken on. In both situations, crossing one threshold increases the likelihood of crossing the other, and crossing both makes it that much harder for the farmer to reestablish the profitable viable identity of the farm.

Specified Resilience, General Resilience, and Adaptive Capacity

If resilience is about a complex system retaining its identity, does it only involve learning more about the system in question, finding out where thresholds might exist, and then optimizing management to prevent the system crossing those thresholds? Learning more about your system is important, but focusing on only known or suspected thresholds can be a trap.

Understanding how a system responds to a known or suspected threshold (and managing for this) is referred to as *specified resilience*. Having a capacity to deal with known thresholds is important, but there is also a need to have a capacity to deal with unsuspected thresholds and unimagined shocks. This capacity is referred to as *general resilience*, the capacity of a system to absorb disturbances of all kinds, including novel ones, so that all parts of the system keep functioning in the same kind of way.

When you prepare your system for a specific disturbance, you may be eroding its capacity to absorb other kinds of disturbances. In other words, there are trade-offs between different kinds of specified resilience. Channeling all your efforts into one kind can reduce resilience in other ways. Therefore, it is necessary to consider how to make a system generally resilient, in all parts of the system and to all kinds of shocks.

What things enhance general resilience? Studies of a variety of social-ecological systems suggest that diversity (especially a diversity of ways for performing the same function, each responding differently to different disturbances), openness (allowing immigration and emigration), reserves, tightness of feedbacks, modularity, a culture of learning and experimentation, and high levels of social capital are all important characteristics of systems with high levels of general resilience.

General resilience is enhanced by high levels of adaptability, sometimes referred to as *adaptive capacity*. It is the ability of the system to change how its parts work in response to a disturbance. You can also think of it as the capacity to reorganize within the limits of any thresholds, to "learn" how to cope with disturbances.

From the point of view of a system stakeholder, adaptive capacity is about working with the system to sustain its present identity or to move it from an undesirable identity to a desirable one. Sometimes, however, it becomes clear that the system is inevitably going to cross a threshold into an undesirable state from which it cannot recover. Further efforts to try to get the system back into the desirable state just make things worse; they amount to digging the hole deeper. In this situation, it is time to *transform* into a new kind of system.

Transformation and Transformability

Transformability is the capacity of a system to become a different system, to create a new identity. An example comes from southeastern Zimbabwe where, in the 1980s after a prolonged drought and consequent unviable cattle ranching conditions, ranchers transformed their cattle ranches to game-hunting and safari parks. They were new enterprises operating in a different way at a different scale, and a new system had been created.

In much of the world today, current systems of resource use—for example, most groundwater use for irrigation in major river basins—are unsustainable and are driving the systems concerned into undesirable states that will be irreversible within human generation timescales. The need for transformation is evident in many of the systems upon which we depend.

Fundamental transformation is painful and costly, however, and no one likes it because it involves a big change and uncertainty. Learning how to build transformability—the capacity to achieve transformation—will be a very important part of future social-ecological systems policy and management.

Transformability is underpinned by three main attributes. They are (1) being able to get beyond *denial* (a belief that the present identity of the system can continue); (2) having the ability to *create options* for a new kind of system (which involves experimenting with different, sometimes novel forms of the system, usually at small, local scales); and (3) having the ability to put one (or more) of these *options into practice* (which will often require help from higher levels).

Adaptive Cycles

The next thing to appreciate with resilience thinking is that the behavior of self-organizing systems changes over time, not only because of external influences, but also through internal processes. The way the components of the system change and interact causes the system to go through cycles in which the capacity of the system to absorb disturbance (its resilience) changes, as does the potential for people managing the system to make changes.

This cycle is described by ecologists as an *adaptive cycle* and is observed in a wide range of self-organizing systems.[1] Its four phases are *rapid growth, conservation, release,* and *reorganization* (or *renewal*).

Think of a forest recovering after a fire or a new business set up to make and sell a new product. As they establish themselves, these systems undergo a period of rapid growth as they exploit new opportunities and available resources. In business, it is the entrepreneurs that can often do well and get ahead. In the forest, it is the fast-growing generalist species that prosper because they can cope well with a bit of variability.

Over time, however, the capacity and potential for rapid growth diminish because the system is no longer operating in an "open field." The availability of resources is reducing as the operating space gets filled. The system moves from rapid growth into a conservation phase. Connections between players (or species) are increasing and becoming stronger. The fast growers in the forest are being displaced by the dominant trees (the stronger competitors, but slower growers) that soak up all the available light and nutrients. The entrepreneurs in the business are being displaced by middle managers who have to improve productivity, usually by increasing the scale of the operation, introducing ever more efficiency, reducing risks, and cutting out perceived redundancies (which are often actually forms of response diversity). The system enters a phase of "conservation" in which net production gets very small and size levels off; the forest or business is no longer getting bigger and is becoming less flexible.

However, just as rapid growth cannot go on forever, so too does this mature conservation phase inevitably come to an end. The forest biomass builds to its maximum (climax) level and becomes ever more inflexible, with nutrients locked up in heartwood; it is more and more susceptible to a disturbance such as fire. The business has grown so complex that it can no longer steer its way through a changing economy or seize opportunities (like new technologies) as they arise. It takes a smaller and smaller disturbance to initiate a collapse, which inevitably happens.

Forests and businesses (and communities and civilizations) all go through cycles of rise and fall, and when they fall, things become very uncertain. Connections between components that were once locked tight break apart. Economic, social, and biophysical capital (e.g., nutrients locked up in trees, financial arrangements and operating units in a business) are released, and as that happens, the equilibrium of the previous conservation phase disappears.

The release can be brutal for some; resources are lost (nutrients are leached out, money and people leave the enterprise), but it also opens the way for renewal in which a new order or new generation rises up. Often, the new order is much the same as the old one, but sometimes it is dramatically different.

As renewal proceeds, a new order, a new "attractor" (potential equilibrium state of a new identity), may emerge. Here, connections begin to grow between the components, and the system is back in a phase of rapid growth.

There are times in the cycle when there is greater leverage to change things, and there are other times when affecting change is quite difficult (such as when things are in gridlock in the late conservation phase). The kinds of policy and management interventions appropriate in one phase do not work in others.

Taken as a whole, the adaptive cycle (figure 9-3) has two opposing modes: a growth and development loop (the fore or front loop) and a release and reorganization loop (or back loop). The fore loop is characterized by stability, relative predictability, and conservation, and this enables the accumulation of capital (which is essential for well-being to increase). The back loop, by contrast, is characterized by uncertainty, novelty, and experimentation. It is the time of greatest potential for the initiation of either destructive or creative change in

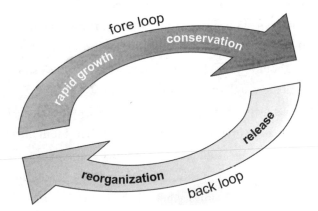

Figure 9-3. A simple representation of the adaptive cycle.
The rapid growth and conservation phases are referred to as the fore loop. This loop has relatively predictable dynamics and a slow accumulation of capital and potential through stability and conservation. The release and reorganization phases are referred to as the back loop. In this loop, which is characterized by uncertainty, novelty, and experimentation, there is a loss (leakage) of all forms of capital.
Source: Brian Walker and David Salt, *Resilience Thinking: Sustaining Ecosystems and People in a Changing World* (Washington, DC: Island Press, 2006).

the system.

The sequential four-phase pattern of the adaptive cycle is not an absolute. A rapid growth phase usually proceeds into a conservation phase, but it can also go directly into a release phase. A conservation phase usually moves at some point into a release phase, but it can (through small perturbations) move back toward a growth phase.

Connections across Scales

Self-organizing systems operate over a range of different *scales* of space and time, and each scale is going through its own adaptive cycle. What happens at one scale can have a profound influence on what is happening at scales above and on the embedded scales below.

When managing a system—whether a forest, a farm, or a community—there is always one scale that is of particular interest to managers; it is known as the scale of concern, or the focal scale. A farmer would be most concerned with what was happening at the scale of the farm. A government department responsible for the region in which the farm is located would be more focused on a much larger scale. When engaging with self-organizing systems, it is critical to acknowledge that you cannot understand the focal scale (the thing that you are interested in) without appreciating the influence from the scales above, below, and often beyond them to larger and finer scales.

When you overlay the concept of linked adaptive cycles, the behavior of the whole system can sometimes make more sense. When the higher scale is in a conservation phase, change is difficult. Components are tightly connected, efficiency in doing the same things is more important than experimentation, and the status quo rules. At other times, when the higher scale is in a growing, active phase, the efforts of reformers are facilitated, not blocked.

Smaller scales will go through their own adaptive cycles, but as they emerge from a back loop, the higher scale may influence them to follow a similar path as the one they have just been through. Higher-scale dynamics constrain and can initiate and guide what is happening at the lower scale. The system as a whole has "memory."

Indeed, it is useful to imagine the system in which you are interested as composed of a hierarchy of linked adaptive cycles operating at different scales. This linked hierarchy of cycles—referred to as a *panarchy* (figure 9-4)—governs the behavior of the whole system.[2]

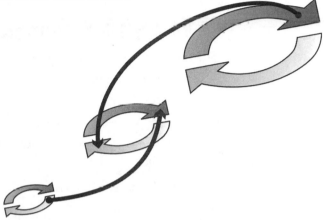

Figure 9-4. Panarchy: hierarchies of linked adaptive cycles.
Source: Brian Walker and David Salt, *Resilience Thinking: Sustaining Ecosystems and People in a Changing World* (Washington, DC: Island Press, 2006).

A Resilience Practice

How are the building blocks of resilience thinking applied to actually manage a system and its resilience? Conceptually, it is a matter of understanding the system at multiple places and scales: recognizing where thresholds might exist and monitoring the appropriate variables, assessing where the system sits in the adaptive cycle, understanding what connections exist across scales and between domains, and having a feeling for how various components of general resilience are tracking over time. Doing all that takes time, effort, and the skills and insights of multiple disciplines, people, and groups. Given these requirements, managing for resilience—really, developing a resilience practice—is more about developing a culture of systems engagement rather than coming up with a one-off solution of what "resilience setting" your system should be at.

There are many guides to how a resilience practice might be approached.[3] Most of them, however, start from the same place: bringing together the key stakeholders in the system (managers, decision makers, representatives of important community segments) and getting them to share their insights on what they think the system is, how they each think the system works, and what is important. More specifically, a resilience practice would get these stakeholders to do the following:

- **Describe** their system. What is the focal scale of the system, and how is it bounded in space and time at different scales? What is its identity? What are the key components of the system that give it that identity? What threatens that identity? Who are the players who have power and influence?
- **Assess** the resilience of their system. Make some determination of specified resilience; general resilience, adaptability, and transformability; and where the system sits in an adaptive cycle.
- **Manage** that resilience. List available options, and choose when and how to implement them.

Keep in mind that because they are self-organizing systems, the systems we are dealing with are always changing and are always adjusting to external pressures and internal connections. So, it is simply not enough for a resilience practice to be a one-off description/assessment/management. Rather, it is an ongoing iterative process, one in which the description/assessment/management is constantly being revisited, updated, and reinterpreted. It is a process in which the system is never precisely and completely known (because that is impossible); rather, it is constantly being probed, interpreted, and better understood as it is managed in an adaptive, learning way.

For this reason, we describe the process more as a culture than a prescription, and we also encourage anyone attempting to "do" resilience practice to be wary of pro-forma templates, standards, and formulas, of which many abound. It is not that these tools are wrong as much as they are almost by definition partial assessments, and they tend to prevent you from figuring out how to engage with the whole system. Rather than encouraging you to engage and work with the complexity of your system, they frequently reduce that complexity to a number, a score, or a standard in an effort to give you some measurable quantity that seems tractable.

Conclusion: Insights from Resilience Thinking

What happens when you try to *engage* with the complexity of a self-organizing system rather than just attempt to "tame" it? First, it becomes apparent that the complexity cannot be tamed and that efforts to do so are not just futile. They can often produce outcomes that are opposite of what was intended, such as crashing fish stocks, shrub-infested rangelands, or regional ghost towns.

Following close on this insight is that working with resilience is not about keeping the system exactly the same; it is not about not changing. Rather, it is about enabling the system to adapt around shocks and disturbances, to self-organize such that the system's identity is sustained. Trying to hold a system in a state that optimizes the supply of goods and services is tantamount to attempting to simplify its complexity. The consequence is that the system's ability to reorganize in response to disturbances or new conditions that might arise is constrained, and it loses its resilience.

Engaging with the complexity of your system helps you appreciate that resilience is not good or bad. It is a characteristic of a system (a *systems property*) reflecting how easy or hard it is to change the system. If the system's identity (like an agricultural region providing food, jobs, and ecological reserves) is valued by people with a stake in it, high levels of resilience are desirable. If it is an economically depressed Rust Belt community with high unemployment and low levels of investment, however, a high level of resilience is very undesirable. Indeed, in such circumstances, high resilience might suggest that the existing system is unsalvageable and that the community should be exploring possible transformations.

An ongoing engagement with the complexity of the system in which you are interested is sure to generate insights into how and why your system functions as it does. It will also provide signposts for where stakeholders need to look to solve growing issues. It is not a panacea or a silver bullet, though, nor is it free. Like any form of management, resilience practice comes with costs in terms of the things you need to do or things you should stop doing. Calculating their direct costs can be challenging, but it is tractable. What is sometimes harder to estimate are the costs of not building resilience, and discovering what those costs are when it is too late can be harder still.

The most important insights arising from resilience thinking in regard to the system in which you have a stake will only become clear to you when you apply the thinking yourself. Some insights will be in accord with what we have suggested above, but some will come as a complete surprise, for that is the nature of complex systems.

For Further Reading

Folke, Carl. "Resilience (Republished)." *Ecology and Society* 21, no. 4 (2016): 44. https://doi.org/10.5751/ES-09088-210444.

Gunderson, Lance, and C. S. Holling, eds. *Panarchy: Understanding Transformations in Human and Natural Systems* (Washington, DC: Island Press, 2002).

Walker, Brian, C. S. Holling, Steven Carpenter, and Ann Kinzig. "Resilience, Adaptability and Transformability in Social–Ecological Systems." *Ecology and Society* 9, no. 2 (2004): 5. http://www.ecologyandsociety.org/vol9/iss2/art5/.

Walker, Brian, and David Salt. *Resilience Thinking: Sustaining Ecosystems and People in a Changing World* (Washington, DC: Island Press, 2006).

———. *Resilience Practice: Building Capacity to Absorb Disturbance and Maintain Function* (Washington, DC: Island Press, 2012).

Notes

1. Lance Gunderson and C. S. Holling, eds., *Panarchy: Understanding Transformations in Human and Natural Systems* (Washington, DC: Island Press, 2002).
2. Gunderson and Holling, *Panarchy*.
3. For example, Brian Walker and David Salt, *Resilience Practice: Building Capacity to Absorb Disturbance and Maintain Function* (Washington, DC: Island Press, 2012); and Carl Folke, "Resilience (Republished)," *Ecology and Society* 21, no. 4 (2016): 44, https://doi.org/10.5751/ES-09088-210444.

CHAPTER 10

Pulling It All Together: Resilience, Wisdom, and Beloved Community

Stephanie Mills

> If times get tough, encourage and support the good; discourage and
> avoid the bad, protect the weak and defenseless.... Many good deeds
> done daily are seeds of a culture of life and love.
> —Bob Waldrop, Oscar Romero Catholic Worker House[1]

L IKE MANY IN MY DAY, I have from time to time sought counsel and insight
in psychotherapy. Back in the 1970s when I was a young ecology activist in
San Francisco, I had a few thought-provoking sessions with Sterling Bunnell, a
Jungian psychiatrist and naturalist. Many years later, *Gnosis* magazine published
an interview with him, which caught and has held my attention to this day. It
was titled "Nature and the Numinous."[2] The conversation ranged widely and
was revelatory and realistic, a learned man's consideration of the cosmos and
microcosmos, of evolution, extinction, climate change, and cultures; of human
purposes and human prospects within the matrix of the living world. Each of
us, of course, must glean wisdom whence we can. It may be idiosyncratic, but
these thoughts from my long-ago shrink have stayed with me.

"We're in for some pretty rough bumping over the next century," observed Bunnell in that interview. "The important thing is that we don't totally lose our bearings and become degraded by it."[3]

I appreciated the frankness of that. It's hard to admit, but an easy skate into an intersectional photovoltaic full-green employment millennium was never really among our options. Difficult, confusing times confront us, times that threaten to degrade individuals and communities materially and morally. We need to find and maintain our bearings locally, collectively, and personally, and the latter is inner work. Way-finding is continuous; it is the making of a life. A sense of self, compassion for numberless sentient beings, humility and curiosity, and loyalty to place are stars to steer by. They can orient us to the good, the true, and the beautiful.

"What would I recommend?" continued the sage. "Don't panic. Appreciate your own lives; and try to help a little loveliness to continue." I will invoke those aphorisms—longtime touchstones for me—in reverse sequence to order these thoughts on fostering community resilience.

When a naturalist speaks of helping "a little loveliness to continue," it is an invocation of the wild beauty and mystery of the living creatures animating the planet's ecosystems—and an injunction not to dismiss aesthetics. We need to reclaim the ability to perceive and defend the integral quality and wholeness of natural beauty. The loveliness emerging from nature is a mark of resilience. Work to help natural beauty continue implicates people—body, mind, and spirit—in their local ecosystems and larger bioregions. Awareness of natural history, a multidimensional tale of the land, informs systems thinking.

"Helping a little loveliness to continue" means saving species at a time when extinction rates are a thousandfold greater than they were pre–*Homo sapiens*. Saving species means saving habitats—preserving the wild. "In wildness," said Thoreau, "is the preservation of the world."[4] Without the preservation and protection of our fellow life forms, all is lost.

This is not just because life on this planet depends on the near-infinite numbers of interactions among distinct beings (pollinators, for instance; bees in peril are teaching us that ecology lesson) or that all those species have as much right to exist as we do. These beings are more than backdrop, metaphor, or menagerie; their example, instruction, and company made us what we are. As culture historian Thomas Berry has observed, if human consciousness had evolved on the moon, it would be as barren as the moon.[5]

Involving our human communities with the continuance of undomesticated creatures means doing good deeds of evolutionary significance, reestablishes our kinship with the other, and confronts us with the self-willed dynamics of their lives and relationships, and the fact of their varied forms of consciousness. It makes "sense of place" more sensory and more participatory. It is a cultural proposition. Wherever we may dwell, in whatever kind of community— urban, suburban, or rural—resilience is contingent on natural diversity.

Bunnell's second precept, "Appreciate your own lives," means not just knowing, respecting, and savoring one's own personal existence, although that is an essential point of beginning. It also means realizing that our lives—*plural*— appreciate (in the sense of achieving fuller worth) in community. We are social animals. Just as the biotic community of the savanna shaped us as a species and myriad landscapes shaped the thousands of cultures of *Homo sapiens'* diaspora, so the more intimate community—kindred, village, neighborhood, town, team, party, or congregation—shapes individuals.

History is adorned with visionaries and groups who have aimed at establishing virtuous, self-responsible, convivial, and right-sized geographic communities; they were advocates of what in resilience-speak would be *diversity* and *modularity*, being highly alert to the crucial matter of scale. The interwar and postwar decades in the United States were periods of immense economic, ecological, and political upheaval and stress. Perhaps inevitably, they were times when initiatives in cooperation, homesteading, and, especially in the first third of the twentieth century, regional and community planning sparked public and private projects.[6] Decentralism, by many a name, has a long history as an American countercurrent. Great American decentralist thinkers aspired to shape communities—dynamic self-organizing entities—that enhance and dignify the lives of their members, guided by the living principle of mutual aid and by knowledge of what a willing, cooperative group of citizens can accomplish. However rough the bumping gets, it is good to keep those ideals to the fore.

Pan, the great nature god of ancient Greece, is invoked in resilience think-ing's idea of *panarchy*, which describes the vast, all-encompassing, ever-cycling self-organization of social-ecosystems. Yet at the vernacular level, a sudden encounter with Pan—the unfettered, ungovernable power of nature—can trig-ger a stampede. At an historic cusp when shocking events and long emergencies provoke unthinking reactions, many of us are studying how not to panic or suc-cumb to other derangements. A look at the larger question—of how to cultivate an inner resilience that can meet such forces with equanimity and courage—will conclude this chapter.

Loveliness

Resilience science is a fresh understanding presaged in many a cyclical myth and origin story. Its precepts are meaningful at several scales, from the granular to the global. Its ideas of ecosystem dynamics and precepts for resource managers were first posited by C. S. Holling from observations of spruce fir forests as they cycled through insect and fire disturbance to mixed regrowth.[7] Nature reliably, if not regularly, dishes out calamity. Although they exact their toll on living systems, windstorms, earthquakes, mudslides, storm surges, and even social upheaval may be vitalizing within certain thresholds. New social-ecological communities and balances can ensue.

The science implies that the stable, climax ecosystem once thought of as a sort of landscape epitome is illusory. In reality, biotic communities—being open, dynamic, self-organizing systems—are always gaining and losing species (although how many and how quickly are open, nontrivial questions). However satisfying our models, they incorporate the biases and blind spots of their mak-ers. Social-ecological systems stripped of diversity—by economic exploitation, by monoculture commodity production, or by invasive alien organisms—may cross a threshold only to endure rudimentary stasis, a grim resilience.

Climate chaos, with human overpopulation and our long history of habitat disruption, are dramatically changing the face and fate of Earth. The ultimate outcomes are unpredictable and, with respect to extinctions, unpromising. We can nonetheless bet that for a while, ailanthus and Siberian elms will sprout on neglected rooftops, that peregrine falcons will nest on skyscraper ledges, that the occasional Cooper's hawk will lurk near suburban bird feeders or wherever plump rock doves gather,[8] and that indigenous and transplanted medicinal and edible plants—plantain, dandelions, goosefoot, and chicory—will pop up through urban crusts. Even in a so-called vacant lot, we can connect with what the philosopher David Abram calls "more than human" nature.[9] Coyotes have loped about in Central Park and are increasingly common in residential areas.[10] Those weedy, adaptable beings have their own stubborn beauty, but represent only the tiniest fraction of Earth's biodiversity.

Given the breakneck pace of anthropogenic geophysical change, *nature* and *wildness* are about as contested as terms can be; yet the wilder, fuller, hinterland terrains where our species has been discreet or sparse on the ground bespeak their reality, value, and qualities, not least as refuges of biodiversity. Long-term community resilience anywhere is inconceivable without wild lands for they are the ground of all being. If wild beings and wild places, keystone species and migration paths, open spaces, verdant watersheds, and sacred groves perish, so, in essence, do we.

Resilience thinking may relinquish idealized, static versions of social and ecological communities, but it retains ideals and concepts of wholeness. Community resilience entails living consciously with flux. In life, there is no standing still and no turning back, but there is learning from history, naturalists, elders, field biologists, and the answering wildness within. We cannot petrify or command any complex self-organizing system, but we can still learn much from terrains rich and poor and see that when the natural community abounds in diversity, panarchy has more to play with.

Living Appreciation

Day-to-day relocalization can only be particular, in actual places with distinct inhabitants (not all of them human). Good precepts, lessons, successes, failures, bright ideas, and good practices conducive to community resilience should be widely shared; but without systems thinking, local knowledge, and empowerment, brilliant top-down schemes are generic at best and oppressive at worst.

For millennia, humans' mode of persisting and even flourishing was to subsist in small groups within watersheds and biomes and depend on the seasonal pulse and yield of the land. Modernity's half-millennium war against subsistence forcibly and sometimes persuasively supplanted that land-based ethos. Colonialism, trade, the exploitation of fossil fuels, rapid urbanization, and the twentieth century's world wars massively disrupted life places and life ways, yet indigenous peoples and peasantry persist. Their knowledge is a reserve of cultural diversity.

The first foundation of community resilience, we say, is people: neighbors, friends, kin, authorities, dependents, the skillful and unskilled, young and old and middle-aged, learned and ignorant, willing and timid, hateful and kind, winners and losers, old settlers and newcomers.[11] We are the crooked timber of humanity, constantly shaping one another and interdependent whether we will or no. No two perspectives are identical; no person is self-same throughout the day, week, or year. There is no way to approach community resilience without encountering the whole gamut of human possibility and finding ways to collaborate in the space and time we share.

The E^4 crises (ecological, energy, economic, and equity; see chapters 2 through 5) and this unfolding climax, if not collapse, of global industrial civilization are ferociously material, having physical consequences from the streets to the pantry and from the polar ice caps to the ubiquitous microbial realm. It looks like much of the work of building community resilience will be work in the elemental sense of the word: physical effort such as topsoil building, retrofitting, repurposing, repairing, revegetating, and reclaiming the responsibility of craft and care. Can arranging such work so that it restores suppleness and sustenance in the places where we live be a participatory, democratic process?

Citizenship, activism, and self-governance are strenuous, essential, and rewarding. Civil society groups, voluntary organizations, religious congregations, political parties, and ad hoc campaigns are legion. Never has there been a greater occasion for public engagement with a growing array of survival issues, and never has there been a greater need for civility, grit, compassion, and clarity. We are unevenly endowed with these virtues. It is a rare soul with the whole kit, so we must practice them and encourage them in others. This is face-to-face learning. Nonviolent communication is ever more crucial. Showing up, listening more than speaking, and engaging hopefully, imaginatively, and imperfectly are the duty. If cultures of resilience emerge, it will be from hard-won agreement about the meaning, purpose, and right conduct of community life in real places, under circumstances of increasing stress.

Relocalization is a contemporary term for efforts to decentralize and scale today's communities sustainably. Centralization is a social arrangement whose marginal costs tend to exceed any equitably distributed social benefits. The center can hold only at great expense of topsoil, blood, and treasure. The twentieth century saw the dismantling of empires and the aggrandizement of super powers. Small wonder that it also spurred decentralist thinking. These thinkers are worth knowing about now.

In his 1942 classic *The Small Community*, Arthur Morgan, who was celebrated for both his civil engineering and his works on utopias, education, and community, provided an august and eloquent argument for the worth of the small community, especially in cultivating civility, mutual aid, and shared purposes. Visionary, scholarly, and rooted in his convictions, Morgan sifted through history, sociology, and his own working experience to distill a modern program for the development of communities that would function as organically as villages. *The Small Community* speaks to the interplay of scale and freedom:

> The genius of democracy is to eliminate compulsion to uniformity, whether that compulsion be physical force or social pressure, and to develop common outlooks and aims by mutual inquiry, mutual interest, and mutual regard. That process seldom if ever takes place on a large scale. Rapid large-scale changes generally come by ignoring individual variations and by enforcing large-scale uniformities. True democracy results from intimate relations and understanding, with the emergence of common purposes. The community is the natural home of democracy, and it can be the home of tolerance and freedom.[12]

Morgan's urbane and vastly erudite contemporary, the philosopher Lewis Mumford, was magisterial in his critique of patterns of technics, organization, ownership, design, or planning that in any way sapped or inhibited the life force. "We must erect a cult of life," Mumford declared (in an early work, *The Culture of Cities*), sounding a note that would reverberate throughout his writings.[13] A resilient community will be much more like a living organism than a unilaterally engineered device.

Mumford was a Manhattanite who loved cities as they had been and again might be. He took civilization as his purview and also concerned himself with questions of scale and power. His paradigm was organism, not mechanism; it was human scale and distributed power:

> Small groups: small classes: small communities: institutions framed
> to the human scale are essential to purposive behavior in modern
> society.... We have overlooked the way in which large units limit
> opportunity all along the line.[14]

Like Morgan, Mumford was a figure in the twentieth-century regionalist movement, which envisioned and advocated urban growth by budding off and reproduction rather than sprawl, and urged planning compact, convivial, self-reliant communities to be dispersed through the countryside and surrounded with generous expanses of open land. Wrote Mumford:

> In its recognition of the region as a basic configuration in human
> life; in its acceptance of natural diversities as well as natural asso-
> ciations and uniformities; in its recognition of the region as a per-
> manent sphere of cultural influences and as a center of economic
> activities as well as an implicit geographic fact—here lies the vital
> common element in the regionalist movement. So far from being
> archaic and reactionary, regionalism belongs to the future.[15]

These were prophetic minds. Although going forward we will need materially to do more with less, as long as libraries endure there will be ample stores of knowledge and insight, certain fruits of civilization to nourish deep thought and intellectual continuity. We will have every reason to seek them, for our troubles were not born yesterday. Our creative responses can be up-to-date, widely inspired, and ecologically and historically informed.

Resilience science speaks, realistically, of "social-ecological systems," correcting the misconception that society and nature can be independent of each other and thus reasserting a fundamental fact: human animals are interdependent with natural habitats. Bioregionalism, a place-aware philosophy of ecological action that developed in the 1970s, foreshadowed relocalization and continues to influence local initiatives and movement rhetoric. Bioregionalism attends to organic life, to the perception of natural terrains (like watersheds), and to the knowledge of their native flora and fauna, of weather and geology, first peoples, layerings of history, and renewable flows of energy and substance.

"Who am I? Where am I? And what am I going to do about it?"[16] was Peter Berg's basic bioregionalist catechism, entwining identity, place, and agency. Berg, a teacher, writer, and organizer, was eloquent, pithy, and prolific. Among the many axioms of bioregionalism he articulated was, "Restore natural systems, satisfy basic human needs, and develop support for individuals."[17] Helping more than just a little loveliness to continue in cities, exurbs, and hinterlands, Berg and other bioregionalists practice ecological restoration: land healing with endemic species. Artisanal, homegrown provision for local needs, and valuing the genius of every person were and are bioregionalist approaches to building community resilience.

Courage and Equanimity

For the few thousand years that human beings have been sedentary and then civilized, we have been chronicling the stories and glories, the conquests and tribulations of states, nations, and sovereign peoples colliding with kingdoms, cults, world religions, revolutions, and economic ideas. Our vast and varied past and the state of the world today hardly argue much for unalloyed progress.

It is a momentous, perilous time to be alive. We are, as the cartoon character Pogo said, "confronted by insurmountable opportunities." The systemic threats resulting from humanity's arrival at the limits to growth are interpreted and explained in multifarious and partial ways. The babel of proposals—good, bad, and ugly—for tackling, trouncing, and evading these crises can be overwhelming. Civilization's history is full of inequality and conflict, spells of peace and plenty, uprisings, enlightenments, reformations, and resurgence. Arcadian idylls are exceptional. Inevitably for individuals and communities, the going gets tough, and not panicking is essential to survival.

Relinquishing the linear plot of progress in favor of the cycling dynamic of resilience thinking or the venerable Tao—its image a swirl of darkness, with a light at its center, shading into the swirl of light with its center dark—might help us move from the rude shock of crisis into the inescapable process of change. Such an inward shift is not apt to be easy or final; solitude, philosophy, fellowship, and practice, practice, practice may all be required. The quotation at the very beginning of this chapter suggests that self-seeking limits what we can see or do.

How do individuals and communities persist and even grow through crises? Courage is an emergent virtue that can grow from within a community or sometimes be discovered through lonely resistance to the community's error. It is not mere toughness. Compassion, honor, and a sense of the sacred animate courage.

Skillful means—preparation, study, and training—can get us past panic. Steady courage does not deny fear; rather, it acknowledges the inevitability of suffering and the end of suffering. If we regain our focus in the moment, and remember that we are hardly alone in this mighty time, we can respond, to good purpose. Spiritual traditions (and not only those) offer an array of practices for strengthening integrity and presence of mind. Whether the opportunity is to face the truncheons serenely, to keep a clear objective during endless negotiations, or to be of good cheer during a long uncomfortable stretch of privation, self-knowledge, self-discipline, a nature connection, a faith, or devotion to the beloved community can serve.

Perhaps it is difficult for people in cultures whose mythos is of glorious heroic, linear and causal, or divinely foreordained trajectory toward an omega point—be it heaven, hell, or apocalypse—to regard the world as an infinite mesh of interrelated dynamic self-organizing systems. It may be a gross oversimplification to characterize linear, teleological models as Western, but it is fair

to say that the notion of limitless material growth guaranteeing future progress has modern European origins. From Asia come other possible metaphors
for life's dynamics. We have glimpsed ancient China's Tao. Hinduism first wove
Indra's cosmic net of gems, each knot bejeweled, each jewel reflecting all the
others; and the Buddha knew impermanence and understood the spontaneous
and simultaneous arising of phenomena.

Our expectation now may be of relentless discontinuity: social, physical,
political, and emotional. Cultivation of inward resilience—of self and community—must be part of organizing and working to meet basic needs. Some
people call this *culture repair*. We do not lack for means. The diversity of ways
for seeking a center, meeting the numinous, coming to terms with death, and
asserting existential meaning is as lavish an evolutionary phenomenon as ants
or orchids. We have been facing the mystery, creating ceremonies, philosophiz-
ing, congregating in faith, and discovering and refining spiritual practices since
humanity began.

Individuals, societies, fellowships, parishes, sects, affinity groups, and sang-
has—not to mention ethicists, agnostics, and free-thinkers—have striven vari-
ously, and always with mixed results, to transcend the smaller self, the self that is
so easily isolated and entangled by fears, wants, needs, and illusions. Of course,
none of the world religions' belief systems can predict or guarantee individual
or group behavior, good or ill. In our moment, though, even for the agnostic,
they can enrich the work of personal and community resilience. It is what they
have always been for.

A time like ours demands an outward focus, energetic organizing, greater
and more intelligent collective action, civic participation, and urgent, hands-on
work toward local self-reliance. So much is now at stake amid such a tumult
of forces—there is so great a need for us to join together as neighbors, friends,
workers, and allies—that to speak in and of the first person and to address the
inner life may seem an indulgence. It goes without saying that inner work alone
cannot suffice. How, though, can we maintain conscience and integrity without
reflection and self-examination?

To be sitting alone, in a familiar dwelling on a winter's night, far away from
the town, out of earshot of the nearest neighbor, hoping to write something in

service of *community* resilience is paradoxical. Still, I think of the many times someone's writing has spoken to me, bucked me up, clarified a belief, uncovered a prejudice, corrected my ignorance, or rejoiced me with poetry, and I find in my solitude that I belong also to a resilient community, one that crosses space and time.

As I pondered our moment, the meaning of resilience, and the challenge of offering something helpful to the reader, a quotation from the *Bhagavad-Gita*, sent to me long years ago by a pacifist friend, would not quit my mind. An episode in a vast epic of dynastic and supernatural conflict, the *Gita* is the gospel of Hinduism and a perennial wisdom book. (Reading it while studying law in England was a life changer for young Mohandas Gandhi, for instance.)

The nugget my friend shared is uttered when the hero, the glorious warrior prince Arjuna, stands poised in his chariot to ride into a battle against forces that include friends and kin. Arjuna is seized by doubts about his warrior duty. His charioteer, who will reveal himself as the god Krishna,[18] calls for an end to Arjuna's hesitation, saying:

> Thou hast a right to action, but only to action, never to its fruits; let not the fruits of thy works be thy motive, neither let there be in thee any attachment to inactivity.... Do thy actions, having abandoned attachment, having become equal in failure and success.[19]

It is not a counsel of heedlessness or indifference but of consecrating awareness to the situation at hand, of detachment from pride and fear. As we head in to social and material turbulence with every intention of sustaining the beloved community, the resilience of persons and places will be greatly served by both rapt attention and a certain humility.

Notes

1. Bob Waldrop, "Building Community during a Major Disaster," accessed April 3, 2017, http://www.energyconservationinfo.org/community.htm.

2. Jay Kinney and Richard Smoley, "Nature and the Numinous: The Gnosis Interview with Sterling Bunnell," *Gnosis Magazine* 33 (Fall 1994): 30–37.

3. Kinney and Smoley, "Nature and the Numinous."

4. Henry David Thoreau, "Walking," in *The Works of Thoreau*, ed. Henry Canby (Boston: Houghton Mifflin, 1937), 672.

5. Berry expressed this notion in various ways over the years. See, for example, Mike Bell, "Thomas Berry—An Earth Spirituality Out on the Edge," *Watershed Sentinel*, January 6, 2017, https://watershedsentinel.ca/articles/thomas-berry/; and Michael Dowd, *Thank God for Evolution: How the Marriage of Science and Religion Will Transform Your Life and Our World* (New York: Plume, 2009).

6. David Shi, "Prosperity, Depression, and Simplicity," chap. 9 in *The Simple Life: Plain Living and High Thinking in American Culture* (New York: Oxford University Press, 1985), 214–47.

7. Brian Walker and David Salt, *Resilience Thinking: Sustaining Ecosystems and People in a Changing World* (Washington, DC: Island Press, 2006), 80.

8. David Allen Sibley, *The Sibley Field Guide to Birds of Eastern North America* (New York: Knopf, 2003) 97.

9. David Abram, *The Spell of the Sensuous: Perception and Language in a More-than-Human World* (New York: Pantheon, 1996).

10. Dan Flores, "Coyote Coexistence Is a Lifestyle California Should Export," *Los Angeles Times*, July 24, 2016, http://touch.latimes.com#section/-1/article/p2p-87921025/.

11. See chapter 1, "Six Foundations for Building Community Resilience," by Daniel Lerch.

12. Arthur Morgan, *The Small Community: Foundation of Democratic Life* (New York: Harper and Brothers, 1942; Yellow Springs, OH: Community Service, 1984), 282. Page reference is to the 1984 edition.

13. Lewis Mumford, *The Culture of Cities* (New York: Harcourt, Brace, Jovanovich, 1938), 11.

14. Mumford, *The Culture of Cities*, 306.

15. Mumford, *The Culture of Cities*, 306.

16. Peter Berg, *The Biosphere and the Bioregion: Essential Writings of Peter Berg*, ed. Cheryl Glotfelty and Eve Quesnel (New York: Routledge, 2015), 139.

17. Peter Berg, *Envisioning Sustainability* (San Francisco: Subculture Books, 2009), 162.

18. Richard Waterstone, *India* (Boston: Little, Brown, 1995), 60–61.

19. Sri Aurobindo, *Bhagavad Gita and Its Message* (Twin Lakes, WI: Lotus Press, 1995), 38–39.

PART III

Community Resilience in Action

CHAPTER 11

Energy Democracy

Denise Fairchild and Al Weinrub

W HAT DOES IT MEAN TO BUILD the resilience of our communities with regard to energy? What energy alternatives represent real solutions to the economic, environmental, and equity crises confronting our civilization?

Although still in its formative stages, *energy democracy*—a growing current in the clean energy and climate movements—is attempting to address these very questions. Energy democracy is rooted in long-standing struggles for social and environmental justice and is a key component of the evolving economic democracy movement. It goes beyond calls to simply "transition to 100 percent renewables" by advocating for local, democratic control of renewable energy production and use within a framework of environmental sustainability, social justice, and a regenerative economy. It offers a deeper understanding of the cultural, political, economic, and social dimensions of our energy and climate challenges.

This chapter presents the history, converging perspectives, strategies, and practices of the emerging field of advocacy that defines energy democracy. It specifically focuses on the promising ideas and efforts of community-based organizations and leaders active in the climate and clean energy struggle. These groups differ radically from the mainstream environmental community about how to get society off fossil fuels.

Energy democracy advocates do not simply focus on decarbonizing the economy. They see resistance to the centralized, corporate control of energy as an affirmative struggle for social, racial, environmental, and economic justice. Energy democracy advocates see opposition to fossil-fuel-powered capitalism as a key front in a crucial battle to transform our economic system, which has used fossil fuels as the driver of capital accumulation, ecosystem destruction, and social exploitation. In energy democracy, the struggle against the fossil fuel agenda is a struggle for a transformation to a more sustainable, resilient system. It is a struggle for community health and well-being. It is a struggle for social justice and an opportunity for building community empowerment.

In case it is not obvious, let us be clear. The struggle to achieve that kind of transformation is fundamentally a struggle for democracy.

The Energy Democracy Movement

An international labor union roundtable in October 2012 in New York City framed the struggle for a global energy transition as an issue of democracy: "An energy transition can only occur if there is a decisive shift in power towards workers, communities and the public—energy democracy. A transfer of resources, capital and infrastructure from private hands to a democratically controlled public sector will need to occur in order to ensure that a truly sustainable energy system is developed in the decades ahead."[1]

Energy democracy is a way to frame the international struggle of working people, low-income communities, and communities of color to take control of energy resources from the energy establishment—the large corporate energy producers, utility monopolies, and federal and state government agencies that serve their interests—and use those resources to empower their communities: literally (by providing energy), economically, and politically. It means bringing energy resources under public or community ownership and/or control, an essential step toward building a more just, equitable, sustainable, and resilient economy. Thus, the energy democracy movement—represented by a growing number of organizations and organizing campaigns worldwide—seeks to replace our current corporate-controlled fossil fuel economy with one that puts racial, social, and economic justice at the forefront of the transition to a 100 percent renewable energy future.

In particular, energy democracy acknowledges the historical and contemporary perspectives and experiences of "frontline communities," those most directly affected by the fossil fuel economy as well as by the impacts of climate change. This framing prioritizes the needs and concerns of working families, indigenous communities, and communities of color in the struggle to define a new energy future. It seeks comprehensive and effective solutions to the full impact of the fossil fuel economy.

Energy democracy is a critical framework for addressing the economic and racial inequalities that a decarbonized economic system would otherwise continue to perpetuate.

A New Energy Paradigm

The energy democracy movement implies a profound shift in how we think about and relate to energy. Energy is an essential enabler of all human activity: from producing the essentials of life, to transportation, to communication, to the creative arts. We cannot survive without it. In that light, given the existential threat we now face from the burning of fossil fuels, our relationship to energy must be reevaluated. Doing so involves a major paradigm shift. The new energy paradigm must address three major aspects of our energy system: its relationship to the environment, to social justice, and to a new economy.

Energy and the Environment

Energy democracy represents a new environmental paradigm. It emphasizes the core values and related strategies needed to protect the ecosystems that support life on Earth. It seeks the historical and cultural precedents for making our energy systems environmentally sustainable, relying on ecological principles from preindustrial, traditional, and land-based societies.

Much is now understood about the impact of fossil fuel use on the environment. The extraction of these fuels from Earth's crust causes enormous damage, through mountaintop-removal coal mining, deepwater drilling, tar sands mining, hydrofracturing ("fracking"), and other forms of extreme fossil fuel extraction. The burning of these fuels—which increases the concentration of greenhouse gases in the atmosphere and the acidification of the oceans—is modifying Earth's climate and altering the biosphere, causing the extinction of an ever-increasing number of species and now putting human populations in jeopardy as well.

This ecosystem destruction is a product of the industrial fossil fuel economy, which has accelerated mass production and consumption and the accumulation of wealth. Its origins, however, lie in a Western civilization worldview of human beings as masters and exploiters of the natural world for the betterment and progress of human civilization, without regard for the fragile ecosystems that sustain life on the planet.

Energy democracy seeks to reframe energy from being a commodity that is commercially exploited to being a part of the "commons," that is, a natural resource that everyone has a right to use and to help sustainably manage. It means that we can utilize energy resources to serve human needs, but in a way that respects the ecosystem services provided by the biosphere as well as rights of others to both access those resources and not have their environment polluted or destroyed. The new energy democracy paradigm calls for reducing and ultimately eliminating the environmental damage of energy resource extraction, production, and consumption. From this perspective, energy—both fossil fuel and renewable—is a communal resource requiring democratic ownership structures and sustainable, ecological management.

The concept of the commons provides a different way to value the environment and a pathway from commodification of our energy resources (which implicitly underlines many clean energy strategies today) toward energy democracy. For example, the Center for Earth, Energy, and Democracy in Minnesota sees energy democracy as a human rights issue; it bases its work on indigenous notions of the commons as a cultural frame for rebuilding our economy in which natural and human resources are respected, protected, and equitably shared.

In addition, the work of the national Our Power Campaign (a project of the Climate Justice Alliance) recognizes ecosystems as the heart of all solutions related to climate change, the economy, and social equity. Its approach to community-based organizing for clean energy focuses on people's basic needs, particularly their economic needs. The campaign attempts to address the economic burdens of the energy transition for the current (centralized, corporate-owned, fossil-fuel-based) energy labor force and ensure that the new local and renewable energy economy adequately supports family-sustaining employment.

Bronx Cooperative Development Initiative in New York emphasizes energy as a service rather than a commodity. The initiative works with community anchor institutions (e.g., hospitals, schools) in low-income communities and communities of color. It uses the procurement and investment capital of these anchor institutions to mobilize community-based energy projects by supporting the development of local start-ups, social enterprises, and cooperatives, all of which help improve the community's physical, economic, employment, and environmental health.

Energy and Social Justice

Energy democracy represents a new social justice paradigm. It recognizes the racialized impacts of the fossil fuel economy and of climate change, and it sees them as threat multipliers: they deepen the daily economic, health, and social justice challenges of vulnerable communities. The new energy democracy paradigm harnesses the lived experiences of low-income and communities of color to reverse that impact and to design an alternative energy system.

The fossil fuel economy has had a disproportionate negative impact on people of color in the United States. The rise of fossil fuel power was a key factor in replacing the slavery-based system of production and in industrializing and commercializing the US economy. The result was westward expansion, the growth of urban centers, the rise of monopoly capitalism, concentration of wealth, migration and immigration of working-class people and people of color, segregation, impoverishment, and the creation of urban slums.

In the period following World War II, government policies supporting highway construction, car ownership, and single-family-home ownership had the effect of encouraging middle- and upper-class whites—but not others—to move from the cities to the suburbs. Thus, many black, Latino, and poor white communities—generally with little political power—were left behind to live in "sacrifice zones" near coal-burning power plants, oil refineries, and other toxic sites. The health impacts of this segregation are very real: the burning of fossil fuels emits particulate matter and toxic chemical pollutants that lead to respiratory ailments, cancers, and mental- and stress-related disorders. Moreover, federal and local land use, housing, and transportation policies, along with widespread racist bank lending policies ("redlining"), trapped low-income populations in these toxic communities, ultimately spurring the rise of the US environmental justice movement.

Not only do the negative impacts of the fossil fuel economy disproportionately affect low-income communities and communities of color, but the impacts of climate change do as well. In particular, those hit hardest by the extreme weather conditions induced by climate change—the floods, the droughts, the hurricanes—are communities of color.[2] Hurricane Katrina and Superstorm Sandy stand out as examples of how the poorest populations and neighborhoods were least prepared to withstand and recover from these storms, thanks to weak levees, inadequate energy infrastructure, contaminated water, and failed sewer and transportation systems. The long-term direct impacts of climate change—such as greater extremes in temperature and precipitation, stronger storms, and sea-level rise—will tend to affect low-income and vulnerable populations the most.

Energy democracy addresses these challenges by emphasizing community-based renewable energy development to build the economic strength, resilience, wealth, and power of low-income communities and communities of color. It focuses on those most negatively impacted by the fossil fuel economy. It stresses equity and the need to redress historical harm in finding solutions that achieve social justice.

For example, the California Environmental Justice Alliance focuses on a state policy framework for moving financial and technical resources into historically disadvantaged or overburdened communities ("just transition" or "green" zones). This redistribution of energy development resources promises to transform economic life for communities that have borne the brunt of the fossil fuel economy. The legislative victories of the green zone policy framework have served to define what equity means with respect to energy development.

The new energy democracy paradigm also recognizes and raises up the leadership of low-income communities, indigenous communities, and other historically marginalized communities in the struggle for environmental justice and in envisioning and shaping an energy system that can meet the needs of all people. For example, the Asian Pacific Environmental Network (APEN) in California employs its community-building and leadership development activities to build the political power needed to advocate for and win programs and policies that support local renewable energy and climate action. For APEN, energy democracy is not a top-down enterprise; rather, it is rooted in the experience, capacity, voice, and power of local resident immigrant communities. APEN is building knowledge and leadership among its constituents, helping them become key stakeholders in energy policy and planning.

In a similar vein, One Voice in Mississippi focuses on the organizing work taking place in rural communities in the South to reclaim community ownership of existing energy cooperatives—the rural electric co-ops—and transform them into authentic community-owned and controlled energy service providers. The rural electric co-ops are key to the economic revitalization of low-income communities in the South, and the implications of this work for the hundreds of rural electric co-ops around the United States are significant.

Energy and the Economy

Energy democracy represents a new economic paradigm. It sees renewable energy resources as enabling a new, alternative economy; it sees a regenerative rather than an extractive economy, one that builds the economic strength and resilience of the nation's communities. This new economic model is characterized by community-based development, nonexploitive forms of production, socialized capital, ecological use of natural resources, and sustainable economic relationships. It emphasizes the need for meaningful work and for family-sustaining jobs for all workers.

By contrast, the current economy (built on the back of fossil fuel energy), though it has allowed for vast increases in labor productivity, exploits resources and human labor to accumulate capital and create huge corporate empires. The most affluent Americans ("the 1 percent") are wealthier than ever, yet most of us continue to experience economic distress, and many communities—particularly communities of color—are literally in a state of economic crisis. Acute economic inequality and exclusion are becoming the new normal.

With the growth of a deregulated low-wage economy, maximizing profits and maximizing growth are the only binding standards. In some ways, big business and financial institutions have assumed state-like powers over workers, communities, and democracy itself. Under this economic regime, we have witnessed a chronic failure to create fair-wage jobs, an increasingly regressive tax system (lower taxes for the wealthiest, higher taxes for everyone else), accelerating income inequality (not only increasing, but doing so at an increasing rate), rising housing costs and increased homelessness, increasingly costly health care, defunding and privatization of the educational system, an eroding retirement system, growing corporate control over government and politics, increasing surveillance, and restrictions on civil rights and civil liberties.[3] We have also witnessed exponentially expanded material consumption over the last century and a half, to the point where it is now colliding with the material limits of Earth's resources and its capacity for ecosystem restoration.

The fossil fuel economy is at the root of many of these global economic, social, and environmental disruptions. The fossil fuel industry receives massive public subsidies to fuel the overproduction and consumption of our natural resources and to invest in extreme extraction and processing that produce significant negative externalities. Researchers at the International Monetary Fund determined that the world's governments are providing subsidies to the highly profitable oil industry to the tune of an astonishing $5.3 trillion in benefits per year, including direct subsidies and the cost of health impacts, environmental spills, and other environmental calamities.[4] This figure represents $10 million every minute, every day.

Simply decarbonizing the current economic system—as hard as it might be—by transitioning to a nonfossil, renewable energy base would not challenge the fundamental logic or economic power relationships of this extractive global economy. It does not affect the growth imperative of the capitalist system, nor does it stop Wall Street and the largest US corporations from extracting wealth from working people. It does not address income and wealth inequality. Simply decarbonizing this economic system would only extend the system's life.

A regenerative, life-sustaining economic alternative, like any economic model, needs an energy model attuned to its values and needs. We cannot build a new economy on an old energy model. Energy democracy—bringing energy resources under public or community ownership and control or other forms of cooperative economics—promotes a more democratized, equitable, sustainable, and resilient economic system.

One approach to advancing economic democracy is through the development of energy cooperatives. The national Community Power Network, for example, promotes community-based solar purchasing cooperatives to further community ownership of renewable energy resources and, in doing so, build a political base of support for creating new energy policy and transforming the utility sector. Within this approach, communities participate in the financial benefits of the shift from big, centralized energy systems to distributed systems of locally owned community energy resources.

Taking this one step further, Co-op Power in New England and New York is engaged in building a new kind of energy cooperative, one representing an alternative economic development model for advancing a new renewable energy economy. In this model, the energy cooperative becomes an economic development engine for new community-based businesses that provide economic, social, and environmental benefits to low-income communities.

The Local Clean Energy Alliance in the San Francisco Bay Area takes the democratization of energy to a municipal scale, in particular through Community Choice energy programs, which are now available in a number of states. Community Choice enables local jurisdictions to form public energy service provider agencies, somewhat akin to municipal utilities. The possibilities for democratized, decentralized energy through Community Choice are huge. This alliance is pursuing organizing strategies to ensure community control, equity, local wealth creation, and other community economic benefits.

From a Centralized to a Decentralized Energy Model

The paradigm shift represented by energy democracy is more than a new set of values and principles to guide our energy system. It calls for a new energy model, one in sync with the environmental, social justice, and new economy paradigms described above.

The dominant model for renewable energy today is large-scale, centralized generating systems such as big solar plantations and large wind farms. It is an extension of the legacy model of centralized, fossil-fuel-based electrical energy production, a product of concentrated financial and economic power. It is currently the model of choice for decarbonized economic growth, but it predominantly benefits corporations and emphasizes a transition to industrial-scale carbon-free energy resources without challenging the growth of energy consumption, material consumption, rates of capital accumulation, and concentration of wealth and power in the hands of a few. In rare cases, centralized energy developments are the result of democratic action of communities and can provide economic wealth-building and political democracy for those communities. In most cases, however, centralized energy development represents the interests of powerful economic forces aided by state and federal governments heavily influenced by large, nonlocal corporations.[5]

An alternative model—the decentralized renewable energy model—places control and ownership of renewable energy resources in the community rather than in remote corporate board rooms. This decentralized energy model represents an opportunity for community empowerment and allows for the new economic and ecologically sound relationships needed to address the current economic and climate crisis. In particular, democratic control of renewable energy resources is facilitated by the fact that renewable resources are distributed: solar energy, wind, geothermal energy, energy conservation, energy efficiency, energy storage, and demand response systems are resources that can be found and developed in all communities. These resources provide a basis for community-based energy development at the local level through popular initiatives.[6] The decentralized renewable energy model is part of a global energy realignment that has begun to gain traction around the world.[7]

Conclusion

Throughout the United States, initiatives to transform the large-scale, corporate-controlled, dirty-energy economy into a community-owned and controlled clean energy economy are emerging. These energy democracy initiatives, some of which have been mentioned above, include communities that are participating in planning, building, and benefiting from an alternative decentralized renewable energy model. They focus on community control of, access to, and ownership of energy assets. In addition, they intentionally address the health and economic conditions of communities most impacted by fossil fuel energy, and they include strategies for workers and communities affected by the downsizing of the fossil fuel industry.

In essence, this energy democracy movement is a comprehensive community resilience initiative to address the existential consequences of the extractive economy through the creation of a new regenerative economy—one based on a decentralized renewable energy model that advances ecosystem health, economic sustainability, and social justice through the empowerment of our communities and the democratization of our society.

Notes

1. Sean Sweeney, *Resist, Reclaim, Restructure: Unions and the Struggle for Energy Democracy*, Rosa Luxemburg Stiftung–New York Office, April 2013, http://www
   .rosalux-nyc.org/resist-reclaim-restructure/.
2. Rachel Morello-Frosch et al., *The Climate Gap: Inequalities in How Climate Change Hurts Americans and How to Close the Gap* (Los Angeles: USC Dornsife, 2009), http://dornsife.usc.edu/pere/climategap/.
3. Jack Rasmus, "America's Ten Crises," June 30, 2012, http://www.kyklosproduc
   tions.com/posts/index.php?p=160.

4. Baoping Shang et al., "How Large Are Global Energy Subsidies?," International Monetary Fund Working Paper No. 15/105, May 18, 2015, http://www.imf.org /external/pubs/cat/longres.aspx?sk=42940.0.

5. Two days after the historic 2014 climate march in New York City calling for climate action, federal and California officials released an 8,000-page proposal for private renewable energy development on 22.5 million acres of California desert. See Carolyn Lochhead, *Energy Plan Calls for Big Renewables Projects in State's Deserts,* September 23, 2014, http://www.sfgate.com/green/article/Sprawling-solar-farms -OKd-near-desert-national-5775871.php.

6. Former US Federal Energy Regulatory Commission Chairman John Wellinghof said the nation's electrical future may well belong to distributed generation such as rooftop solar rather than central power stations and generators far from demand. "It's going to be a race between the two types of renewable resources," said Wellinghof. "Right now, I'd put my money on distributed resources." Quoted by Chris Clarke, September 6, 2012, http://www.kcet.org/news/rewire/the-grid/federal -energy-expert-backing-distributed-generation.html.

7. A ten-minute video describing decentralized energy systems and their community benefits can be found at http://www.youtube.com/watch?v=HvuXxyKSh3A.

CHAPTER 12

Building Community Resilience at the Water's Edge

Rebecca Wodder

Water is H$_2$O,
Hydrogen two parts
Oxygen one
But there is also a third thing that makes it water
And nobody knows what that is.
—D. H. Lawrence, "The Third Thing"[1]

Our Story as Told by Water

Water is essential to life, from the inner space of our bodies to the outer space of planetary bodies. When we explore distant planets, we look for evidence of water as a sign of possible or past life.

Earth is known as the "blue planet" because water covers more than 70 percent of its surface, giving our home a brilliant blue color when viewed from space. Without water, humans can live only a few days. The search for water in a drying world likely drove human evolution.[2] Despite enormous technological advances, human society is still entirely dependent on water to sustain our families, communities, businesses, agriculture, and industry as well as all ecological systems. Quite simply, there is no substitute for water.

A Triple Threat to Community Resilience

Despite water's unmatched importance to community resilience and despite our standing as the richest nation on Earth, the reliable provision of clean, affordable water is not a given in the United States in the twenty-first century. Serious water problems confront American communities daily. Some are the result of an extreme event like a storm or an industrial accident. Others are slow-moving and insidious, like contaminated drinking water or a long-lasting drought. Tens of thousands of poor households routinely lose water service, and, according to the US Census Bureau, "about a half a million American households lack basic plumbing amenities like hot water, a tap, or toilet."[3] No matter what kind of water crisis looms, it nearly always hits poor and disenfranchised communities hardest.

Despite great strides in controlling water pollution since rivers routinely burned in the 1960s, our water resources still face a triple threat. First, much of our water infrastructure is outdated and suffers frequent age-related failures, threatening public health and safety. Second, our water systems are stressed by unsustainable choices we have made in our use of land and water resources: suburban sprawl, population growth in drought-plagued parts of the country, increasing demands on water supplies by energy and high tech industries, and severely overallocated surface and groundwater resources. Third, a changing climate presents extreme hydrologic conditions that exacerbate challenges to water infrastructure and sustainable resource use.

Climate Impacts on Water

From devastating floods to withering droughts, "water is the primary medium through which climate change influences Earth's ecosystem and thus the livelihood and well-being of societies."[4] The Third National Climate Assessment, issued in 2014, describes observed and expected impacts on the quality, quantity, and distribution of water that threaten human and natural communities in multiple ways. In addition to increased risk of floods and droughts, scientists predict reduced surface- and groundwater supplies, increased demands for water, and decreased water quality.[5]

Climate change is affecting precipitation patterns, leading to more extreme (in size, frequency, and duration) hydrologic conditions. In the Northeast and Midwest, precipitation is increasing; in the South and West, it is decreasing; and all parts of the country are experiencing a higher frequency of the most intense precipitation events. The frequency of extreme downpours could grow by more than 400 percent in much of the United States by the end of the twenty-first century, requiring "fundamental reassessments of planning approaches to intense precipitation, local flooding, landslides and debris flows."[6] In the Southwest, once-in-a-millennium megadroughts, lasting more than thirty-five years, are also likely to occur.[7]

Headwater forests that are the source of much of the nation's water supply are succumbing to disease and fire. Snowpacks that once provided a natural water reservoir for western communities are disappearing. Warmer temperatures increase evaporation and transpiration, leading to water loss from reservoirs and decreased soil moisture. Meanwhile, more water is needed for irrigation and increased power demands for cooling.

Water quality is negatively affected by these climate-intensified changes to the hydrologic cycle. Runoff from more frequent and intense storms regularly overwhelms combined sanitary and stormwater systems, dumping raw sewage into rivers and lakes. Water quality is also affected by higher water temperatures, which encourage toxic algae growth and degrade habitat for fish and wildlife.

Toward Water Resilience

As a result of outdated water infrastructure, unsustainable resource use, and changes to the hydrologic cycle, younger generations are inheriting rapidly growing water management challenges. When today's young adults were born, water parameters were still relatively predictable. Now, engineers face an alarming reality of greater extremes[8] in designing water supply and containment, wastewater disposal, and stormwater systems. Communities need new principles and practices not only for adapting their aging water systems to a new climate reality, but also for advancing the rights and responsibilities that enable an ethical and sustainable approach to water. Community resilience will come from an integrated approach to water that taps and builds both the natural capital inherent in healthy hydrological systems and the social capital needed for diverse, inclusive, and collaborative local efforts to equitably manage our freshwater wealth.

Water: The Universal Solvent

Water plays a critical role in almost all processes and systems: biological, chemical, and physical. It is called the universal solvent because it dissolves more substances than any other liquid, making it essential to life.[9] Water can be a blessing or a curse, a threat or an opportunity, a privately owned commodity or the foundation of our common wealth. Water delivers essential social, economic, and ecological benefits to people and communities. It can also threaten life and property in times of flooding, drought, and toxic water pollution. We structure our communities to cope with the dual nature of water.

Water for People

People depend on a reliable supply of clean water to support their daily activities and enhance their quality of life. We use it in our homes for drinking, cooking, and cleaning; for commercial purposes such as restaurants and manufacturing; for public services such as firefighting; and regionally, in our food and energy production systems. Its visible presence in our communities—as rivers, streams, beaches, and lakes—provides cultural, social, and even psychological benefits.[10]

Water can be a medium for increasing social cohesion, bringing disparate groups of people together around common interests. Its relevance to broadly shared concerns such as health, welfare, and quality of life explain why clean water is consistently ranked more highly in public polls than other environmental issues.[11] Nearly every community has a river, lake, or other fresh-water resource that offers opportunities for community projects (like replanting streamside vegetation or collecting trash) that expand civic engagement and build collaborative skills.

Water sustains critical ecosystem services for human communities. Healthy freshwater systems provide habitat to support recreational and commercial fisheries. Groundwater supplies private and public wells. Wetlands filter water pollution, soak up floodwaters, and enhance floodplain fertility. Rivers and streams transport sediment and deliver water supplies. Healthy watersheds sustain water supplies during droughts, control erosion, and stabilize slopes. Riparian vegetation maintains stream banks and moderates water temperatures. Coastal marshes and floodplain forests buffer wind and wave damage from hurricanes and other extreme weather events.

Water converges with our energy, economic, equity, and environmental challenges:

- Collecting, treating, and delivering water take an enormous amount of *energy*. Similarly, *energy production* requires enormous amounts of water, whether for resource extraction, power generation, or cooling processes. For example, in drought-prone California, 20 percent of electricity is used for water-related purposes,[12] and 17 percent of water withdrawals go to thermoelectric energy generation.[13] Efforts to conserve water reduce energy use and vice versa.
- The United States is a water-rich nation, giving us an *economic* advantage over nations constrained by too little water to sustain high levels of industry, commerce, and agriculture.[14] At the local level, healthy hydrologic features and nature-mimicking green infrastructure save money by reducing energy consumption, diminishing flood damage, and avoiding water-borne illnesses and lost productivity as well as reducing the construction and operating costs of water-related infrastructure.[15] Thus, more money is left for other community priorities.
- Despite the hydrological wealth of the United States, water is a frequent source of *inequity* and environmental injustice. In California, farm

workers are sickened when nitrates from fertilizer contaminate ground-water. Children in Alabama are infected with hookworm due to inadequate sanitation. Poor neighborhoods are frequently the site of polluting factories, while their access to the social and recreational benefits of being near healthy water bodies is often limited.

- In addition to local ecosystem services described above, water is essential to planetary *environmental* parameters such as biodiversity, soil productivity, and nutrient and sediment transfers. In the United States, phenomena such as the "dead zone" in the Gulf of Mexico and extinction rates for freshwater species that are four to seven times higher than for terrestrial or avian species provide clear evidence of the global ecological consequences of damaged water systems.

Systems Thinking for Managing Community Water

As the universal solvent, water is part of every human and natural system and is best approached through the lens of systems thinking. Human communities are complex adaptive systems responding to the energy, economic, equity, and environmental challenges that stress them. Human communities are also social-ecological systems, depending for their survival on ecosystem services provided by nature while often degrading those services through actions that impact nature.

The collection, treatment, distribution, and regulation of water for human purposes is accomplished through a mix of built, natural, and human systems.

America's *built infrastructure systems* supply water, remove wastewater and stormwater, protect against floods and droughts, and provide for power generation and transportation. The system components include dams and levees, canals and reservoirs, treatment plants and water pipes, water pumps, wells, and irrigation systems. Built infrastructure is generally large-scale and concentrated; expensive to construct, operate, and maintain; inflexible in the face of increasingly extreme conditions; and most often, engineered for a single purpose rather than providing multiple benefits.

Management boundaries of built water systems are defined by where their water comes from, how it is used, and where it goes after use. Source waters can be rivers, lakes and reservoirs, and groundwater. Service areas are defined by the homes and businesses reached by pipes, protected by pumps and levees, and served by water bodies that receive discharged wastewater and stormwater.

Much of the water infrastructure in the United States is old, outdated, and inefficient, leading to disasters ranging from devastating levee failures to contaminated drinking water. Across the nation, water leaks waste trillions of gallons of treated water every day. In many cities, even minor rainstorms result in combined sewer overflows that dump 860 billion gallons of raw sewage into US lakes and rivers annually.[16] Larger storm events submerge neighborhoods and roads, averaging more than eighty lives lost and $8 billion in property damages per year since the mid-1980s.[17] Engineering experts estimate that to repair and upgrade our built drinking water systems will require an investment over the next quarter century.[18] Given the enormous price tag and the long design life of built systems, the choices we make now will lock us onto a fixed path for many decades to come.

Natural hydrological systems have always been a key part of built systems, whether or not people appreciate their fundamental roles in water supply and management. Components of natural hydrological systems include headwater forests, streams and rivers, estuaries and lakes, aquifers and wetlands, riparian areas and floodplains, and watersheds.[19]

The characteristics of natural water infrastructure are generally the opposite of built infrastructure. Natural water infrastructure is mostly small-scale and distributed, provides "free" services, is flexible and adaptable in the face of changing conditions, and provides many other benefits such as wildlife habitat, natural beauty, and recreational opportunities. Many freshwater ecosystems, however, are severely stressed by land use changes, polluted runoff, drainage of wetlands and farm fields, and hardening or burying stream channels.

Healthy natural water systems are resilient and adaptable, but they have thresholds beyond which their natural capacities are undermined and even destroyed. For example, when 10 percent to 15 percent of a watershed is paved over, it no longer sustains its ecological functions.[20] When an aquifer is overused, the water-bearing rock structures can collapse, irreversibly diminishing storage capacity. When a river's water is oversubscribed, the river can go completely dry.

The failure of many state laws to protect "nature's right" to water is starting to change, with instream flows that maintain ecosystem integrity being recognized as a "beneficial use" in more and more places.[21]

Human systems for using, storing, and sharing water can be formal or informal, private or public, competitive or cooperative. Formal components—including federal and state water laws, water rights and treaties, water adjudication boards, and other legally binding systems and rules for managing water—have developed over centuries. They are usually aimed at maintaining existing water rights, uses, and technologies and are sometimes constrained by outdated conceptions of hydrological science. They can present significant barriers to collaborative, sustainable, and equitable approaches to water.

Informal components include social networks for collective action, local knowledge of water-related issues, and voluntary commitments to maintain, monitor, and provide feedback on the performance of water management systems. Communities come together informally in times of crisis, such as when neighbors work together to fill sandbags when flooding threatens or to deliver bottled water during incidents of water contamination or reduced supplies. Communities also set terms for water use, such as the collective development of water budgets and community agreements on groundwater use. One of the oldest examples of cooperative effort comes from Hispanic communities in the Southwest that, beginning in the late 1500s, formed irrigation associations called *acequias*.[22] A contemporary example is the formation of the People's Water Board in Detroit, Michigan, a local organization that advocates for fairness in water delivery to poor families.[23]

All three systems—built, natural, and human—operate in every community, but they may not be well integrated or may even be working at cross-purposes. Meeting today's water-related challenges requires better integration to achieve greater equity, sustainability, and adaptability.

Bounce Back or Bounce Forward

In February 2008, the foundational water management concept of stationarity was declared "dead" in an article in the influential journal *Science*. By this pronouncement, the authors meant that engineers could no longer base their designs and operating instructions for water supply and containment systems on the assumption that the natural hydrological system would continue to function within historical ranges. Instead, the "new normal" is higher highs and lower lows, with climate change altering hydrological parameters such as precipitation, evapotranspiration, discharge rates of rivers, and water stored in snowpacks.[24]

Crossing this threshold into the new normal affects built, natural, and human systems for managing water. Due to their inflexibility, size, cost, and, in many cases, poor condition, built systems are impacted most by the changing climate. Dams and levees fail when stronger storms exceed their design capacity. Deep tunnels dug to store stormwater are overwhelmed by ever-larger rainstorms. Reservoirs built to provide a reliable water supply shrink steadily in the face of prolonged drought. These conditions go beyond the design capacity of much of the existing built infrastructure in the United States.

Climate change impacts natural systems as well. Higher temperatures are contributing to increased evaporation rates and loss of natural water storage in snowpacks and glaciers. Rising sea levels are contaminating aquifers with saltwater. Insect infestations—more extensive and robust under warmer conditions—are killing forests and creating conditions for raging fires, followed by erosion and landslides that diminish the forests' capacity to provide community water supplies.

Human systems are also at risk. Many poor neighborhoods and public housing are located in low-lying areas vulnerable to flooding because the land is cheap. Thus, those who have the least ability to prepare, avoid, or recover from a natural disaster are also more likely to be hit by such a disaster.[25]

When a disaster occurs, there is great urgency to "bounce back," to put things back the way they were (the simplest definition of resilience); but prior choices may have contributed to the disaster and its consequences. A more effective way to spend recovery funds is to "bounce forward," using the momentum and awareness generated by the disaster to make transformative changes that position the community for better outcomes in the future.[26] For example, in 2008 in Port Arthur, Texas, Hurricane Ike destroyed public housing that was already impacted by a neighboring oil refinery. When the housing was replaced, it was moved away from the refinery to a safer place.[27]

Adapting Community Water Systems to a Changing Climate

At the most fundamental level, building the water resilience of our communities means increasing the water system's *adaptive capacity* to function under a wider range of hydrologic conditions by changing how we manage the built, natural, and human components.

Communities can increase adaptive capacity by reducing demand to free up built system capacity to deal with extremes. Water conservation—using (and reusing) water more efficiently and wasting less of it through fixing water leaks—is relatively quick and cheap for a community to achieve through incentives, regulations, and repairs. Raising the elevation of homes and businesses or moving them out of harm's way altogether can reduce the need for expensive flood protection systems like levees and pumps. Replacing aging infrastructure with built systems better designed for the new normal conditions is comparatively much more expensive and time-consuming. Some communities are experimenting with smaller, modular, and distributed water treatment systems, designed for multiple benefits, with feedback loops built in to guide continuing adaptation to changing conditions.[28]

Incorporating nature-mimicking elements into built systems is another effective approach. Examples include permeable paving, rain gardens, and constructed wetlands. For example, during a record-setting drought in 2007–2008, one Atlanta suburb avoided major water shortages by using a constructed wetland to maintain an abundant water supply.[29]

Natural hydrological systems are the foundation of built systems, providing water supply, receiving wastes, and maintaining a first line of defense against extreme weather events. When natural water systems reach a tipping point (e.g., watershed imperviousness, water pollution, wetland losses), the built system can break down, too. Protecting healthy systems from harm, restoring damaged components to good condition, and repairing ecological functions are strategies that communities can use to move toward greater resilience.

Communities can also strengthen the human assets involved in managing their built water systems. Engineers of all types need training in climate uncertainty and variability. Scientists and water managers need more and better means of communication to ensure timely and effective information transfer. Climate models need to provide a higher level of resolution to guide local land and water use decisions. Volunteers can help monitor and maintain green infrastructure and collect data to inform adaptive management of water resources as conditions change.

Transforming Community Water Systems

Ultimately, piecemeal repairs to a community's water system will not be enough. Instead of putting things back the way they were after a water crisis, a better strategy will be to use opportunities presented by natural disasters, infrastructure failures, or court orders to transform the system through integrating built, natural, and human elements. Patching together aging infrastructure is expensive and ineffective. Investing in *transforming* the water system will pay higher dividends.

Transforming water systems requires extensive collaboration and integration at many scales and in many locations: across disciplines, departments, and decision makers; across diverse stakeholder interests within a community; and among the many users and uses of water. The connectivity and scalability of freshwater hydrology can be used to link the concerns of communities up- and downstream, making watershed-wide plans extremely useful for thinking and acting at multiple scales in pursuit of sustainable and equitable water outcomes. A transformed community water system must seek flexible, adaptive, and integrated approaches with built-in feedback loops. It must recognize and incorporate the full costs of water and ensure safe, affordable water for all citizens.

With these principles in mind, many communities are experimenting with Integrated Water Management, which "promotes the coordinated development and management of water, land, and related resources, in order to maximize the resultant economic and social welfare in an equitable manner without compromising the sustainability of vital ecosystems."[30] This approach, also known as

"One Water,"[31] recognizes that all water is valuable and interconnected, whether in nature or in built systems, and should be managed in conjunction with energy, land use, and other key resources. Benefits of this approach go beyond ensuring reliable, affordable water services to enhancing recreation, property values, human health, and wildlife habitat. An early and successful adopter of this concept is the City of Los Angeles, where wastewater and drinking water utilities collaborated on wastewater, stormwater, water recycling, and water conservation needs.[32] As a result, the city saved an estimated $500 million in construction costs over the first five years of implementation and is on track to meet 50 percent of its water needs locally by 2035.[33]

Building Resilience at the Water's Edge

What approaches will best serve communities over the long term? The concept underpinning efforts to manage water for greater resilience is simple: work with nature and work together. Our actions must be ecologically sustainable, meeting the needs of natural systems that support life; and they must be socially equitable, meeting the needs of the most vulnerable members of society as well as the needs of future generations. Fortunately, in working with water systems, there are inherent synergies between the natural and human components that make these dual goals achievable.

Community resilience requires adequate stocks of natural and social capital[34] to prepare for, avoid, and recover from natural disasters and other twenty-first-century challenges. Water can be a strong platform for building a common identity to support social capital, whether because of a shared asset (e.g., water supply) or a shared threat (e.g., flood or drought). It can also provide opportunities to cultivate a sense of *agency* (the ability to make choices and act upon them) in a community through shared success in projects to protect or restore water-related natural capital. Further, the social capital built or strengthened through such natural capital projects will be available to address other community problems. In a mutually reinforcing cycle, tapping and building the benefits of healthy ecosystems and inclusive cooperation can help communities meet their water challenges and enhance their resilience.

Building Resilience by Working with Nature

To sustain a clean, ample water supply and protect communities from extreme weather events, communities need to protect and restore the components of their natural hydrological systems: surface and underground source waters, water quality and quantity, and streamside riparian areas.

Surface waters depend on forested watersheds for most of their supply (the forest system of trees, groundcover, roots, and soil retains water and slows evaporation). As previously noted, when more than 10 percent to 15 percent of a watershed is covered by impervious surfaces, ecological services are curtailed. Lakes and reservoirs in arid, hot climates are subject to high evaporation rates. In such areas, many communities are turning to underground storage, recharging their aquifers with treated effluent or storing excess water allocations. *Groundwater* supplies depend on precipitation falling on intact recharge areas and pumping rates that do not exceed recharge. Source waters can be overallocated to the point that even big rivers like the Colorado fail to reach the sea. Water conservation initiatives can help reduce the demand burden on source waters, even in times of growth; for example, communities can leverage the investment of new development by requiring developers to sponsor retrofits of existing homes and businesses with water conservation technologies, achieving a "net zero" in overall water use.[35]

Water quality can be protected through low-impact development ordinances that limit or slow stormwater runoff from developed areas, the largest source of pollution of surface waters. Major water pollution accidents can be avoided by keeping industrial and agricultural waste storage facilities out of floodplains and by limiting pipelines that cross under rivers. *Water quantity*— too much, too little, or at the wrong times—can be managed through floodplain mapping and zoning, water storage and use efficiencies, and modifying operations of dams and reservoirs.

Streamside riparian areas are impacted by development, hardening and channelizing stream segments, and heavier-than-usual volumes of stormwater that erode stream banks and undercut trees. In places that are still mostly natural, ecological services can be maintained through private conservation easements along river corridors and protected public lands, especially upland forests. For hydrological systems that are partially degraded, stream and watershed restoration projects can revive some ecosystem services. For example, wetlands and floodplains can be restored to store floodwaters and to filter pollution before it reaches the water supply. Riparian areas can be replanted with trees and native vegetation, lowering water temperatures for fish. Concrete and riprap can be removed, side channels can be reopened, and long-buried streams can be "daylighted." Thousands of river restoration projects are undertaken every year, guided by growing scientific understanding[36] of what constitutes ecologically successful river restoration and practical examples of effective approaches.[37]

Building Resilience by Working Together

Projects to protect or restore water resources, however, are too often scoped, designed, and implemented by scientists, engineers, and planners working for government agencies and environmental organizations without the participation of local citizens. When that happens, important civic engagement opportunities are missed, and valuable human resources are ignored. A 2015 report finds that "promoting social cohesion—in which a society's members cooperate to achieve shared well-being—in communities is an additional and overlooked tool for strengthening climate resilience, with particularly good outcomes in low-income communities."[38]

Another part of the problem is that the US legal system treats water as property that can be bought and sold, often at a cost beyond the reach of lower-income families and neighborhoods. An alternative view—of water as a basic human right—is emerging. For example, following the recent lead-tainted drinking water scandal in Flint and skyrocketing numbers of water shutoffs in Detroit, members of the Michigan legislature proposed a bill to ensure that every citizen in the state "has the right to safe, clean, affordable, and accessible water for human consumption, cooking and sanitary purposes."[39] Establishing a right to clean water is a key step in restoring public trust and environmental justice.

Successful collective water management efforts require the development of trust, shared values and behavioral norms, and social networks. Trust is most important and depends on equity and fairness,[40] but it is undermined by poverty, inequality, and environmental injustice. To create conditions that enable people to work together effectively, communities must first recognize and redress injustices such as the siting of polluting facilities in or near poor neighborhoods, poorly maintained or inadequate water infrastructure, water unaffordability and shutoffs, and lack of access to quality-of-life benefits that come from being near water.

Water management outcomes improve when community members can participate in a diverse and inclusive process to identify mutual concerns and shared values. Social scientists recognize that "crafting cross-cutting identities is a powerful way to enable connection across perceived diversity."[41] The common identity of living in the same watershed and depending on the same water resources and hydrological functions offers important opportunities for building bridges between different groups. Through community participation, information flows more easily, which increases awareness of our linked fates and effects of our actions (or inactions) on upstream and downstream neighbors.[42] Communities that invest in diverse, inclusive civic engagement are better at solving large, complex problems like water management than communities that do not embrace it.[43]

Conclusion

In 2005, Hurricane Katrina made landfall near New Orleans, killing more than eighteen hundred people and causing $151 billion in regional damages.[44] This was no natural disaster; rather, it was a human-made one brought on by poorly constructed levees, homes, and businesses built in extremely vulnerable low-lying areas and by inadequate means of evacuation. Today, New Orleans is transforming its relationship to water. The heart of New Orleans' award-winning resilience plan is "living with water,"[45] a combined strategy of working with nature—in this case, the Mississippi River—and working together as a community to restore water-related natural and social capital. Rather than abandon their city to extreme storms and rising seas, New Orleanians are leading the way in building community resilience at the water's edge and learning lessons that will benefit us all.

Notes

1. Robert Montgomery, *The Visionary D. H. Lawrence: Beyond Philosophy and Art* (Cambridge: Cambridge University Press, 1994), 187.
2. Clive Finlayson, *The Improbable Primate: How Water Shaped Human Evolution* (Oxford: Oxford University Press, 2014).
3. George McGraw, "For These Americans, Clean Water Is a Luxury," *New York Times*, October 10, 2016, http://www.nytimes.com/2016/10/20/opinion/for-these -americans-clean-water-is-a-luxury.html?emc=eta1&_r=0.
4. United Nations, "Climate Change Adaptation: The Pivotal Role of Water," UN Water Policy Brief (2010), 1, http://www.unwater.org/publications/publications -detail/en/c/206477/.
5. Aris Georgakakos et al., "Water Resources," in *Climate Change Impacts in the United States: The Third National Climate Assessment* (Washington, DC: US Global Change Research Program, 2014), 69–112, http://nca2014.globalchange.gov /report/sectors/water.
6. Andreas F. Prein et al., "The Future Intensification of Hourly Precipitation Extremes," *Nature Climate Change Journal Advance Online Publication*, December 5, 2016, www.nature.com/natureclimatechange.
7. Toby R. Ault et al., "Relative Impacts of Mitigation, Temperature, and Precipitation on 21st-Century Megadrought Risk in the American Southwest," *Science Advances* 2, no. 10 (October 5, 2016), http://advances.sciencemag.org/content/2/10 /e1600873.full.
8. P. C. D. Milly et al., "Stationarity Is Dead: Whither Water Management?" *Science* 319 (February 2008): 573–74.
9. USGS Water Science School, "Water Questions and Answers," last modified December 2, 2016, http://water.usgs.gov/edu/qa-solvent.html.
10. Wallace J. Nichols, *Blue Mind: The Surprising Science That Shows How Being Near, In, On or Under Water Can Make You Happier, Healthier, More Connected, and Better at What You Do* (New York: Little, Brown, 2014).
11. Polluted drinking water and the pollution of rivers, lakes, and reservoirs have consistently topped Americans' concerns throughout Gallup's twenty-seven-year trend measuring these environmental issues. Gallup, "Americans Concerns about Water Pollution Edge Up," March 17, 2016, http://www.gallup.com/poll/190034/ameri cans-concerns-water-pollution-edge.aspx.

12. California Energy Commission, "Water-Energy Nexus," accessed April 4, 2017, http://www.energy.ca.gov/research/iaw/water.html.

13. US Geological Survey, "California Water Use, 2010," last modified March 28, 2017, http://ca.water.usgs.gov/water_use/2010-california-water-use.html.

14. Steven Solomon, *Water: The Epic Struggle for Wealth, Power and Civilization* (New York: HarperCollins, 2010).

15. American Rivers et al., *Banking on Green: A Look at How Green Infrastructure Can Save Municipalities Money and Provide Economic Benefits Community-wide*, April 2012, https://www.americanrivers.org/conservation-resource/banking-on-green/.

16. American Rivers, "How Sewage Pollution Ends Up in Rivers," accessed April 4, 2017, https://www.americanrivers.org/threats-solutions/clean-water/sewage-pollution/.

17. National Weather Service Hydrologic Information Center, "Flood Loss Data," last modified May 14, 2015, http://www.nws.noaa.gov/hic/.

18. American Water Works Association, "Buried No Longer: Confronting America's Water Infrastructure Challenge," February 2012, http://www.awwa.org/Portals/0/files/legreg/documents/BuriedNoLonger.pdf.

19. Watersheds define the boundaries of natural water systems, collecting the precipitation that falls within the drainage basin and delivering it to a single outlet.

20. Center for Watershed Protection, "Impacts of Impervious Cover on Aquatic Systems," March 2003, http://owl.cwp.org/mdocs-posts/impacts-of-impervious-cover-on-aquatic-systems-2003/.

21. Sandra Postel and Brian Richter, *Rivers for Life: Managing Water for People and Nature* (Washington, DC: Island Press, 2003).

22. Natural Resources Conservation Service, US Department of Agriculture, "The History of the Acequia," accessed April 4, 2017, https://www.nrcs.usda.gov/Internet/FSE_DOCUMENTS/nrcs144p2_067306.pdf.

23. People's Water Board, accessed November 9, 2016, https://peopleswaterboard.org/about.

24. Milly et al., "Stationarity Is Dead."

25. Alice Fothergill and Lori A. Peek, "Poverty and Disasters in the United States: A Review of Recent Sociological Findings," *Natural Hazards* 32 (2004): 89–110, http://www.cdra.colostate.edu/data/sites/1/cdra-research/fothergill-peek2004poverty.pdf.

26. *Bounce Forward: Urban Resilience in the Era of Climate Change*, Strategy Paper from Island Press and the Kresge Foundation, 2015, 14, https://www.islandpress.org/resources/KresgeBrochure-framing-doc.pdf.

27. Christopher Flavelle, "Climate Change Is Already Forcing Americans to Move," *Bloomberg View*, October 31, 2016, https://www.bloomberg.com/view/articles/2016-10-31/climate-change-is-already-forcing-americans-to-move.

28. Charles River Watershed Association, Water Transformation Series, 2014, http://www.crwa.org/water-transformation-series.

29. American Rivers, "Natural Security: How Sustainable Water Strategies Are Preparing Communities for a Changing Climate," 2009, 48–55.

30. Global Water Partnership, "What Is IWRM?," accessed April 28, 2017, http://www.gwp.org/en/GWP-CEE/about/why/what-is-iwrm/.

31. Carol Howe and Pierre Mukheibir, *Pathways to One Water: A Guide for Institutional Innovation* (Alexandria, VA: Water Environment Research Foundation, 2015), http://www.werf.org/c/_FinalReportPDFs/SIWM/SIWM2T12a.aspx.

32. Water Environment Research Foundation, "Snapshot Case Studies: Los Angeles: Integrated Water Resources Plan," accessed April 4, 2017, http://www.werf.org/c/KnowledgeAreas/IntegratedInstitutionsinfo.aspx.

33. City of Los Angeles, *pLAn: Transforming Los Angeles: Environment/Economy/Equity*, April 8, 2015, http://plan.lamayor.org/about-the-plan/.

34. According to the International Institute for Sustainable Development, natural capital is "the water, land, air, living organisms and all formations of the Earth's biosphere that provide us with ecosystem goods and services imperative for survival and well-being" (https://www.iisd.org/wic/research/ecosystem/, accessed April 28, 2017). Social capital consists of the social relationships, information exchange networks, and behavioral norms used to advance the collective good.

35. Alliance for Water Efficiency, "Water Offset Policies for Water-Neutral Community Growth," January 2015.

36. Margaret Palmer et al., "Standards for Ecologically Successful River Restoration," *Journal of Applied Ecology* 42 (2005): 208–17.

37. Ann L. Riley, *Restoring Neighborhood Streams: Planning, Design, and Construction* (Washington, DC: Island Press, 2016).

38. Danielle Baussan, *Social Cohesion: The Secret Weapon in the Fight for Equitable Climate Resilience* (Washington, DC: Center for American Progress, 2015), 2, https://cdn.americanprogress.org/wp-content/uploads/2015/05/SocialCohesion-report2.pdf.

39. House Bill 5101 (Plawecki)/Senate Bill 643 (Young): Michigan Human Right to Water Act, introduced November 12, 2015, http://affordablewaternow.org/wp-content/uploads/2016/02/2015-HIB-5101.pdf. See also http://www.uusc.org/press_release/water-affordability-legislation-landmark-move/.

40. Elinor Ostrom and T. K. Ahn, "The Meaning of Social Capital and Its Link to Collective Action," October 1, 2007, in *Handbook on Social Capital*, ed. Gert T. Svendsen and Gunnar L. Svendsen (Cheltenham, UK: Edward Elgar, 2008; Indiana University, Bloomington: School of Public and Environmental Affairs Research Paper No. 2008-11-04), available at http://ssrn.com/abstract=1936058.

41. Robert Putnam and Lewis M. Feldstein, *Better Together: Restoring the American Community* (New York: Simon and Schuster, 2003), 279–82.

42. Robert D. Putnam, *Bowling Alone: The Collapse and Revival of American Community* (New York: Simon and Schuster, 2000), 288–89.

43. Ostrom and Ahn, *The Meaning of Social Capital.*

44. Data Center, "The New Orleans Index at Ten: Measuring Greater New Orleans' Progress toward Prosperity," July 2015, https://s3.amazonaws.com/gnocdc/reports/TheDataCenter_TheNewOrleansIndexatTen.pdf.

45. City of New Orleans, "Resilient New Orleans: Strategic Actions to Shape Our Future City," August 2015, http://resilientnola.org/wp-content/uploads/2015/08/Resilient_New_Orleans_Strategy.pdf.

CHAPTER 13

Food System Lessons from Vermont

Scott Sawyer

HUMAN ACTIVITIES ARE UNDERMINING the life support systems of the planet and triggering catastrophic changes. Today, on land, sea, and in the air, the signs of resource depletion, ecosystem degradation, and anthropogenic climate change are widespread. Food system activities are both a major driver of these changes and particularly vulnerable to them. The ability of food systems to prepare, mitigate, and adapt will be a major challenge for all societies.

What Is a Food System?

Food systems encompass the *processes* (e.g., planting, producing, harvesting, processing, packaging, transporting, marketing, consuming, and disposing of food), *resources* (e.g., land, soil, crops, animals, and machinery), and *people* (e.g., farmers, bakers, and policy makers) involved in providing nourishment to humans and many species of animals. Food systems are commonly understood and visible in the crops, cuisines, lingo (e.g., "pop" versus "soda"[1]), and products that are manifestations of the history, culture, and ecology of specific communities. We must also understand food systems as being linked at local, regional, national, and global scales, however. Every time you buy a cup of coffee, you are engaging a highly complex web of relationships.

How are food systems driving the changes that undermine the life-support systems of the planet? Today, the way food is produced, processed, sold, consumed, and disposed of for more than seven billion people and many billion more livestock[2] has transformed communities and ecosystems at every scale, from the loss of family farms and mom-and-pop diners to the ecological reengineering of much of California's Central Valley and the Midwest. Globally, the enormous scale of industrialized food production contributes to soil erosion, deforestation, water overuse and pollution, air pollution, climate change, and a wide range of social problems, from migration to obesity.

Although agriculture has affected ecosystems for millennia, the globally perilous scale of its current impacts is a relatively recent phenomenon. As Mark Kurlansky illustrates in *The Food of a Younger Land*, before supermarkets, chain restaurants, and frozen food, most people ate local, regional, seasonal, and traditional foods.[3] After World War II, however, a few critical and relatively quick developments radically transformed our relationship to food in the United States and ultimately much of the rest of the world: the replacement of human- and animal-based labor with fossil-fuel-based inputs and mechanized equipment; the construction of nationwide limited-access highway networks; and technological improvements in production, processing, and storage.

On one hand, the benefits of this transition have been enormous: the world is fed today by an extremely productive global food system that employs many millions of people and makes a wide variety of relatively affordable food consistently available in nearly every city, town, and village. On the other hand, the successes of the industrialized global food system have had substantial unintended consequences, impacting public health (e.g., increased obesity), social stability (e.g., decline of family farms), the economy (e.g., corporate monopolies of many food products), and the environment (e.g., soil erosion).

Everything Is at Stake, including Steak

The burning of fossil fuels to power society—together with the clearing of car-bon sinks such as forests for housing, agriculture, and other purposes—has cre-ated dangerous conditions for the resilience of food systems. Two reports from the US Department of Agriculture describe the anticipated detrimental effects of climate change on most crops, livestock, ecosystems, and human workers (these effects will vary somewhat by region):[4]

- Rising temperatures and altered precipitation patterns will affect agri-cultural productivity. Crop sector impacts from weather in the United States are likely to be greatest in the Midwest, and these impacts will likely expand due to damage from crop pests. Moreover, because the impacts of climate change are global, the availability of food products that we have been accustomed to enjoying—and that US companies use as key ingre-dients—will diminish. For example, cocoa production in Ghana and the Ivory Coast is expected to decline,[5] as is coffee production.[6]
- Livestock production systems are major contributors to greenhouse gas emissions and are also vulnerable to temperature stresses. Temperature stresses can be mitigated for animals raised indoors, but hotter summer temperatures may require new thermal environment control systems, and the cost and availability of animal feed will likely be a problem.
- Climate change will exacerbate current stresses from weeds, diseases, and insect pests on plants and animals; it will also alter pollinator life cycles, which will impact all types of crop and livestock production.
- Ecosystem services (e.g., flood control) that food systems depend on will be damaged. Increased incidences of extreme weather events will affect food production around the world.

In addition, the possible human health effects of climate change are large, and farmers and farm workers will be especially affected because they spend most of their days outside. These effects include the following:

- Injuries, illnesses, and deaths related to extreme heat and weather events.
- Infectious diseases related to changes in vector and zoonotic biology (e.g., Lyme disease) as well as risks from water and food contamination.
- Allergy and respiratory symptoms related to increasing plant and mold allergens and irritants in air.[7]

Emergence of Alternative Food Systems

Among the goals of resilience management is to "nurture and preserve the elements that enable the system to renew and reorganize itself following a massive change."[8] Over several decades, pockets of alternatives that aim to transform industrial food systems have emerged at all scales, from global movements like Slow Food and practices like organic farming, permaculture, and fair trade certification, to local grocery cooperatives and community gardens. These alternatives are often premised on the *relocalization* of food supply chains as well as on values such as authenticity, trust, soil health, sense of community, and sustainability.[9] In particular, advocates of alternative food systems envision a world in which the following occur:

- Agricultural activities preserve, reinforce, and revitalize the sustainability of working lands by farming in nature's image: recycling nutrients, maintaining soil health, promoting crop diversity, and protecting water quality.
- The elements of food systems—from soils, seeds, crops, and livestock, to processing, marketing, distributing, consuming, and composting—and the communities that depend on them are all systematically advanced by cooperation that expands the profitability of all involved partners.
- Farmers, farm workers, and food system workers are accorded safe and welcoming working conditions and are properly compensated for their work.
- All people have a greater understanding of how to obtain, grow, store, and prepare nutritional food.
- All people have access to healthy food they can afford, and food-related health problems decrease.

Consumer purchasing behaviors—particularly among millennials, the largest, most diverse age cohort in US history—have demonstrably shifted in recent years in favor of natural ingredients, locally sourced food, and better health.[10] Because the emergence of alternatives to conventional food system practices "spells doom for outdated food products and behind-the-times retail outlets and restaurants trying to sell them,"[11] the food industry is quickly moving to catch up. For example, even large corporations are now eliminating antibiotics in chicken or are selling cage-free eggs (e.g., McDonald's), dropping artificial colors and flavors (e.g., Kraft Macaroni & Cheese), and investing in organics (e.g., Walmart). Some product lines and corporations are experiencing declining sales (e.g., soda[12]), whereas others are acquiring companies that exemplify the values of alternative food systems (e.g., Post bought Mom's Best Cereals). Even so, some businesses and associations are fighting back by undermining regulations.[13]

More recently, alternative food systems are also emerging in the form of *systems-level* planning initiatives organized by cities, counties, regions, and states. One of the most advanced and comprehensive—and most relevant for building resilience at the level of communities—is Vermont's Farm to Plate initiative, the subject of the remainder of this chapter. Although Vermont is a state, its relatively low population (about 650,000) makes its experience applicable to many communities and regions across the country.

Farm to Plate: Transforming Vermont's Food System

In 2009, the Vermont state government passed legislation directing our organization, the Vermont Sustainable Jobs Fund (VSJF), to develop a ten-year strategic plan to strengthen Vermont's farm and food sector.[14] The threefold aim was to increase economic development in Vermont's food system, create jobs in the farm and food economy, and improve access to healthy local food for all Vermonters. Over the next eighteen months, VSJF and partnering organizations interviewed stakeholders, held regional public input events, and initiated new research on the major elements of Vermont's food system.

As a result of this effort, in 2011 we released the *Farm to Plate Strategic Plan,* identifying twenty-five goals and dozens of strategies to strengthen and grow Vermont's food system as well as the progress to reach those goals.[15] Also in 2011, we launched the Farm to Plate Network, which now includes more than 350 businesses, nonprofit organizations, government agencies, capital providers, and educational institutions collaborating and aligning their activities in support of the strategic plan's goals. The strategic plan, the network, and related projects are now collectively known as the Farm to Plate Initiative, with a common online home.[16]

By many accounts, Vermont has developed the most comprehensive food system plan in the United States. How did Vermonters do it? We harnessed the power of networks to build trust, pursue new opportunities, and tackle long-standing problems across the state and have developed a comprehensive data collection, analysis, and visualization system for tracking progress and telling stories. All our products (from network reports to the Farm to Plate website) and processes (from the two-day annual gathering to network meetings) are designed to be great experiences and facilitate relationship building. In short, the Vermont legislature asked, "If more of what we ate was locally or regionally produced, would this strengthen our local economy, create more jobs, and lead to greater food security for all Vermonters?" The Farm to Plate Initiative answered "Yes!" by establishing the value proposition that *food system development is sustainable development.*

As with many alternative food systems, the foundation of Vermont's food system is built on personal relationships among producers and consumers plus a collective desire to eat food that is healthy, is fresh, tastes good, and supports those who produce it. In many respects, Vermont had a head start: the social fabric of the state's communities is largely intact, and Vermont has long been a national leader in promoting sustainable agriculture practices and local food. There are no billboards in Vermont, very little traffic, and farms, forests, rivers, lakes, and independent businesses are easily experienced in daily life. Local raw and processed food is easily accessible and available to the majority of Vermonters through farmers' markets, community-supported agriculture (CSA) farm subscriptions, farm stands, co-ops, specialty food stores, restaurants, and, increasingly, institutions, independent grocers, and chain grocery stores.

Guidance for Food System Resilience

It is tempting to approach the resilience of a community food system by asking the question, "Can we feed ourselves with local food?" One should avoid that temptation as an end in itself because the answer is almost certainly no (not a very desirable answer if you need coffee to start your day). Strengthening your food system will necessarily require a broader focus, with special attention paid to working with gatekeepers, analyzing linked systems, and using frameworks that will make your work more efficient and effective.

Who Opens the Door?

In a review of earlier food system plans, it became clear that the entity that asked for the plan played a large role in the long-term success of the effort. That the Vermont legislature asked for *the Farm to Plate Strategic Plan* to be developed opened every door for VSJF to cultivate relationships, secure buy-in, and raise funds. Initiatives that do not have official sanctioning or institutional support appear to diminish over time.

Many governmental officials are waking up to the risk posed by climate change as well as the opportunities presented by food system development. To the extent possible, one should cultivate relationships with public policy and other food system organizations, local officials, and state legislators that are interested in food system issues and encourage them to pass state- or region-wide multiyear food system planning initiatives. Regional or statewide plans are preferable because they are more likely to encompass agricultural regions that city-specific plans normally cannot account for. We do not discount the effectiveness and passion of single issue or smaller scale initiatives like community gardens; literally every scale of change is needed. Rather, promoting comprehensive resilience requires *sustained, networked action* with the power to keep the door open while reconfiguring the rules and resources governing food systems.

Analyze Linked Human and Environmental Systems

Our ongoing analysis of Vermont's food system is built around the system operating within—and being influenced by—social, political, economic, and environmental contexts that are local, regional, national, and global in scope. This concept is reflected in our "soil to soil" model of the elements of the Vermont food system (figure 13-1). The model begins with the soil and other farm inputs that go into various types of food production; it follows these food products as they go through additional processing and are distributed to local, regional,

Figure 13-1. The elements of Vermont's food system.
Source: Vermont Sustainable Jobs Fund.

national, and international market outlets; and, finally, it considers what happens to these products when they are returned to the environment (e.g., back to the soil as compost).

A systems approach required us to dig deeper into topics beyond the economic development, jobs, and food security priorities originally identified by the legislation that started the Farm to Plate Initiative. In developing the *Farm to Plate Strategic Plan*, we focused on cross-cutting issues that affect the major elements of Vermont's food system: financing, education, labor and workforce development, technical assistance, energy, and public policy. Based on our analysis of strengths, weaknesses, opportunities, and threats facing the major elements of Vermont's food system, we developed the twenty-five goals of the plan plus many objectives and strategies. The Farm to Plate Network is now addressing these topics and is using indicators and data visualizations to monitor and report progress.

Frameworks and Networks Work

Organizational silos have historically dogged the cultures and processes of individual organizations, let alone large-scale change initiatives. However, food system enterprises, technical assistance providers, advocacy organizations, and government agencies need highly networked communication and coordination regarding land access, product availability, market data, rules and regulations, distribution systems, and many other issues.

We found the framework for *collective impact* ("the commitment of a group of important actors from different sectors to a common agenda for solving a specific social problem"[17]), developed by John Kania and Mark Kramer, to be a useful approach for organizing the Farm to Plate Initiative. There are five conditions of collective impact:

1. **Backbone support.** Collective impact initiatives require organizations (like VSJF) that can plan and manage the initiative as well as support it with facilitation, technology, communications, data collection, reporting, logistics, and administration.

2. **Common agenda.** A common agenda is a shared vision for change that includes a common understanding of challenges and an approach to solving them. Here, the *Farm to Plate Strategic Plan* is the common agenda being implemented by the 350-plus member organizations of the Farm to Plate Network.

3. **Continuous communication.** The Farm to Plate website contains all our food system research and strategic plan sections as well as job listings, news, events, stories, maps, projects, and more than a hundred data visualizations of Farm to Plate goals. Network groups also use the website to share notes and documents.

4. **Mutually reinforcing activities.** The Farm to Plate Network creates the space for strategic conversations and coordination among multiple stakeholders to make systematic food system changes that no one organization can accomplish alone. Working groups are at the core of the Farm to Plate Network. Each working group takes responsibility for a set of goals, strategies, and indicators from the *Farm to Plate Strategic Plan* to further develop, implement, and monitor annually.

5. **Shared measurement system.** Although the collective impact framework does not specify a shared measurement system to use, we have found the results-based accountability[18] system to be very helpful. This system simplifies indicators by differentiating between results for whole populations (i.e., population indicators) and results for particular programs, organizations, or services (i.e., performance measurements). This distinction is key because it both explains and determines which organizations are accountable for what results. In other words, organizations are responsible for the programs and services they administer. They are not responsible for results for whole populations. Rather, it is the collective impact of many organizations *working together* that influences population indicators.

The collective impact framework does not specifically identify funding as a condition, but involving funders in the process from the beginning was fundamental to the success of our initiative. So, a sixth condition was added:

6. **Funding.** Develop broad support from state government, foundations, corporate donors, and fee–for-service revenues by actively involving funding organizations in the planning process.

Getting alignment among so many organizations is challenging at first, but it evolved as more organizations in the network built trusting relationships with one another. Much of the trust building comes from quarterly working group meetings and other experiences shared together throughout the year. It is worth the effort to build a strong, trusting network. Your network is your Swiss Army knife: a key feature of networks is the ability to simultaneously attack problems from many angles.

Actions for Food System Resilience

Successful and mutually reinforcing activities in a food system initiative are the manifestations of systems thinking, useful organizing frameworks, and relationship building. Farm to Plate activities have included new research and analyses, data visualizations, case studies, career profiles, presentations, workshops, trainings, videos, and matchmaking events. The remainder of this chapter uses the elements of the food system diagram (see figure 13-1) to describe processes and actions that communities can explore to build the resilience of their food system. In our experience, a handful of fundamental challenges for each element of Vermont's food system rose to the surface and demanded multiyear, sustained action.

Farm Inputs: Increasing Farmland Access

Before food production can occur, a number of critical inputs are required, from land to labor and from seed to feed. In Vermont, a long-term decrease in land in agriculture, the challenge of affordable access to farmland (particularly for young farmers), and soil health are identified as major farm input resilience challenges. The Farmland Access and Stewardship Working Group[19] has pursued a variety of strategies for conserving land, expanding access to land (e.g., conservation easement programs, cooperative land management arrangements, and farm incubator programs), matchmaking efforts (e.g., via the Land Link farm property clearinghouse website[20]), farmland investment and leasing models, farm succession planning, protecting soils and reducing runoff, improving forage management and storage, and increasing on-farm energy production. None of these types of programs on its own can ensure that farmland is accessible to future generation of farmers or that soil health is improved. Rather, it is the *totality* of these programs—and the network of service providers that coordinate the deployment of these programs—that can ensure that healthy soils and farmland are available to future generations.

Food Production: Addressing Scale Asymmetries

Vermont's small size, relatively short growing season, and topography are barriers to generating large volumes of food products typical in other states. For example, our estimates indicate that Vermont food production for in-state consumption is likely short—by hundreds of millions of pounds—with regard to most fresh and lightly processed food products. This scale asymmetry represents Vermont's food production resilience challenge, but it is also endemic in America's food system. For example, small family farms make up 88 percent of all US farms but only 20 percent of sales, whereas large family farms (which generally produce commodities like dairy products, grains, and meats) make up 3 percent of the total but account for 45 percent of sales (figure 13-2).

Farm viability, then, is at the heart of Farm to Plate efforts to improve the resilience of food production in Vermont. Farm input costs, market access, food safety, business management, infrastructure and equipment, distribution, and environmental impacts all play roles in farm viability and can be particularly challenging for smaller scales of production. The Production and Processing Working Group[21] addresses these variables by aggregating and developing standardized information on the viability of various business models and scales as a way to increase diffusion of best practices and industry benchmarks, diagnosing the viability of individual businesses and larger industries as a whole, and providing farms with indicators and tools for more thoroughly

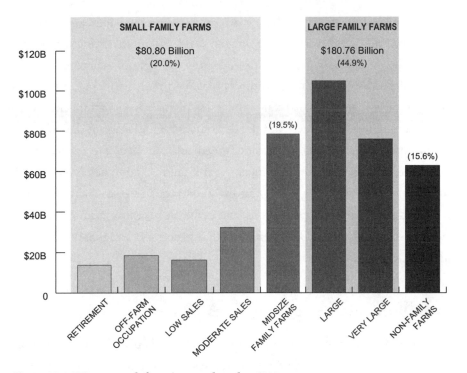

Figure 13-2. US gross cash farm income by sales, 2012.
Source: Vermont Sustainable Jobs Fund. Data: USDA 2012 Census of Agriculture, https://www.agcensus.usda.gov/Publications/2012/Online_Resources/Typology/typology13_us.pdf.

assessing and self-examining the viability of new enterprises, current operations, or expansions.

Food Processing and Manufacturing: Tailoring Support

Vermont produces world-class cheese, maple syrup, beer, ice cream, and many other products, and food manufacturing in Vermont is growing at a faster rate than overall manufacturing. The presence of a diverse range of food processors and manufacturers is one of your best clues to determine the health of your food system. Local breweries, bakeries, specialty food manufacturers, and cheese makers use local ingredients—and push producers to increase the availability of local ingredients—as well as ingredients from around the world, so they have a vested interested in the resilience of other food systems. Food processing and manufacturing jobs also typically pay better wages than retail jobs, and they help create buzz and brand awareness about your food system. In addition, entrepreneurs of these businesses often provide leadership throughout their communities.

Food processors and manufacturers have common financing, infrastructure, equipment, technical assistance, business planning, education, and workforce training needs; however, but the diversity, size, and stage of development of food processing and manufacturing categories (e.g., Ben & Jerry's ice cream compared to a small jam maker) means that a tailored approach is warranted. To that end, the Financing Cross-Cutting Team[22] has assessed financing gaps, identified new funding opportunities, and promoted creative funding arrangements across the "capital continuum"[23] so that processors and manufacturers of all scales can be successful.

Food Distribution: Facilitating Transactions

The scale of production of alternative food systems is usually such that small and medium-sized farms and food enterprises have a hard time gaining access to the volume-oriented, low-cost environment of traditional retail markets. Instead, they have excelled at direct sales via farmers' markets, CSA farms, and farm stands, but these sales represent a very small percentage of overall food sales. A key insight of our research is that, to be successful, food enterprises must align their stage of development (e.g., startup stage) and the type and scale of their operations with suitable market outlets.

Local and national distributors—who provide "first mile" (i.e., helping farmers and other producers prepare for wholesale production) and "last mile" (i.e., finding creative solutions to buyer needs) services—have recently stepped up to facilitate local transactions at colleges, hospitals, and government institutions. For example, Sodexo, a large national distributor to higher education food service operations in Vermont, has made buying local a priority and has developed and staffed a "Vermont First" program to facilitate this process. This program is widely seen as having made the process more streamlined and efficient and having increased local procurement by connecting vendors and buyers and then reporting back sales figures.

Retail: Finding Niches

The presence of local food products on menus and store shelves is another big clue about the health of your food system. Although it is comparatively easier now to access local raw and processed food at many market outlets in Vermont and elsewhere than it used to be, the share of total home food sales in the United States that takes place in supermarkets and supercenters increased from 37 percent in 1958 to 81 percent in 2014.[24] Most producers and processors in Vermont and other alternative food systems are *not* at a scale to supply supermarkets and supercenters. With that in mind, the Aggregation and Distribution Working Group[25] has focused on independent retail food outlets, including country stores, convenience stores, and smaller grocery stores. Independent stores occupy the middle ground *above* direct sales but *below* chain supermarkets. The Farm to Plate Network seeks to make local food in these market channels more available and affordable to consumers through marketing assistance, consumer incentive programs, procurement policies, and more efficient supply chain logistics.[26]

Consumption: Increasing Inclusion

The adoption of local purchasing behaviors has shifted dramatically as consumers, chefs, and food manufacturers have demanded more locally sourced meats, produce, and minimally processed ingredients. One of the biggest concerns of alternative food systems has been ensuring that all segments of society have access to local, healthier food. Vermont is not racially or ethnically diverse, but there are class and region-based differences. The resilience challenge, in this case, is to include all Vermonters in the opportunities presented by local food. Research conducted by the Consumer Education and Marketing Working Group[27] found that many Vermonters want local food to be more connected to Vermont traditions and communities. After all, Vermonters were farming, gardening, fishing, and hunting long before there were craft beers and gourmet burgers. The "Rooted in Vermont"[28] statewide grassroots marketing campaign uses social media to celebrate all Vermonters' entry points to local food and is geared toward engaging Vermonters not usually characterized as part of the local food movement.

Nutrient Management: Creating Synergies

The *Farm to Plate Strategic Plan* asks Vermonters to embrace the adage "waste equals food" by recycling and redistributing the nutrients we use rather than overly relying on importing nutrients (e.g., fertilizers) or sending nutrient-rich food scraps to the landfill. In 2012, Vermont passed a *universal recycling law* that requires that certain recyclable and organic materials, including food residuals, be diverted from landfills by 2020. By banning the disposal of all organics by 2020, Vermont is heavily relying on its food system to meet these diversion goals. As a result, innovative synergies have emerged between Vermont's waste management, farm inputs, food security, workforce development, and renewable energy communities. For example, Salvation Farms' Vermont Commodity Program—a food hub for aggregating surplus crops and distributing them to food-insecure Vermonters—pairs postharvest handling experience with job training for refugees, formerly incarcerated people, and youth in transition.[29]

Food System Resilience in Practice

On August 28, 2011, Tropical Storm Irene swept through Vermont, killing six people, destroying or damaging 311 bridges, and flooding 20,000 acres of farmland.[30] Vermont's close-knit food system community sprang into action: as neighbors helped farmers dig out of the muck, dozens of agencies, institutions, and food system nonprofits collaborated to help affected farms. Thanks to an outpouring of donations from individuals and organizations, grants and loans were soon offered to farmers who had suffered damage.

Vermont was able to recover quickly after Irene thanks to resilience-building patterns—like trusting relationships, information sharing, and spare capacity—that Vermonters have been cultivating in their food system for decades. The Farm to Plate Initiative is simply a continuation of that Vermont culture of resilience, an effort by the community to ensure that our food system continues adapting to meet the challenges of a changing world.

Notes

1. Nikhil Sonnad, "*The Great American Word Mapper,*" Quartz, accessed April 5, 2017, http://qz.com/862325/the-great-american-word-mapper.
2. Timothy P. Robinson et al., "Mapping the Global Distribution of Livestock," *PloS One* 9, no. 5 (2014): e96084.
3. Mark Kurlansky, *The Food of a Younger Land* (New York: Riverhead Books, 2009).
4. *Climate Change and Agriculture in the United States: Effects and Adaptation,* USDA Technical Bulletin 1935 (Washington, DC: US Department of Agriculture, Office of the Chief Economist, 2012), www.usda.gov/oce/climate_change/ effects_2012 /effects_agriculture.htm; Scott Malcolm et al., *Agricultural Adaptation to a Changing Climate: Economic and Environmental Implications Vary by U.S. Region,* USDA Economic Research Service, Economic Research Report No. (ERR-136), July 2012, https://www.ers.usda.gov/publications/pub-details/?pubid=44989.
5. Peter Läderach, "Predicting the Impact of Climate Change on the Cocoa-Growing Regions in Ghana and Cote d'Ivoire," International Center for Tropical Agriculture, September 2011, www.eenews.net/assets/2011/10/03/document_cw_01.pdf.
6. Jeremy Haggar and Kathleen Schepp, "Coffee and Climate Change: Impacts and Options for Adaptation in Brazil," University of Greenwich National Resources Institute Working Paper Series: Climate Change, Agriculture and Natural Resources No. 4, February 2012, www.nri.org/docs/ promotional/D5930-11_NRI _Coffee_Climate_Change_WEB.pdf.
7. US Environmental Protection Agency, "Climate Change Indicators: Health and Society," last updated November 2, 2016, https://www.epa.gov/climate-indicators /health-society.
8. Brian Walker et al., "Resilience Management in Social-ecological Systems: A Working Hypothesis for a Participatory Approach," *Conservation Ecology* 6, no. 1 (2002): 14, http://www.consecol.org/vol6/iss1/art14; Brian Walker and David Salt, *Resilience Thinking: Sustaining Ecosystems and People in a Changing World* (Washington, DC: Island Press, 2006), 1.
9. Steve Martinez et al., "Local Food Systems: Concepts, Impacts, and Issues," USDA Economic Research Service, Economic Research Report No. 97, May 2010, https:// www.ers.usda.gov/webdocs/publications/err97/7054_err97_1_.pdf.
10. James Rushing, *Ripe for Grocers: The Local Food Movement,* A. T. Kearney, May 2014, https://www.atkearney.com/consumer-products-retail/featured-article/-/asset_pub lisher/S5UkO0zy0vnu/content/ripe-for-grocers-the-local-food-movement/10192; *What's Hot: 2017 Culinary Forecast,* National Restaurant Association, accessed April 5, 2017, http://www.restaurant.org/News-Research/Research/What-s-Hot.
11. Technomic, *Food Industry Transformation: The Next Decade,* May 5, 2015; see https:// blogs.technomic.com/how-the-next-decade-will-make-or-break-food-brands/.

12. John Kell, "Soda Consumption Falls to 30-Year Low in the U.S.," *Fortune*, March 29, 2016, http://fortune.com/2016/03/29/soda-sales-drop-11th-year/.

13. Michael Pollan, "Big Food Strikes Back: Why Did the Obamas Fail to Take on Corporate Agriculture?," *New York Times Magazine*, October 5, 2016, http://www.nytimes.com/interactive/2016/10/09/magazine/obama-administration-big-food-policy.html.

14. Vermont Sustainable Jobs Fund, "Enabling Legislation," appendix A in *Farm to Plate Strategic Plan*, updated February 2015, http://www.vtfarmtoplate.com/plan/chapter/appendix-a-enabling-legislation.

15. Vermont Sustainable Jobs Fund, "Getting to 2020," chap. 2 in *Farm to Plate Strategic Plan*, updated July 2013, http://www.vtfarmtoplate.com/getting-to-2020.

16. Vermont Sustainable Jobs Fund, "The Farm to Plate Network," Farm to Plate, accessed April 28, 2017, http://www.vtfarmtoplate.com/network.

17. John Kania and Mark Kramer, "Collective Impact," *Stanford Social Innovation Review*, Winter 2011, https://ssir.org/articles/entry/collective_impact.

18. "What Is Results-Based Accountability?," Clear Impact, accessed April 5, 2017, https://clearimpact.com/results-based-accountability/.

19. Vermont Sustainable Jobs Fund, "Farmland Access and Stewardship," Farm to Plate, accessed April 28, 2017. http://www.vtfarmtoplate.com/network/farmland-access-stewardship.

20. Vermont Land Link, http://vermontlandlink.org/.

21. Vermont Sustainable Jobs Fund, "Production and Processing," Farm to Plate, accessed April 28, 2017, http://www.vtfarmtoplate.com/network/production-and-processing.

22. Vermont Sustainable Jobs Fund, "Financing," Farm to Plate, accessed April 28, 2017, http://www.vtfarmtoplate.com/network/financing.

23. Flexible Capital Fund, *Capital Continuum*, http://flexiblecapitalfund.com/wp-content/uploads/2016/09/Flex-Fund-Vermont-Capital-Continuum.pdf.

24. Vermont Sustainable Jobs Fund, "Population Indicators: Share of Food Sales at Grocery Stores and Supercenters Increased from 1983 to 2014," in "Getting to 2020," chap. 2 in *Farm to Plate Strategic Plan*, May 2013, http://www.vtfarmtoplate.com/getting-to-2020/13-local-food-availability#indicator-population-indicator-6.

25. Vermont Sustainable Jobs Fund, "Aggregation and Distribution," Farm to Plate, accessed April 28, 2017, http://www.vtfarmtoplate.com/network/aggregation-distribution.

26. Vermont Sustainable Jobs Fund, "Independent Grocers," Farm to Plate, accessed April 28, 2017, http://www.vtfarmtoplate.com/network/independent-grocers/activity.

27. Vermont Farm to Plate, "Consumer Education and Marketing," http://www.vtfarmtoplate.com/network/consumer-education-marketing.

28. Rooted in Vermont, www.Facebook.com/RootedinVermont.

29. Marcella Houghton, "Training Workers, Rescuing Food," Vermont Farm to Table, http://www.vtfarmtoplate.com/features/training-workers-rescuing-food#.WFntjv krJEY.

30. Vermont Long-Term Disaster Recovery Group, *We're Going to Get It Done*, accessed April 5, 2017, http://www.vermontdisasterrecovery.com/sites/www .vermontdisasterrecovery.com/themes/vdr/uploads/pdfs/tropical_storm_irene_re port.pdf.

CHAPTER 14

Learning Our Way toward Resilience

William Throop

IN THE SIMPLEST TERMS, resilience education is about building our individual and community capacities to flourish in times of tremendous transition. It strengthens our ability to weather the inevitable adversity that comes with system transformation. It gives us a systems lens through which to understand the forces driving change at multiple scales. It harnesses the creative energy of people, enabling work across cultural divides to increase the sustainability of our social-ecological systems. At its heart, it cultivates virtues like courage, humility, and frugality, which help us preserve what we most value in our communities.

Communities must *learn* their way toward greater resilience. Resilience education provides a toolkit with different approaches to learning. Some of the tools are easily used and widely available, but many others require significant institutional change and are underutilized. For example, it is fairly easy to design user-friendly materials that explain resilience thinking to various audiences, but information alone tends to produce little change in thinking patterns and behavior.[1] To truly build community resilience, we need to change the ways we deal with problems; thus, resilience education must cultivate new sets of interlocking skills, concepts, habits, and relationships. Unless curricula are embedded into resilience-oriented school cultures, their effect on behavior will be limited.

Deep resilience learning will require systematic change in the way that education has traditionally been delivered. How, though, do we create such cultures, and over what kind of time frame is this possible? Because schools primarily touch the younger generation, we must move beyond the classroom and create powerful learning opportunities that serve groups across our communities. Ultimately, we must all become teachers of a sort, master learners of the art of systems adaptation and transformation.

In this chapter, our most important educational tools for resilience building are described, some examples of their effective use are provided, and some of their limitations are indicated. Each tool can be used to cultivate the six foundations of community resilience (see chapter 1): people, systems thinking, adaptability, transformability, sustainability, and courage—but some tools are better suited to certain of these foundations. To strengthen community resilience with the speed necessary to handle the challenges we face, we must use all the tools simultaneously and skillfully. We cannot wait for a new generation that has had a large enough dose of resilience schooling to shift our cultural practices.

∼

When we speak of education in the United States, we often mean formal, institution-based schooling: kindergarten through twelfth grade (K–12) and the postsecondary system. Here an institution sets both the goals of learning and the means by which learning is conveyed. Because the early stages of this system affect almost everyone in the United States, it has high potential to influence the habits of the populace over time—but that means that its impact has a time lag, which we can ill afford. Postsecondary formal education has less of a time lag, but reaches a smaller portion of the population. When we move beyond formal education, we find a dizzying array of kinds of nonformal and informal education.[2]

In nonformal education, the learner selects the educational goals, but the institution determines the means by which these goals are met. These programs include continuing education courses, skills trainings, and after-school programs. Adult education avoids the time lag problem mentioned above, but because its programs cater to those who already have an interest in a topic, they often do not reach a diverse audience. In informal education, there is no formal curriculum at all. The learner chooses the means for acquiring knowledge or skills, but an organization typically produces the materials. Such materials may be sought out by a potential learner, or they may simply be stumbled upon. Because the information is often accessed by chance, informal education has a somewhat broader reach than nonformal education. Some theorists also distinguish self-directed learning, in which someone selects both the goals and the means of acquiring knowledge.[3] Ultimately, the distinctions between these different forms of education blur, but their potential for reaching different audiences is crucial for accelerating resilience education.

K–12 Education

The K–12 formal education system has always taught some elements of resilience, although only recently has it used that label. The social skills taught in early grades, the literacy and critical analytical skills emphasized throughout schooling, the ability to learn from failure, and the civic engagement curricula in high schools all build resilience capacity. Such schooling emphasizes the "people" and "adaptability" foundations of building community resilience, which are essential for enabling people in a community to work together to solve problems.

Teachers often add place-based experiential components to a curriculum to build greater understanding of local system dynamics and empower students to contribute to their communities. For example, more than three thousand schools in the United States use community gardens as learning laboratories. In 2014, more than a fourth of all public elementary schools had a school garden.[4] Such gardens are easily started, although they need the commitment of multiple teachers for their benefits to be fully realized. Without such support, they often become an optional activity for after school rather than a multifaceted means of educating about systems thinking.

Water quality monitoring in local streams and other forms of service learning can have similar benefits. As students experience problems in one part of a system, they begin to ask questions about other parts of the system, drawing connections and seeking solutions. Some schools use volunteers to aid teachers in offering such programs, which enhances community connections and trust. Some schools also use building renovations and operations to demonstrate sustainable design and management. Increasingly, schools are using their own buildings and grounds as learning laboratories, helping students understand energy flows, cycles of resource utilization and waste, sustainable purchasing, and local flora.[5]

As curricula shift to embrace more hands-on resilience engagement, the role of the teacher must shift as well. The pedagogy of place- and project-based education requires teachers to relinquish some control over students, to adapt to student interests and community goals, and to learn along with students. This process can be exhilarating but also exhausting. Schools that make such pedagogy routine have come together to form the Green Schools National Network and similar groups to support the enterprise of transforming K–12 education to meet the needs of a sustainable future. A similar initiative, the National Wildlife Federation's Eco Schools program, included more than 4,700 schools in 2017.[6]

Indeed, "green schools"—institutions that specialize in environmental education—have tremendous potential for systematically building community resilience because they can serve as educational hubs that extend far beyond the student body. For example, the Common Ground School, an environmental charter high school in Connecticut with 185 students, offers after-school programs, summer camps, and adult education.[7] It runs a sizable urban farm that engages the local community and that employed ninety-three youth in 2015. The school estimates that fifteen thousand community members have joined in its educational programs. The curriculum and facilities serve as models for a holistic treatment of the foundations of community resilience, where the culture and operations of the school reinforce the classroom learning. Parents and other family members are likely to be indirectly influenced by what students are learning and to be engaged with other community members in the school's nonformal educational programs.

Almost inevitably, such schools cultivate character traits in their students, but they rarely do so explicitly, which is a missed opportunity. Character traits like courage, humility, and grit are crucial for both personal and community resilience. In recent years, US public education has been highly focused on developing students' basic communication and quantification skills and testing these skills as a means of improving education, but development of students' character has received less attention. KIPP public charter schools are one exception; they have made character development central to their mission. More than two hundred KIPP schools around the country have taught more than eighty thousand students with a curriculum grounded in positive psychology's work on virtue cultivation.[8] Of course, character should be developed in the home and reinforced in major institutions like businesses and places of worship, but the centrality of citizens' character to their community's resilience makes it risky to leave character development out of resilience education.

Despite some excellent work being done on developing K–12 resilience education, many schools are only teaching basic resilience skills or offering an occasional special program that is not integrated into a holistic resilience curriculum or the school culture. It is hard to change the majority of schools without a change in state level educational standards and a lot of teacher development. By late 2016, sixteen states had adopted the new Next Generation Science Standards (a set of standards developed by the National Research Council and other institutions), which include some resilience-learning outcomes, but much more needs to be done in this area.[9] Teachers are often constrained by competing demands for their time, evaluations based on test results, and budget issues, so even if they see the value of resilience education, they may not pursue it. It can be very difficult to motivate robust resilience education in one's local schools. Sometimes, though, all it takes is one visionary and energetic teacher or principal, with some public support, to demonstrate how experiential resilience education can begin to transform children and a region.

Higher Education

Higher education provides skills and knowledge for most of the people who will lead communities, businesses, governments, and other institutions, so it should be among the most useful tools in the resilience education toolbox. It is just beginning to live up to this promise. The sustainability movement in colleges and universities has taken off lately. From 2005 to 2016, the Association for the Advancement of Sustainability in Higher Education (AASHE) grew to include more than 20 percent of the country's approximately four thousand higher education institutions, most of which are trying to integrate sustainability into curricula and operations. The association introduced the Sustainability Tracking and Rating System (STARS), which sets standards for sustainable practices throughout an institution. These standards—the higher education equivalent of LEED building standards—have guided institutional transformation. Sustainability rankings such as *Princeton Review*'s "Guide to 361 Green Colleges" and *Sierra* magazine's "Cool Schools" issue have created friendly competition between universities and helped students find schools that are on the sustainability vanguard.

This sustainability movement was built on the foundation of popular environmental studies programs and the growing interest in justice studies. It explicitly embraces a systems focus, which seeks to understand social and economic systems within their ecological contexts. Many schools started with a few sustainability courses, but soon these courses grew into interdisciplinary sustainability minors, majors, and graduate programs, which often focus on a topic like energy, food, or justice. The pedagogy tends to be interdisciplinary and project-based, using the campus and the surrounding communities as learning labs. As with K–12 schooling, the development of a campus culture informed by sustainability has much greater effect on behavior than a few academic programs.

Student interest has been an important driver of this more holistic approach to sustainability. The *Princeton Review* estimates that almost two-thirds of students applying to college are concerned about an institution's sustainable practices, no matter what they intend to study. Higher education leadership has also galvanized action. More than seven hundred higher education presidents have signed the American College and University Presidents Climate Commitment to achieve climate neutrality and to integrate sustainability across the curriculum. A few institutions have already achieved climate neutrality, and 61 percent of institutions have reduced total greenhouse gas emissions by 3.77 million metric tons of carbon dioxide equivalent.[10]

Good sustainability education addresses most of the foundations of community resilience, although with some differences. For example, the resilience lens highlights the needs for redundancies and modularity in systems rather than the ruthless pursuit of efficiency that often characterizes sustainability approaches.[11] It looks at the general characteristics of systems that enable them to cope with a range of disruptions and adjust to new realities. The need to help communities adapt to climate change, water shortages, energy transitions, economic disruption, and mass migrations of peoples has recently motivated a new resilience emphasis in higher education. In 2015, Second Nature, an organization that works with leaders in higher education to promote sustainability, added resilience to its climate commitment: signatories will work with their local communities to develop and implement plans that assist the region in adapting to the impacts of climate change, and they will include resilience education in the curriculum for all students.

To see how comprehensive resilience learning in a higher education environment can function, it is helpful to see what holistic sustainability/resilience education looks like from the student point of view. It varies, of course, but I will use my own institution, Green Mountain College in Vermont, as an example of what twenty years of work on the thorough integration of sustainability into the curriculum and operations can yield (similar stories could be told about many institutions).

During orientation at Green Mountain College, new undergraduate students are introduced to the campus and the region as a learning laboratory for sustainability. They begin to learn the campus norms regarding energy use, recycling and composting, and social interactions; they begin the process of acculturation. Most of them spend time on the farm that supplies food to the dining hall; they tour the biomass combined-heat-and-power

plant that—along with efficiency retrofits, solar installations, and carbon off-
sets—has enabled the college to become climate neutral. In their first semester,
students start taking sustainability-themed general education courses, which
explore the dynamics of human and natural systems at multiple scales while
teaching standard college-level skills. Instead of college algebra, for example,
they might take quantitative environmental analysis. First-year composition
courses explore diversity and inclusion issues and the role that our images of
nature play in structuring our relation to natural systems. Students start to
understand the dynamics of the regional social-ecological system and begin to
tell their own sustainability stories.

Soon they select majors, some of which reflect traditional liberal arts and
preprofessional disciplines, but many of which address dimensions of sustainability, such as renewable energy and ecological design or animal conservation and care. Students will probably take some one-credit sustainability skills
courses on topics like solar panel installation, home energy audits, food preservation, and cheese making. These popular short courses taught by professionals in the region aim at the reskilling of people necessary for flourishing in
a post-carbon economy. Students work with faculty on sustainability projects
for stakeholders in the region. As they advance, they may take courses in our
graduate programs in sustainable and resilient communities, sustainable business, and sustainable food systems. By their senior year, students will have taken
a capstone general education course in which they plan and execute a project
that serves a genuine community need, and they will develop their own vision
for how they will contribute to creating more just and sustainable communities.
Alumni surveys and other data suggest that this kind of holistic education cultivates the skills necessary for change agents.[12]

What are the limitations of educating for resilience through higher education, aside from higher ed reaching only about 59 percent of the adult population?[13] Green Mountain College is strongest in cultivating four of the six
foundations for building community resilience discussed in chapter 1: people,
systems thinking, sustainability, and transformation; more work is needed with
adaptability and character ("courage"), and I suspect that the college is not alone
in this area. Lately, Green Mountain College has been focusing on building the

trust and associations linked to social capital and generalized resilience, but in this age of deep social polarization, there is much more to do to cultivate the dispositions necessary for working effectively with many different kinds of people. We work on character traits associated with academic success, but could do much more to cultivate traits like courage, hopefulness, and humility that are necessary for flourishing in times of massive transition.[14] We also need to be more explicit about resilience theory throughout the curriculum. This is just one story of a collegiate experience, but there are many more like it, including at some of the largest institutions in the United States, like Arizona State University. If its promise for advancing community resilience is to be fulfilled, the movement must continue to spread across all of higher education.

Nonformal Education

Much of our learning, especially as adults, occurs outside of formal educational contexts. We learn by attending programs, working together to achieve some community goal, doing our own research, and talking to our neighbors. We can think of such opportunities as being on a continuum from more- to less-structured educational experiences. The more structured they are, the more the content is controlled and results are predictable. The more a program is structured to meet explicit learning goals, however, the more likely it is to speak only to those who want the knowledge. Because resilience education also needs to reach beyond those who seek it, less-structured education is important.

On the more-structured end of the nonformal education continuum, there exists a plethora of programs aiming to teach specific resilience skills or knowledge. For example, one can earn certificates in sustainability or take a self-paced course (see the International Society of Sustainability Professionals for both options). Many massive open online courses (MOOCs) are offered on resilience and sustainability topics, and most are free. Such programs can provide strong theoretical understanding of the foundations of resilience, but often their effect is short term and merely intellectual. The deeper learning required for behavior change tends to be directly proportional to the time and effort required by the learner and the application of learning in a place. General information provided through literature or in online formats rarely engages learners in mastering the systems dynamics at work in their own communities, but it may be the first step toward more experiential learning.

For more place-focused short educational programs, people often look to nonprofit organizations that offer experiential learning in their regions. For example, families may attend programs at nature centers to learn about the local ecosystem. It is much rarer for families to engage with programs about local social or economic systems, in part because few exist. If citizens do not learn much about adaptive governance, the role of voluntary associations and trust in lubricating social problem solving, and the debilitating effects of deep social injustice in a region, however, they will be less equipped to use their knowledge of ecological systems to strengthen resilience. Thus, there is an important gap in this education sector that needs attention. Another limitation is that many smaller communities cannot economically support face-to-face learning opportunities, which diminishes the reach of such programs.

We often think that less-structured learning is less effective, but one of the most powerful forms of resilience education occurs when citizens participate together in community planning and problem solving.[15] Here, much of what is learned comes from community members who share their perspectives on local system dynamics, on threats to what they value, and on desirable transformations. Expert knowledge needs to inform such processes, but citizens have their own expertise about where they live, and when shared with peers, it contributes powerfully to the social learning required for deep resilience. Participatory processes can be a powerful means of generating social learning and shifting behavior, and they can also build social capital that helps cushion shocks to a community. Indeed, Bryan Norton argues that we can only know what sustainability is in a community after we have entered into collaborative processes to decide what community attributes must be preserved for future generations.[16] (This approach is very similar to what we mean in resilience thinking by the "identity" of a community system.)

Social learning processes can occur at multiple scales. Some long-term, large-scale processes like the Chesapeake Bay restoration program have had dramatic effect on a region in part through their educational efforts, but smaller-scale processes often engage a broader range of participants. The hundreds of small community energy committees in Vermont towns are transforming citizens' thinking about our energy future. Watershed groups in California and elsewhere have had great success educating a wide range of stakeholders while restoring salmon to rivers like the Klamath.[17] This kind of collaborative decision making often generates local learning at its best. Of course, participatory processes can go badly. They can be hijacked by powerful interests, they can be frustratingly slow, or they can result in compromises that few support and that increase enmity. They require strong facilitation and strong participant motivation. Sometimes, the motivation comes from external threats, but often it comes from a desire to join together to make positive change in a community.

Informal Education

At the least-structured end of the education continuum, we find ourselves: master learners and disseminators. We access information wherever we can find it, whether in books, online, or from friends. We try new ventures and relearn skills that our grandparents took for granted. Along the way, we build community by sharing what we know, encouraging resilience in one another, modeling sustainability in our lifestyles, and challenging one another to grow into this great transition. The vast majority of education occurs in these hyperlocal interactions, so each of us has a critical role in the community education process.

With this opportunity also comes serious responsibility. The "quality control" in informal conversation can be very low. Part of our task must be to raise the standards for knowledge in our discourse, emphasizing the importance of data, scientific consensus, and careful systems thinking. This form of education is also haphazard and unevenly distributed. If we only share with those like us, our communities can fragment and resilience can decrease. We must bridge divides and use nonpolarizing mechanisms to build a shared reservoir of understanding in a community. Finally, a didactic approach to such education rarely achieves its potential. People generally do not like to be taught without their consent. This learning must be multidirectional, with listening being as important as speaking.

I am a teacher by training, and I love the challenge of designing a powerful learning experience for students, but I find the serendipity of the informal education process at least as rewarding. The neighbor who stops by and asks whether I like my solar panels gives me an opportunity to talk about the incentives and the short payback period. I learn from her about her composting system. As each of us shares our resilience practices, we influence our friends to act similarly. Our conversations at church suppers or local basketball games can influence people who would never read a book on resilience and would reject sustainability as mere liberal politics. The reach of our informal education can be as broad as the formal K–12 system, and its cumulative impact can change culture at greater speed.

⌒⌇

If we are to rapidly learn our way toward greater resilience, our communities will need to use most of the above educational tools. Although for clarity I have treated them as separate kinds of education, ideally they are integrated into a system of mutually reinforcing and adaptive learning processes. We cannot know in advance what combination of educational tools will work best in a region, although we can determine where to invest our energies based in part on what the tools have achieved elsewhere. It may help to have an idealized image of how the tools work together. In this image, K–12 schools will lay the groundwork for community resilience, serving as a learning hub for the immediate area and reaching through children to educate adults. Regional colleges prepare the teachers and other community leaders, who will integrate resilience practices throughout community institutions. These institutions also help reinforce the social norms that characterize resilient communities. Nonformal education will add specific resilience knowledge and skills that cannot be learned in schools and motivate further curiosity. Informal education will pique the interest of those less engaged with other forms of resilience education and strengthen the social learning process across the community.

So far, I have taken for granted that society has (or soon will have) a shared view of what, in general, community resilience requires. As we work toward more robust resilience education, however, we will encounter hard questions about who decides which practices will build resilience and how citizens can determine which learning opportunities to pursue. In system transformations, there may be deep disagreements about which paths forward will be most productive. We are certainly experiencing such debates in the United States today. In such contexts, the use of education to teach people specific ways of thinking, valuing, and behaving is likely to generate resistance and may further polarize communities. Resilience education must achieve a balance between fostering specific skills and knowledge and developing citizens' capacities to make good decisions under conditions of uncertainty. To achieve this balance, educators must have humility about what should be learned without losing confidence in what they believe. They must be as good at listening to others as they are at communicating. They must be master learners, people with the curiosity and courage to question current social norms and the skill of engaging people in learning their way to new norms. We are, each of us, on the way to becoming master learners of resilient living.

Notes

1. See, for example, Mark Costanzo et al., "Energy Conservation Behavior: The Difficult Path from Information to Action," *American Psychologist* 41 (1986), 521–28. For a general discussion of research on behavior change, see Doug McKenzie-Mohr, *Fostering Sustainable Behavior: An Introduction to Community-Based Social Marketing*, 3rd ed. (Gabriola Island, BC: New Society, 2011).
2. For an insightful account of different kinds of educational programs, see Donald Mocker and George Spear, "Lifelong Learning: Formal, Nonformal, Informal, and Self-Directed," Information Series No. 241, ERIC Clearinghouse on Adult, Career, and Vocational Education, 1982 (ED220723).
3. Mocker and Spear, "Lifelong Learning."
4. L. Turner, A. Sandova, and F. J. Chaloupka, "School Garden Programs Are on the Rise in US Public Elementary Schools, but Are Less Common in Schools with Economically Disadvantaged Student Populations," Bridging the Gap Program, Health Policy Center, Institute for Health Research and Policy, University of Illinois at Chicago, 2014.
5. For more information about green schools, see Green Schools National Network, "The Teaching Building: Current Practices in Sustainability in the 21st Century

Classroom," https://greenschoolsnationalnetwork.org/teaching-building-current -practices-sustainability-21st-century-classroom/.

6. National Wildlife Federation, "Eco-Schools USA Spring 2017 Snapshot," accessed April 28, 2017, https://www.nwf.org/~/media/PDFs/Eco-schools/Snapshots/Spring 2017Eco-SchoolsUSASnapshot.ashx.

7. See Common Ground, http://commongroundct.org/community-programs/.

8. See KIPP, http://www.kipp.org/approach/character/.

9. See Next Generation Science Standards, http://www.nextgenscience.org/.

10. The Second Nature annual reports detail this progress; see http://secondnature.org /our-impact/annual-reports/.

11. Brian Walker and David Salt, *Resilience Practice* (Washington, DC: Island Press, 2012).

12. For an outsider's perspective on Green Mountain's sustainability education, see Cosette M. Joyner Armstrong et al., "When the Informal Is the Formal, the Implicit Is the Explicit: Holistic Sustainability Education at Green Mountain College," *International Journal of Sustainability in Higher Education* 17, no. 6 (2016): 756–75.

13. According to Ryan and Baumann, 59 percent of adults have some postsecondary education, whereas 43 percent earned an associate's degree and 33 percent a bachelor's degree. Camille Ryan and Curt Baumann, "Educational Achievement in the United States: 2015," March 2016, www.census.gov/content/dam/Census/library /publications/2016/demo/p20-578.pdf.

14. For a discussion of the role of cultivating virtues related to building sustainable and resilient communities, see William Throop, "Flourishing in the Age of Climate Change," *Midwest Studies in Philosophy* 60 (2016): 296–314.

15. Stephen Sterling, "Learning for Resilience, or the Resilient Learner? Towards a Necessary Reconciliation in a Paradigm of Sustainable Education," *Environmental Education Research* 16 (2010): 511–28.

16. Bryan Norton, *Sustainable Values, Sustainable Changes* (Chicago: University of Chicago Press, 2015).

17. J. T. Woolley, M. V. McGinnis, and J. Kellner, "The California Watershed Movement: Science and the Politics of Place," *Natural Resources Journal* 42, no. 1 (2002): 133–83. See also Michael V. McGinnis, *Science and Sensibility: Negotiating an Ecology of Place* (Oakland: University of California Press, 2016).

CHAPTER 15

Beyond Waste: Sustainable Consumption for Community Resilience

Rosemary Cooper

O UR CURRENT GLOBAL SYSTEM of production and consumption of goods and services is not working for the planet, nor for its people and communities. Economic growth demands ever greater levels of consumption of newer, better, and cheaper products. Such consumption, however, undermines environmental quality, compounds inequity, and burdens communities with mounting waste management costs. It also leaves people increasingly overworked and anxious to keep up, not just with the Joneses down the street but with the wealthiest elite across the globe.

To feed consumption as profitably as possible, production systems have become increasingly global and automated. In the United States, once a manufacturing powerhouse, this change has left many communities vulnerable to capital flight, disinvestment, and unemployment. With ownership of production systems (including manufacturing, distribution, marketing, and sales) increasingly concentrated in large and influential multinational corporations, wealth is trickling up and exaggerating inequities both within the United States and across the globe.

What can we do to transform the way goods and services are consumed and produced in a globalized system with many powerful, vested interests? Fortunately, communities across the United States are innovating and cultivating the seeds of such a transformation. These efforts provide hope that even at the local level, we can change the way we produce and consume and, in doing so, build community resilience for an uncertain future.

This chapter draws from original research as well as from *Local Government and the Sharing Economy Roadmap*, which I cowrote as senior associate with the sustainability "think and do tank" One Earth.[1] It also draws from the *Sustainable Consumption Toolkit* published by the Urban Sustainability Directors Network.[2]

What Is Sustainable Consumption?

Sustainable consumption is a new systemic framework that challenges consumption-based growth and proposes new ways for people and communities to prosper. It is about consuming differently and changing the way goods and services are provided so as to improve quality of life for all within ecological limits. To genuinely promote sustainable and resilient communities, the *Sustainable Consumption Toolkit* contends that sustainable consumption must call for the following:

1. Absolute **reductions in the material goods and energy** we consume.
2. **A shift in values** away from material wealth and consumerism toward new measures of progress and well-being.
3. **Technological innovation and efficiency gains** that help us refine the production process, creating less impact on the planet.
4. Recognition that consumption will need to increase for those **individuals and communities whose needs are not being met**.
5. **A transformation of our economy** from one defined by continuous growth to one that functions within the very real limits of a finite planet.[3]

These values differentiate sustainable consumption from mere waste management efforts and also from similar notions like the "circular economy." Waste management focuses just on products' end of life through recycling, composting, and disposal; the circular economy emphasizes "cradle-to-cradle" product design and values such as reuse and repair. In contrast, sustainable consumption looks at both the physical product life cycle (from design and production to disposal and reuse) and transforming consumer behavior. These distinctions are important. Research clearly shows that the majority of carbon emissions from US communities is generated upstream of consumers.[4] Moreover, significantly reducing consumption and waste outright—which is essential for long-term resilience—can only be achieved through changes in cultural norms and personal actions.

Although technological efficiency is important, as the third point above stipulates, global growth in consumption is predicted to outpace even the greenest, most efficient design and production methods. According to Paul Gilding, even at reduced levels of resource usage we would need to consume over three times Earth's resources by 2050 so as to keep pace with expected global growth in gross domestic product.[5] As it is, if the whole world population consumed at the level of the current US ecological footprint, we would need the resources of more than four planet Earths. (See chapter 8 for more on ecological footprints.)

Rather than communities continuing to rely on consumption-fueled growth, sustainable consumption shifts the focus to a broader notion of economic development and prosperity. As stated in the *Toolkit*, "A sustainable consumption lens emphasizes the 'value delivered' rather than 'the amount of stuff' or the material components of the goods we consume."[6] Sustainable consumption provides new ways for people to access goods and services to meet their basic needs, reduce income pressures, and enhance social connections. It also offers new opportunities for job creation in areas such as reuse and remanufacturing, food gleaning, and energy retrofitting. In addition, it highlights alternative economic and business models that minimize environmental impact and support more inclusive and equitable community economies.

Although the field of sustainable consumption is still evolving, the following six specific practices are generally emphasized:[7]

1. **Reduction of the amount of materials and energy consumed:** Smaller homes, more efficiently made products, absolute reductions in the amount of goods purchased, streamlining or eliminating product packaging, food waste prevention.

2. **Reuse of products and materials:** Reused building material stores, remanufacturing businesses, online direct-trade marketplaces (e.g., Craigslist), repurposing things you have to meet a new need.

3. **Repair and maintenance of products to extend their useful life:** Repair businesses, repair cafes and fix-it clinics, the do-it-yourself (DIY) repair movement.

4. **Sharing of products, services, and land, including via borrowing and renting:** Tool and other lending libraries, clothing swaps, food gleaning programs, community gardens.

5. **Use of durable, long-lasting, and upgradable products and materials:** More durably made goods, goods that are more repairable, leasing versus purchasing, extended product warranties.

6. **Use of lower-impact, equitably sourced products made using materials and resources that are rapidly renewable, able to be replenished, and less toxic than conventional materials:** Institutional sustainable purchasing policies, consumer education programs.

Ensuring Relevance to Everyone

For sustainable consumption practices to thrive, they must be relevant and appealing to a diversity of people and households. Included are those who consume too much as well as those struggling to meet their basics needs.

Juliet Schor, author of *True Wealth* and cofounder of New Dream (a nonprofit organization that promotes alternatives to consumerism), envisions a postconsumer lifestyle she calls the "plenitude economy" in which households have diverse sources of income, shorter (e.g., four-day) workweeks, or both.[8] This lifestyle frees up time to access goods and services outside consumer society, such as by trading services and assets; it also allows more time and creative opportunities for do-it-yourself projects. Not only does this model provide a way out of the "productivity trap"[9] (i.e., our current economy's structural need for ever-greater labor productivity) by sharing available employment, it also gives people more time to spend with friends, build social connections, be creative, and enjoy life. Moreover, in the process of working less and self-provisioning more, households consume less and reduce their ecological footprints.[10]

The plenitude model has undeniable appeal to many Americans, particularly those in professional and managerial positions with longer work hours and relatively high pay. Marketing expert Doug Holt contends, however, that if sustainable consumption[11] is to scale, it must be relevant to "new Main Street USA," a metagrouping that combines the middle class and the working poor with annual household incomes of $30,000 to $80,000, which together make up 60 percent of the US population.[12] Rather than working less, Main Street USA needs decently paid, secure, and sustainable work alternatives. Instead of consuming less, people need access to basic household goods and services at a reasonable level of quality. Shifting the narrative and emphasis of sustainable consumption strategies to meet these everyday, practical needs can help ensure that they are embraced by the majority of Americans.

Cities Focusing on Sustainable Consumption

A growing number of cities in the United States are recognizing that sustainable consumption can meet the needs of different households and help them achieve multiple sustainability goals. Included among these goals are climate action, social equity, sustainable economic development, social connection, and well-being.

Local Government Sets the Stage

Cities can help set the stage for meaningful action through up-front self-assessment and analysis. The *Sustainable Consumption Toolkit* provides a simple self-assessment tool to help communities identify the most promising entry points for sustainable consumption activities and create initiatives that are relevant, timely, and well received.[13] If job creation is a community concern and modernizing waste management is a local government priority, for example, it could be opportune to develop programs to support local thrift, reuse, and repair businesses. If the community is grappling with concerns over affordable housing, a better focus might be to promote smaller, less costly homes with reduced levels of energy and material consumption.

If sustainable consumption activities are going to meet the interconnected crises of equity, economy, energy, and environment, cities will need to undertake critical, systems-based analysis. A sustainability filter is another such tool to help communities select, design, and implement sustainable consumption initiatives, but with an eye to addressing root causes and drivers of sustainability challenges and to advancing multiple benefits. A sustainability filter poses questions that help users identify interconnected sustainability issues and related opportunities.[14] As outlined in the *Sustainable Consumption Toolkit*: "An example of developing an integrated approach to sustainable solutions around housing, mobility, food and consumer goods is the implementation of [policies] that support complete, compact communities to reduce the need for vehicle transport (fuel use) and larger housing sizes while improving access to food and consumer goods."[15]

It is also key for communities to understand the carbon profile of local consumption patterns so as to reduce the greenhouse gas emissions they are responsible for no matter where they occur. New methods of consumption-based greenhouse gas emissions analysis estimate the total global emissions from local consumption, including those associated with imported goods and food.[16] These analyses have found that more than half the carbon footprint of US cities is associated with the consumption of food, goods, and services. Considering that 75 percent of consumption emissions come from households, community-level sustainable consumption actions are clearly an untapped strategic opportunity to reduce global emissions.

Sustainable Consumption Initiatives and Actions

Depending on community makeup and goals, resources, partners, and perspectives, sustainable consumption strategies vary in scope and focus. They can involve local government, grassroots innovators, university researchers, local foundations or business, nonprofit organizations, and other institutions as leaders or partners. The following section provides a sampling of promising sustainable consumption initiatives in the areas of consumer goods, transportation, economic development, food, and housing that can make our communities more resilient.

Consumer Goods:
Sharing and Repairing Instead of Owning and Discarding

Although much of the so-called "sharing economy" has been criticized for its failure to reflect sustainability values (e.g., low pay for drivers of ride-sourcing services like Uber), there are some sharing practices with promise for communities.[17]

Community sharing innovators are people who start up new sharing-focused initiatives and businesses at the local level.[18] Although various organizational structures are used, nonprofit or informal grassroots models dominate. Prominent examples include community swap meets for clothing, toys, media, and more; local lending libraries for tools, clothing, toys, and seeds; repair cafes or fix-it clinics; and food-related sharing such as food buying clubs, community kitchens, and community gardens.[19] Some community sharing transactions require money for buying or renting goods, whereas others based on swapping or bartering are free exchanges.

Community sharing activities are exactly what Schor had in mind as part of her plenitude model for households. Such activities can also help provide lower-income people with access to needed basic household goods for no or low cost. For community sharing to be a truly transformative path to community resilience, it will need to scale widely across American communities as well as change consumer behavior fundamentally so that overall levels of consumption are reduced: lower for those consuming too much, and adequate for those who do not have enough. Together with grassroots innovators and other partners, city governments can play key roles in fostering this transformation.

Scaling Community Sharing

The efforts of community sharing innovators are challenged by limited funds, space, volunteer time, and profile. Innovators are exploring ways to address these challenges on their own by adopting digital platforms to make transactions more convenient, using crowdfunding to raise money, and becoming cooperatives or social enterprises.[20] Some local governments are providing additional support by developing web platforms to profile sharing activities, providing grants, and connecting sharing innovators with relevant partners and resources. Portland, Oregon, and Flagstaff, Arizona, have both undertaken such supportive roles.[21]

Shifting the emphasis from individual to community-based behavior change is another opportunity to scale community sharing.[22] In practice, it means bringing goods sharing to existing communities with natural potential. For example, university students with limited funds only need certain goods for a short time, so they tend to purchase cheap goods that wear out and end up in the waste stream quickly. Some schools, like Portland State University, have reuse rooms for household and other goods whose inventory and use by students could be greatly expanded and then replicated at other universities.

Multifamily buildings are another opportunity because they house many people in close proximity who could relatively easily share kitchen gadgets, tools, camping gear, and more. City dwellers are increasingly faced with smaller, more costly housing where accessing shareable goods instead of owning them could address the problem of limited storage space while being gentler on household budgets. For example, Vertical Living Libraries, an idea developed by Ryan Dyment, founder of the Toronto Tool Library and Sharing Depot, are being explored by some Canadian and US cities.[23] Such a library would provide a shared space in a multifamily development with a wide range of household items, power tools, and entertainment equipment and products that could be borrowed using a digital app.

Affordable space is another key need of sharing innovators. Local government already has a history of providing space for community sharing. Tool libraries, community kitchens, and swap meets are often located in community centers, old firehouses, and public libraries, and community gardens can be found in parks and vacant city lots. Linking underutilized public space more systematically with the needs of community sharing innovators could really scale things up, though. For example, imagine if every public library in the United States also housed a lending library for tools, toys, seeds, and kitchen appliances, all cataloged and accessible online just as with books. Because research shows that people do not want to travel far to borrow items, the public libraries peppered across neighborhoods are perfectly suited to provide the easy access that is needed for wider adoption of these programs.[24]

Ensuring Community Sharing Leads to Less Consumption Overall

To ensure that sharing actually leads to reduced consumption overall, community sharing needs to be complemented with educational efforts focused on consuming less. The latter is key because research shows that accessing secondhand or shared goods does not necessarily lead to lower household consumption levels;[25] lower costs can simply prompt people to spread out their household budget and consume more. Resourceful PDX, a program of the Portland (Oregon) Bureau of Sustainability and Planning, achieves this goal by promoting sharing, reuse, and repair activities and by offering tips on how to consume less (e.g., by "creating memories instead of excess stuff by planning ahead" for both ongoing needs like food and major transitions like having a baby).[26] Resourceful PDX mentions the benefits of conserving natural resources, but less prominently than lifestyle benefits such as saving money, reducing clutter, building community, and spending more time with friends and family.

Another important but perhaps less obvious role for local governments to help encourage sustainable consumption is to invest in high-quality public assets such as green spaces, parks, recreation facilities, libraries, festivals, and community events. Improving the quality of life for middle- and lower-income households, which often rely on free public spaces and events for their leisure time, is increasingly seen as the motivation for such public investment.[27] As Tim Jackson pointed out in his book *Prosperity without Growth*, public assets provide the space for cultivating a common citizenship, which is one of the great casualties of consumer society. He wrote, "The less we share in terms of common endeavor, the more powerful the social logic of private affluence."[28]

Repair Cafes

Repair cafes or fix-it clinics are free events where people bring broken belongings—everything from computers and electronics to clothing, furniture, bicycles, toys, and more—to be repaired by volunteer fixers.[29] They are organized by grassroots innovators, local governments, or nonprofit organizations and are held at various locations, such as tool libraries, community or recreation centers, churches, and businesses. The volunteer fixers might be skilled do-it-yourselfers, professionals with repair businesses, or apprentices interested in repair-related careers. Cafe attendees meet fixers and often learn something about repair, which can bring new customers to local repair businesses and empower cafe attendees to undertake their own repairs. The fix-it mind-set developed at repair cafes opens the door to people considering repairability in their purchasing decisions, which is the type of upstream consumer that can ultimately help shift product design.

The keys to the continued growth of repair cafes are similar to those of community sharing innovators more broadly. Having repair cafes coordinated and run by more established organizations like local governments and non-profit organizations can provide needed funds and paid staff to coordinate volunteers. Doing so would help make repair cafes consistent and accessible options for community residents so that repairing rather than discarding and buying becomes a new norm.[30]

Transportation:
Connected, Electric, and Equitable Mobility Systems

The overall community benefits of new mobility providers (such as the ride-sourcing platform Uber) in isolation are questionable.[31] There is, however, tremendous sustainability and resilience potential in the development of integrated mobility systems that combine public transportation with multiple and diverse mobility providers, particularly when they are nonmotorized or are electric and equitable.

Integrated mobility planning connects new mobility modes—such as bike sharing, car sharing, and ride sourcing—with traditional transportation modes like public transit, walking, and bicycling. Websites and apps allow people to choose their preferred travel options in real time based on time and cost. Research conducted by the Chicago-based Shared-Use Mobility Center in 2016 shows that "the more people use shared modes, the more likely they are to use public transit, own fewer cars, and spend less on transportation overall."[32] When effectively planned, shared mobility fills gaps and extends the reach of public transport rather than competing with it.[33]

Further enhancing the ecological and equity benefits of integrated mobility is key to truly realizing their community resilience benefits. In a paper exploring "ecological footprints and lifestyle archetypes," sustainability researcher Jennie Moore explains the characteristics of a city's transportation system that would use one Earth's fair share of resources in 2050: 86 percent of trips would be taken by transit, walking, and cycling, with household travel by personal motorized vehicles averaging 582 kilometers (362 miles) annually and no to low private ownership of cars.[34] In addition, *all* motorized vehicles would be electric. Achieving these strong, one-planet goals for mobility systems will require transportation agencies to transform into mobility agencies that effectively coordinate their efforts with other agencies and community partners in the unremitting pursuit of compact, walkable, and complete community design.

Integrated mobility systems have significant potential to reduce travel times and avoid the high costs of full-time car ownership. Such changes are of particular benefit to low-income households, which typically face longer commute times with poorer job access and a greater reliance on car travel. Although the use of mobility services like car sharing and ride sourcing is lower in low-income communities than in the general population, new projects and partnerships are emerging to build more equitable shared mobility systems.[35] For example, revenues from California's carbon emissions cap-and-trade program are being directed into a three-year pilot project to introduce electric car sharing into low-income communities in Los Angeles. Indeed, renowned economist Jeffrey Sachs predicts a future when all Americans will have mobility apps on their phones to share cars rather than own them individually.[36]

Creating Jobs and Resilient Local Economies

Some sustainable consumption sectors and activities—food gleaning, building deconstruction, and the reuse and repair sectors, for example—are labor intensive. These areas provide good opportunities for communities to develop local, living-wage jobs that are more insulated from the ups and downs of the global economy.[37] Gleaning programs make food that would otherwise have been wasted available to city residents from household and community gardens, local farms, restaurants, and local institutions, helping alleviate hunger while reducing food waste. (Food waste is the largest element of the waste stream by weight and produces methane, a greenhouse gas significantly more potent than carbon dioxide, when it decomposes in landfills). Building deconstruction organizations salvage reusable construction materials and finishings from buildings that would otherwise be demolished, diverting significant debris from landfills and generating revenue from sales. These and other sustainable consumption enterprises have proven to be valuable community resources for job training and workforce development, especially for hard-to-employ workers.[38]

Sustainable consumption activities with cooperative business models have tremendous potential to create high-quality, stable jobs with more community loyalty than corporations. Cooperatives distribute surplus profits to worker-owners and other stakeholders such as producers, customers, and investors, who usually reside locally. This system contrasts with that of corporations, which inequitably direct profits to executives and shareholders, most of whom live outside the communities where business operations occur. As a result, cooperatives are able to create higher-value jobs and build more community wealth.[39] Although cooperatives have been around for a long time, more of them are increasingly focusing on sustainable consumption practices for everything from food gleaning and car sharing to upcycled goods and solar energy technologies.[40] The *Sustainable Consumption Toolkit* points out this emerging trend and encourages local governments to support cooperatives to not only advance sustainable consumption practices but also to foster more equitable and resilient local economies.[41]

Housing: Smaller, More Affordable, and More Connected

A home is arguably the single largest, most significant consumer good that a household will purchase. A sustainable consumption approach to housing naturally promotes smaller homes and downsizing. By limiting the size of new or remodeled homes, fewer materials are used for construction and less energy for home heating and use; and with less storage space, households may also be encouraged to own fewer household goods. Moreover, architect Susan Susanka has demonstrated that people have a natural affinity for the smaller, more personal spaces in a home rather than expansive ones such as marble foyers or seldom used formal dining rooms.[42] McMansion ordinances are one tool that cities can use to encourage smaller homes, particularly when larger homes threaten neighborhood or historic character.[43]

Equally if not more important than the size of one's home, however, is its location. A home in a compact, mixed-use neighborhood—where one can walk, bicycle, or take transit for daily needs like work, school, and groceries—is a home that does not require the expense of a privately owned car or the daily consumption of energy to use it. Such neighborhoods boost social interaction among residents, reduce greenhouse gas emissions, and support a greater variety of housing choices.[44]

Urban cohousing developments can provide the best of both small-home living and compact, vibrant neighborhoods; they are a particularly attractive option in increasingly unaffordable locations.[45] Residents of cohousing developments own or rent individual units that tend to be smaller than in conventional housing, particularly when located in more dense, urban settings; however, they enjoy access to amenities shared with other residents, such an extra kitchen, recreational spaces, laundry, workshop, and guest rooms. Motivated by less storage space and the ease of sharing with nearby neighbors, household levels of consumption in cohousing can be significantly lower than in conventional housing.[46] Because people who live in cohousing choose it in part to be able to have neighbors with shared values, social connections among residents (often of a variety of ages) plus a culture of mutual aid are also usually strong. It is not hard to imagine a life of plenitude flourishing in cohousing.

Conclusion

With 70 percent of the gross domestic product in the United States connected to household consumption,[47] it is no wonder that Americans sometimes seem to think of themselves as consumers first and community members only second. As this chapter demonstrates, however, there are many opportunities for communities across the country to chart a different, more sustainable path based on postconsumer, postgrowth values and strategies. Encouraging affluent Americans to consume and work less through the appeal of a plenitude lifestyle is only one element of the necessary transformation. For sustainable consumption to go mainstream, it will need to meet the practical, everyday needs of the majority of Americans: secure, well-paid jobs and affordable access to basic household goods and public places. It is an opportunity to foster a new shared prosperity that respects the finite ecological limits of our planet and to create more resilient communities that are happier, more connected, and more equitable places for all people to flourish.

Notes

1. See One Earth, http://www.localgovsharingecon.com.
2. See Urban Sustainability Directors Network, "Advancing Sustainable Consumption in Cities," *Sustainable Consumption Toolkit*, accessed April 28, 2017, http://sustainableconsumption.usdn.org.
3. See Urban Sustainability Directors Network, "The Sustainable Consumption Concept," *Sustainable Consumption Toolkit*, accessed April 28, 2017, http://sustainable consumption.usdn.org/concept-overview/.
4. For example, a study in Portland, Oregon, found that of total community carbon emissions, "on average, 56% of emissions were from the production of

goods and services while 31% come from the use phase (e.g., appliances, lighting, personal vehicles)"; see "Climate Action Planning: Estimating Consumption Related to Emissions," Urban Sustainability Directors Network, accessed April 5, 2017, http://sustainableconsumption.usdn.org/initiatives-list/estimating-consumption-related-emissions.

5. P. Gilding, *The Great Disruption: Why the Climate Crisis Will Bring on the End of Shopping and the Birth of a New World* (New York: Bloomsbury, 2012).

6. See the section on Concern/myth: "Sustainable consumption does not support economic development" under "Misconception: Sustainable Consumption Is Anti-Development," http://sustainableconsumption.usdn.org/common-concerns/.

7. Urban Sustainability Directors Network, "The Sustainable Consumption Concept."

8. See J. B. Schor, *True Wealth* (New York: Penguin, 2012); and New Dream, https://www.newdream.org (formerly the Center for a New American Dream and now renamed New Dream for more international appeal).

9. The "productivity trap" is articulated by Tim Jackson, *Prosperity without Growth: Economics for a Finite Planet* (London: Earthscan, 2009), 145. The current economy's need for ever-increasing growth and labor productivity can only be resolved with a growth-based model.

10. See Schor's five-minute video "Visualizing a Plenitude Economy," uploaded September 15, 2011, https://www.youtube.com/watch?v=HR-YrD_KB0M.

11. With the framing of sustainable consumption as one that emphasizes transformation of the dominant growth-based model, it can be argued that it is essentially a sustainable economy model, so Doug Holt's perspective is of relevance.

12. Doug Holt, "Why the Sustainable Economy Movement Has Not Scaled: Toward a Strategy That Empowers Main Street," in *Sustainable Lifestyles and the Quest for Plenitude*, ed. Juliet Schor and Craig Thompson (New Haven, CT: Yale University Press, 2014), 202–32.

13. Urban Sustainability Directors Network, "Self-Assessment Checklist," *Sustainable Consumption Toolkit*, accessed April 28, 2017, http://sustainableconsumption.usdn.org/self-assessment/#.

14. The Sustainability Filter was first developed with six question areas for the *Local Governments and the Sharing Economy Roadmap*; see One Earth, "Sustainability Filter," http://www.localgovsharingecon.com/sustainability-filter.html. It was then revised into one with three categories in the *Sustainable Consumption Toolkit*; see Urban Sustainability Directors Network, "Sustainability Filter," *Sustainable Consumption Toolkit*, http://sustainableconsumption.usdn.org/sustainabilityfilter/.

15. Urban Sustainability Directors Network, "Sustainability Filter."

16. Urban Sustainability Directors Network, "Understanding Consumption-Based Emissions," *Sustainable Consumption Toolkit*, accessed April 28, 2017, http://sustainableconsumption.usdn.org/understanding-consumptionbased-emissions/.

17. To understand the many definitions of the sharing economy, see One Earth, "Defining the Sharing Economy," *Local Governments and the Sharing Economy*, 36–51, accessed April 5, 2017, http://www.localgovsharingecon.com/uploads/2/1/3/3/21333498/localgovsharingecon_report_full_oct2015.pdf; see also Sustainable Economies Law Center, *Policies for Shareable Cities: A Policy Primer for Urban Leaders*, September 9, 2013, http://www.theselc.org/policies-for-shareable-cities/.

18. One Earth, "Community Sharing," *Local Governments and the Sharing Economy*, http://www.localgovsharingecon.com/community-sharing.html.

19. One Earth, "Community Sharing"; New Dream, "Guide to Sharing," accessed April 5, 2017, https://www.newdream.org/programs/collaborative-communities/community-action-kit/sharing.

20. "Sharing Platform Peerby Launches 'Peerby GO'; Renting from Neighbors including Delivery," Peerby International, September 10, 2015, http://press.peerby.com/110784-sharing-platform-peerby-launches-peerby-go-renting-from-neighbors-including-delivery; http://thesharingproject.ca/thingery/; http://www.shareable.net/blog/11-platform-cooperatives-creating-a-real-sharing-economy.

21. See One Earth, "Community Sharing," *Local Governments and the Sharing Economy*, 168–71, accessed April 5, 2017, http://www.localgovsharingecon.com/uploads/2/1/3/3/21333498/localgovsharingecon_communitysharing_oct2015.pdf.

22. One Earth, "Community Sharing," 172–73.

23. One Earth, "Community Sharing," 173.

24. "The Sharing Project: A Report on Sharing in Vancouver," accessed April 5, 2017, http://ponderresearch.co/wp-content/uploads/2015/03/TheSharingProject_Report.pdf.

25. Vancity, "Thrift Score: An Examination [of] B.C.'s Second-Hand Economy," accessed April 5, 2017, https://www.vancity.com/SharedContent/documents/reports/Vancity-Report-Examination-of-BCs-secondhand-economy.pdf; BBMG, *Reclaimism: Aspirational Consumers and Emerging Trends*, June 2014, accessible at http://www.sustainablebrands.com/digital_learning/research_report/next_economy/reclaimism_aspirational_consumers_emerging_trends.

26. See Resourceful PDX, http://www.resourcefulpdx.com.

27. Holt, "Why the Sustainable Economy Movement Has Not Scaled."

28. Jackson, *Prosperity without Growth*, 193.

29. For more information, see Urban Sustainability Directors Network, "Repair Cafés/Fixit Clinics," *Sustainable Consumption Toolkit*, accessed April 28, 2017, http://sustainableconsumption.usdn.org/initiatives-list/repair-cafes-fixit-clinics.

30. See One Earth, "Challenges and Solutions," accessed April 5, 2017, http://www.localgovsharingecon.com/uploads/2/1/3/3/21333498/localgovsharingecon_fixitclinics_oct2015.pdf.

31. Ride sourcing's sustainability is evaluated in One Earth, "Shared Mobility," in *Local Governments and the Sharing Economy*, 71–97, http://www.localgovsharingecon .com/uploads/2/1/3/3/21333498/localgovsharingecon_sharedmobility_oct2015.pdf.

32. Shared-Use Mobility Center, *Shared Mobility and the Transformation of Public Transit: Research Analysis*, prepared for American Public Transportation Association, March 2016, http://sharedusemobilitycenter.org/wp-content/uploads/2016/04 /Final_TOPT_DigitalPagesNL.pdf.

33. Shared-Use Mobility Center, *Shared Mobility*.

34. Jennie Moore, "Ecological Footprints and Lifestyle Archetypes: Exploring Dimensions of Consumption and the Transformation Needed to Achieve Urban Sustainability," *Sustainability* 7, no. 4 (2015): 4747–63.

35. Michael Kodransky and Gabriel Lewenstein, "Connecting Low-Income People to Opportunity with Shared Mobility," Institute for Transportation and Development Policy, December 2014, https://www.itdp.org/wp-content/up loads/2014/10/Shared-Mobility_Full-Report.pdf; Shared-Use Mobility Center, Building an Equitable Transportation System with Shared Mobility webinar, December 6, 2016, http://sharedusemobilitycenter.org/event/webinar-building-an -equitable-transportation-system-with-shared-mobility/.

36. J. Sachs, *Building the New American Economy: Smart, Fair, and Sustainable* (New York: Columbia University Press, 2017).

37. Urban Sustainability Directors Network, "Gleaning Programs," *Sustainable Consumption Toolkit*, http://sustainableconsumption.usdn.org/initiatives-list/urban -gleaning-programs; Urban Sustainability Directors Network, "Encouraging and Mandating Building Deconstruction," *Sustainable Consumption Toolkit*, accessed April 28, 2017, http://sustainableconsumption.usdn.org/initiatives-list /encouraging-and-mandating-building-deconstruction.

38. See, for example, Hidden Harvest (http://www.hiddenharvest.org) and Second Chance (http://www.secondchanceinc.org).

39. "Overview: Cooperatives," Community-Wealth.org, accessed April 5, 2017, http:// community-wealth.org/strategies/panel/coops/index.html.

40. See, for example, Green Worker Cooperatives (http://www.greenworker.coop/our coops), the Evergreen Cooperative Initiative (also known as the Cleveland Model; http://community-wealth.org/content/cleveland-model-how-evergreen-coopera tives-are-building-community-wealth), and Earthworker Cooperative (http:// earthworkercooperative.com.au). See also Cat Johnson, "11 Platform Cooperatives Creating a Real Sharing Economy," Shareable, May 18, 2016, http://www.shareable .net/blog/11-platform-cooperatives-creating-a-real-sharing-economy.

41 See Urban Sustainability Directors Network, "Multi-Stakeholder Cooperatives," *Sustainable Consumption Toolkit*, accessed April 28, 2017, http://sustainable consumption.usdn.org/initiatives-list/multi-stakeholder-cooperatives; and Urban

Sustainability Directors Network, "Worker-Owned Cooperatives—The Cleveland Model," *Sustainable Consumption Toolkit*, accessed April 28, 2017, http://sustain ableconsumption.usdn.org/initiatives-list/worker-owned-cooperativesthe-cleve land-model.

42. S. Susanka, and K. Obolensky, *The Not So Big House: A Blueprint for the Way We Really Live* (Newtown, CT: Taunton, 2009).

43. Urban Sustainability Directors Network, "McMansion Ordinances/Overlay Zones Limiting Square Footage," *Sustainable Consumption Toolkit*, accessed April 28, 2017, http://sustainableconsumption.usdn.org/initiatives-list/mcmansion-ordinances -overlay-zones-limiting-square-footage.

44. To read more and find additional resources, see Urban Sustainability Directors Network, "Creating Walkable Mixed-Use Neighborhoods," *Sustainable Consumption Toolkit*, http://sustainableconsumption.usdn.org/initiatives-list/creating -walkable-mixed-use-neighborhoods.

45. Urban Sustainability Directors Network, "Cooperative Housing," *Sustainable Consumption Toolkit*, accessed April 28, 2017, http://sustainableconsumption.usdn .org/initiatives-list/cooperative-housing.

46. This tendency is strongest in cohousing entities located in less affordable urban areas, which limits unit size, and when cohousers share strong environmental values and ethics. Ericka Stephens-Rennie, cofounder of the Vancouver Housing Cooperative, personal correspondence with author; One Earth, "Shared Spaces," in *Local Governments and the Sharing Economy*, 98–127, http://www.localgovsharingecon. com/uploads/2/1/3/3/21333498/localgovsharingecon_sharedspaces_oct2015.pdf.

47. Urban Sustainability Directors Network, "Economy," *Sustainable Consumption Toolkit*, accessed April 28, 2017, https://usdntoolkit.squarespace.com /economy-introduction/.

CHAPTER 16

Resilient Streets, Resilient Cities

Mike Lydon

W HEN YOU HEAR THE WORD *city* or *community*, the first image that comes to mind is probably of a street: specifically a roadway and sidewalks, framed by buildings and full of people. We intuitively know that a street is more than just pavement and vehicles.

Practically everyone uses the street on a daily basis: by car, bus, bicycle, foot, wheelchair, or stroller. It is where we naturally interact with the people, businesses, and institutions that make up our community. Our streets are both conduits of transportation and cogs of culture. They give communities the linkages and armature for public *and* private life.

The street is literally the public right-of-way, the space we all have a right to use. Whether a public square, a busy urban avenue, or quiet small-town lane, the street is the most immediate place available to connect with both the people and the functions of our community. This quality makes the street an ideal place where community members can experiment and collaborate on projects that contribute to resilience.

To further understand the special role streets play in community resilience building, this chapter attempts to tie two topics together. One is the all-important nexus between transportation and land use, and the other is the emerging tool of "tactical urbanism" as a way for community members and their local governments to collaborate on community resilience building.

Two Types of Cities

Enrique Peñalosa, former mayor of Bogota, Colombia, once said, "We can have a city that is friendly to cars, or a city that is friendly to people. We cannot have both."[1] In North America, our streets, neighborhoods, and cities are no different from those in Bogota. In coarse terms, they are either drivable or walkable, and most are only drivable.

We do not need to recount how and why American communities came to be this way; a university library's worth of materials already tells that story. The stark contrast between these two paradigms, however, underscores that as cities, towns, and suburbs evolve, each street that is built and every land use decision that is legislated influences how far people will have to travel, how they will get to where they need to go, and the "quality of place" they experience once they arrive. In urban planning circles, this phenomenon is known as the *transportation-land use connection,* and the degree to which such decisions are coordinated directly influences the amount of driving people do, thereby affecting the economic, social, environmental, and public health of our cities. In other words, creating stronger links between our land use and transportation decisions must be considered a fundamental underpinning for community resilience.

The Drivable City

From subsidized oil, to local zoning codes that fragment land uses, to traffic engineering "level of service" metrics and design standards that bloat streets, the drivable city is an intentional product. Even if its streets technically accommodate other users, the design—dimensions, distances, signage, materials, landscaping—are designed to favor cars above all else. Altogether, this design makes most streets in the drivable city uncomfortable and inconvenient for anyone not in a vehicle and makes them dangerous for everyone. Indeed, the United States sustained more than 35,000 traffic fatalities in 2015, the most since 2008 and the largest year-on-year percent increase since the 1960s.[2] Although some blame cell phones and other dashboard distractions, few call attention to the root cause: our daily destinations are spread out. People must drive everywhere for everything.

The poor land use and transportation choices that create the drivable city are not only terrible for safety but are also incapable of responding to shocks when they occur. Take the Los Angeles region's five-year, $1.1 billion effort to widen Interstate 405 as an example. Despite the failure of similar projects elsewhere, project proponents promised taxpayers a true reduction in congestion. Since wrapping up the project in 2014, users have actually experienced *more* gridlock.[3] The traveling public's pain was put on full display as news outlets across the country documented miles and miles of gridlock on Interstate 405 the day before Thanksgiving 2016 as an estimated 3.5 million Los Angelenos hopped in their cars for their holiday travel. Some could have bicycled the length of the 405 in a fraction of the time it took to drive that day. What set out to be a project for reducing chronic congestion only made it worse.

Sprawling Los Angeles is not alone. In January 2014, a rare snowstorm depositing a mere two-and-a-half inches of snow in car-happy Atlanta caused thousands of highway commuters to be stranded in their vehicles, with many having to abandon them altogether.[4] The event was referred to locally as "carmageddon" and underscores that if small storms, crashes, or even the holidays shut down our highest-capacity transportation systems, the impacts of a major disaster or unforeseen trauma could be much worse.

The drivable city is wedded to a transportation and land use system that depends on mass private car ownership, billions of dollars of public spending annually on road construction and maintenance, and a vast national network of filling stations and their supporting infrastructure. It is a very resilient system—it has weathered fuel price spikes, public spending crises, and the Great Recession—but it is not a system that is economically, socially, or environmentally sustainable. Fortunately, as the challenges of the twenty-first century come into starker relief, some cities are waking up and realizing that how well their transportation system is linked with supportive land use has everything to do with their long-term resilience.

The Walkable City

Most compact cities were built before the rise of the automobile, so they enjoy a network of sidewalks and a land use pattern (dense, mixed use) with buildings that frame streets and make public transport viable. In the walkable city, streets are often narrower and intersect much more frequently than in the drivable city, providing convenient and safer access for people who have more destinations nearby. When so many things are close by—the drugstore, the school, the grocery store, the neighborhood park—there is less need to drive than when things are spread out. In place of congested highways and giant feeder arterials is a grid of human-scale streets, making buses, streetcars, bikeways, and ample sidewalks the preferred way to get around. No matter the sustainability measure—air quality, cost, resource use, social connectivity—this pattern almost always outperforms the alternative.

Proximity and the transportation choices that flourish with it are what make urban living so convenient and explain why smart-growing North American cities (e.g., Seattle; Portland, Oregon) are able to add thousands of residents and jobs to their city centers without seeing net increases in automobile use.[5] It also helps explain why New York City is one of the safest places to travel, whereas sprawling Fort Meyers, Florida, is literally the most dangerous.[6]

Other than getting people out of their carbon-emitting cars and saving lives, what does coordinating transportation and land use decisions really have to do with community resilience? It means that people are healthier and happier because they are able to walk or bike to many destinations in their neighborhood. It means that low-income people have access to jobs, services, and transportation options to get them there affordably. It means that a city has fiscal stability because efficient land use patterns translate to the efficient use of tax dollars funding the creation and maintenance of the infrastructure systems that make it more resilient. If an evacuation is necessary, it means that people are not stuck in complete gridlock due to the provision of many viable transportation options. It also means that after a traumatic event occurs, communities can come together in well-structured and accessible streets, parks, and other public spaces.

Imagery associated with the "resilient city" or the "smart city" often shows large infrastructure projects or new technologies that will presumably guard against future climate change impacts or reduce fossil fuel consumption. If, however, they reinforce the land use and transportation patterns of the drivable city rather than those of the walkable city, increase dependence on individual technologies rather than enable diverse and adaptable responses to future challenges, or suck up limited public investment dollars for single-purpose solutions rather than build community capacity for ongoing adaptation, they are not initiatives that build true community resilience.

The Role of Local Government

Building community resilience is a long-term undertaking that local government cannot do on its own. Local governments face incredible challenges, many inflicted by outside forces that extend beyond the control of any one jurisdiction. The urgency to balance short-term needs (like dealing with a budget crisis) with long-term needs (like building a much-needed transit line) can be overwhelming, as can be the bureaucratic complexity that must be cut through for projects of any size to be realized. Lack of leadership continuity stemming from staffing turnovers also limits progress, as do economic cycles, ever-changing project scopes and budgets, and politicians' priorities. All told, these challenges can make it difficult—and expensive—for local governments to meet their existing responsibilities, let alone undertake innovative and truly transformative projects.

Urban planning is the process through which local governments scope, develop, and implement policies and projects that deal with land use and transportation (among other things). These days, most local governments try to involve their constituents through a public participation component of the planning process. Public participation is typically limited to a few meetings where people who have the luxury of extra time listen to project proposals on, say, a Tuesday night so that they may provide feedback for consideration. Although meetings do have value, they are a passive process that too often excludes the underserved, the young, and the unaware from the discussion. With so many barriers to progress, it is no wonder that the civil society and city leaders have begun to experience an apathy known as "planning fatigue." Recovering is difficult and explains the frustration citizens feel toward the planning process, to say nothing of those paid to administer it. The result is that communities suffer because there is simply too much *planning* and not enough *doing*.

People who live and work in a community have important roles to play in resilience-building efforts, roles that go beyond mere participation (see chapter 1). Although urban planning is a complex government function requiring trained professionals, one way to break through gridlock and get from planning to doing is to connect top-down governmental goals with community-based, bottom-up actions. In recent years, planners and local governments have started to embrace a method for doing so called *tactical urbanism*, a city-building process that uses short-term, community-focused projects built with low-cost materials to catalyze long-term change.

Sometimes sanctioned by city government and sometimes not, tactical urbanism does not propose one-size-fits-all *solutions* (big infrastructure projects like a new highway or technofixes like driverless vehicles) from the outset. Rather, it stresses the need for flexible *responses* to local needs. The former approach assumes that most variables impacting city life can be controlled now and into the distant future. The latter approach eschews this top-down approach and replaces it with an embrace of the dynamism of cities.

This reframing of how and why we do projects invites a new conversation about what resilience means locally and how local governments *and* community members together explore a more nuanced and nimble approach to building better places to live. As such, tactical urbanism has proven to be a powerful way for local governments and urban planners to gain community trust and create the political focus necessary for investment in larger projects that learn from smaller ones.

Tactical Resilience

According to Michael Berkowitz, "Cities can't just build resilience out of thin air—they need the right tools to do it."[7] *Tactical resilience* is the application of the tactical urbanism methodology to projects that do not just make cities bet ter places to live, but that specifically address communities' resilience challenges. Tactical resilience provides ways for local residents, businesses, and community leaders to collaborate with their local governments in developing the projects with the most potential to build the resilience of neighborhoods and, ultimately and by extension, of cities. The following two case studies offer examples of how tactical resilience works in practice.

Why We Test: Learning to Learn in Burlington, Vermont

Burlington, Vermont (population 42,000), is a small university city known throughout the United States as a forward-thinking community. The city's mobility outcomes reflect its values: 30 percent of Burlingtonians walk, bike, or take the bus to work (which is high by North American standards). This number is not representative of the quality of active transport infrastructure, which is seriously lacking across the city, nor the city's hopes to get many more people moving without a car.

PlanBTV Walk Bike—a project that my planning and design firm Street Plans did with the City of Burlington—is a response to these challenges and serves as Burlington's first citywide effort to improve walking and cycling.[8] Specifically, the project aims to eliminate all deaths and serious injuries caused by traffic incidents while increasing walking and doubling cycling and transit use by 2026. All told, the plan aims to cut the number of driving trips by half.

Achieving these outcomes will be difficult, even in a politically support- ive environment. Thus, the plan places a strong emphasis on high-impact, high-priority investments that can be delivered at low cost using citizen-led demonstration and city-led pilot and interim design projects. The key to this approach is helping all Burlingtonians understand how their short-term actions can translate to the long-term transformation of city streets.

To this last point, a low-cost and iterative approach seemed to be missing from the city's project delivery toolkit. Given the limited resources in a city of Burlington's size, the emerging opportunity became even more obvious when we learned that local citizens, advocacy organizations, and neighborhood groups were already lobbying the city to allow them to implement street safety demonstration projects as a tool for public engagement and education. Although the progressive-minded city government wanted to say yes, there was no city-sanctioned framework for it to do so. Given Street Plans' experience and the timing of the PlanBTV Walk Bike, the Public Works Department asked the firm in 2015 if it could write both a policy for the city to allow the demonstration projects to take place and a guide for citizens to show them how to initiate the demonstration projects legally.

The process kicked off with a big round of public engagement activities and the development of the city policy and the citizens' guide. A month later, we worked with Local Motion, a local active transport advocacy organization, and with the Department of Public Works to develop and implement four demonstration projects along some of the city's busiest streets. We had three weeks to plan the projects and a total of $4,000 for materials.

These projects set out to accomplish two things. The first goal was to engage thousands of people in conversation about creating better walking and cycling conditions by allowing them to physically experience bike and pedestrian infrastructure not currently found in the city. The second goal was to test the city policy and citizens' guide to ensure that it worked for everyone concerned. For maximum impact, the projects were organized in partnership with an arts festival called Art Hop, and Open Streets BTV, an initiative that closes streets to automobile traffic so that people may walk, run, bike, or skate; in other words, they can do anything but drive a car.

Over three days, the team implemented two colorful sidewalk curb extension plazas to alleviate foot traffic that often spills into a highly trafficked street during Art Hop. Three innovative bikeway types and intersection treatments not currently found in the city were added to streets intersecting the two-mile Open Streets route so that people of all ages and abilities could experience safer cycling infrastructure. At each project location, staff set up a tent and gathered feedback about the temporary street designs. A survey gathered hundreds of additional responses, and traffic and speed counts helped us understand the effects that the demonstration projects had on traffic flow.

In the end, we found that people liked the temporary street design changes and wanted them included in the city's regular plans. We learned about details in the designs and the planning process that needed adjustment for future permanent installations to be successful. We engaged hundreds of people who otherwise would not have taken part in the conventional planning process. In addition, the city government learned how quickly it could respond to these types of projects; indeed, within a few weeks, the Department of Public Works went back to the demonstration sites and used long-lasting materials to make some project improvements more permanent.

Scaling up the demonstration project, similar thinking is now being applied to a yearlong, city-led pilot project testing two different types of bikeway barriers along a major corridor in Burlington's northern neighborhoods known to be a dangerous street. The results of this test will also help the city learn which design and materials work best. Overall, the city government is now integrating these experiences into its regular planning process. (As a bonus, the success of this project inspired Local Motion to invest in a digital "Pop-Ups and Demonstration Project Toolkit," supported by a mobile trailer full of project supplies ready to be deployed to unsafe streets around Vermont.)

Everyone knows that urban sustainability can be built into streets physically: think stormwater bioswales, LED streetlights, bicycle lanes, and transit stops. As the Burlington case study demonstrates, however, changing the interaction between local government and citizens from one of simply listening to one of hands-on collaboration can open up opportunities for experimentation, learning, and relationship building, all of which are essential parts of effective community resilience building.

Retain Your Rain: Tactical Resilience in Norfolk, Virginia

When it comes to the effects of climate change, Norfolk, Virginia, may be one of North America's most imperiled cities. Low-lying and largely built on creek beds transformed into concrete, Norfolk experiences periodic flooding during which several neighborhoods partially go under water during high tides or severe rain events. After joining the Rockefeller Foundation's 100 Resilient Cities program, the City of Norfolk released a resilience strategy in 2015 and won a $120 million federal grant to "unite the region; create coastal resilience; build water management solutions; improve economic vitality; and strengthen vulnerable neighborhoods."[9]

Millions of dollars for big projects can only go so far, however. On the other end of the spectrum are all the small things that people can do on their own to build resilience at the level of individual city lots. Organized as the first test of the tactical resilience concept, the Retain Your Rain workshop was organized by the 100 Resilient Cities program, the City of Norfolk, and Street Plans in June 2016. The workshop focused on small, inexpensive stormwater retention techniques, helping more than fifty residents, business owners, and city leaders discover what they can do in the very short term to reduce flooding and become active participants in a citywide, systemic approach to water management.

Attendees from the three Norfolk neighborhoods most threatened by flooding were invited to the workshop, where the use of small-scale, low-cost water management techniques like rain barrels, rain gardens, "blue roofs," and enhanced tree pits was physically demonstrated. (Such projects, when multiplied throughout a neighborhood, help alleviate flooding by holding water on property and thereby slowing down runoff.) In the span of a few hours, the participants installed four rain barrels and one rain garden and depaved a sidewalk for landscaping and water retention. In addition, the fire department helped simulate before-and-after impact by flooding drain spouts from above. Within just minutes of finishing the interventions, workshop participants could see how small-scale actions could, in aggregate, reduce flooding in their neighborhoods.

Feedback from the workshop made clear that Norfolk should also develop a city policy and a citizens' guide to facilitate future rainwater projects. Additional lessons include the need to combine small-dollar city funding matches with neighborhood crowd-sourced funding, a public data dashboard for sharing data about the individual projects, and ongoing training and feedback workshop series for both residents and neighborhood leaders. As in Burlington,

Vermont, the Norfolk project shows how facilitating small, decentralized, independent initiatives can help achieve larger community needs in the short term while cultivating resilience-building capacities (like local skills, knowledge, and experience) for the long term.

What Is Next?

The growth of tactical urbanism—and tactical resilience—has come at a fascinating if not daunting moment in time. As rapid urbanization continues, one thing is clear: as we continue to grapple with the twenty-first century's environmental, energy, economic, and equity crises, the burdens on human, economic, and natural resources will only grow. To build their resilience, communities have to do more with less, with *do* being the operative word.

Tactical resilience holds promise as a way to educate and empower community members to take action. To achieve real lasting outcomes, however, this model of collaborative government-citizen relationship cannot be relegated just to small-scale neighborhood projects; it must spread throughout the city and be applied to other aspects of government responsibility. Tactical resilience on its own cannot solve the enormous challenges that communities face in the twenty-first century. It can, however, get planners, designers, engineers, and elected officials out of their offices and back into the streets with people, where the foundation for social, political, and economic capital is built. It can cut through bureaucracy and break big plans down into manageable projects using many, many small actions that test concepts with quick feedback loops. It can also help cities and citizens collaborate proactively to learn what is needed to sustain high-quality public spaces, to achieve zero-fatality streets, and to simply create engaging, healthier places to live together.

From the outside, working with community members on small projects may seem like an inefficient, hopelessly messy way for a modern city to get things done, but inefficiency is often necessary to create space for the redundancy and experimentation critical to system resilience. Grassroots and neighborhood-scale initiatives are experiments, and multiplied across a city and across the country, they collectively embody important resilience-building functions like diversity, modularity, feedback, and social capital. With a nod to "Carlson's law," the resilient city will not be orderly and neat; rather, it will be chaotic and smart.[10]

Notes

1. Clarence Eckerson Jr., interview with Enrique Peñalosa, Streetfilms, February 1, 2007, http://www.streetfilms.org/interview-with-enrique-penalosa-long/.
2. Bill Chappell, "2015 Traffic Fatalities Rose by Largest Percent in 50 Years, Safety Group Says," National Public Radio, February 18, 2016, http://www.npr.org/sec tions/thetwo-way/2016/02/18/467230965/2015-traffic-fatalities-rose-by-largest-percent-in-50-years-safety-group-says.
3. Adam Gropman, "$1.1 Billion and Five Years Later, the 405 Congestion Relief Project Is a Fail," *LA Weekly*, March 4, 2015, http://www.laweekly.com/news/11-billion -and-five-years-later-the-405-congestion-relief-project-is-a-fail-5415772.
4. "Thousands Still Stranded on Atlanta Highways after Snow Catches South Unprepared," *NBC News*, January 29, 2014, https://usnews.newsvine.com/_news /2014/01/29/22492664-thousands-still-stranded-on-atlanta-highways-after-snow -catches-south-unprepared.
5. Mike Lindblom, "As Jobs Grow in Downtown Seattle, Workers Are Turning More to Transit," *Seattle Times*, February 9, 2017, http://www.seattletimes.com/seattle -news/transportation/as-jobs-grow-in-downtown-seattle-workers-turn-more-to -transit/; Portland Bureau of Transportation, "Health + Vitality," accessed April 5, 2017, https://www.portlandoregon.gov/transportation/66617.
6. "Dangerous by Design 2016," Smart Growth America, accessed April 5, 2017, https://smartgrowthamerica.org/dangerous-by-design/.
7. "100RC Partners with Street Plans, Bringing 'Tactical Resilience' Workshops to 100RC Network Cities," 100 Resilient Cities, May 16, 2016, http:// www.100resilientcities.org/blog/entry/100rc-partners-with-street-plans-bringing -tactical-resilience-workshops-to.
8. Street Plans is currently wrapping up the project in collaboration with the engineering firm Dubois & King.
9. "Norfolk's Strategy Release," 100 Resilient Cities, accessed April 28, 2017, http:// www.100resilientcities.org/blog/entry/norfolk-strategy-release;BrendanO'Hallarn, "Virginia Wins $120.5 Million Resilience Grant Spearheaded by Old Dominion University," January 2016, https://www.odu.edu/news/2016/1/hud_grant.
10. Carlson's law is a term coined by *New York Times* columnist Thomas Friedman based on a observation by technologist and corporate executive Curtis Carlson that, per Friedman, "innovation that happens from the bottom up tends to be

chaotic but smart. Innovation that happens from the top down tends to be orderly but dumb." Charles Marohn, "Chaotic but Smart," *Strong Towns*, November 4, 2013, https://www.strongtowns.org/journal/2013/11/4/chaotic-but-smart.html.

CHAPTER 17

Community Resilience and the Built Environment

Daniel Lerch

THE BUILT ENVIRONMENT—buildings and infrastructure—consists of the most tangible things we associate with a community. Threatened by extreme weather events, earthquakes, obsolescence, and age, the built environment has also been the predominant focus of efforts to build resilience in our communities.

A resilient built environment and a resilient community are not the same thing, however.[1] Structures that are individually "resilient" do not necessarily contribute to overall community resilience and, in fact, can even reduce it. Moreover, a community's built environment and the patterns of human activity it enables and supports (or prevents and discourages) have outsized effects on the resilience of even larger-scale systems like the region, the state, and the country. The configuration of the built environment strongly influences how much energy people use, what opportunities they have access to, and even their health and well-being—all of which are important indicators of community resilience.

The built environment is shaped by decisions at multiple scales, from the individual homeowner's energy-retrofit project to city zoning codes to federal government highway subsidies. It is a complex, churning, and never-ending process of decision making that also tends to shut out those who do not already wield power. To understand how the built environment can best contribute to community resilience, we need to first understand what it is and how it works.

What Is the Built Environment?

The built environment is the sum of all physical structures in a community: buildings, roads, pipes, power lines, bus shelters, parking lots, sewage plants, and so forth. For most people, the built environment is simply the background to their lives: it has been there for a long time, it usually does not change much, and when it does, the process that led to that change is usually unclear.

The built environment is really the physical manifestation of decisions about how we occupy land, played out over decades and centuries. Governments decide who can own land and what it can be used for. Landowners decide what they want to do with the land. Financial institutions decide what kinds of land uses they are willing to lend money for (and who they are willing to lend money *to*). Architects and planners decide how a structure will be designed and situated; engineers decide how a structure will be constructed. Owners and managers decide how a structure will be operated, maintained, repaired, and retrofitted. Most of these actors have a say in how a structure will be demolished or deconstructed at the end of its life. Multiply this pattern by hundreds or thousands of buildings—and many more individual pieces of infrastructure— and you have the built environment of a community.

The decisions that shape the built environment are themselves shaped by many things, in particular, economics, culture (including social norms, law, and politics), and resources. In the 1980s, the streets of major Chinese cities were awash in bicycles, but today they are choked with cars; this is the result of major political decisions and economic changes. European and Latin American cities generally have public squares whereas US cities west of New England generally do not; this is the result of different land ownership structures, social norms, and political priorities. Since World War II, countless neighborhoods and suburbs around the world have been built that are only accessible by automobile;

this is the result of economic and energy conditions (particularly the affordability of energy-dense oil resources) that enable hundreds of millions of people to afford owning, operating, and maintaining their own car.

The built environment also influences itself. The roads that are first laid down on undeveloped land can persist for centuries, even millennia, as structures accrete around them and push new structures into the same pattern. A railroad—or a highway—makes land accessible to people and enables development that then orients itself on that particular piece of transportation infrastructure (and likely not to others) for many years to come. Structures and their uses attract and repel other kinds of structures and uses: the bustling, beautiful downtown public market building attracts other vendors to set up shop and landowners to build more retail space and housing nearby, whereas the gray, looming downtown parking garage often does the opposite.

You can think of the built environment—or really, the built environment plus our use of it, as structures without human use are little more than sculptures—as a very complex, potentially very long-lived system that is constantly changing based on our choices. In the United States, because of how the built environment is regulated at the state and local levels, regular people—in theory—have a say in many of those choices through public participation processes regarding land use planning, building codes, public investments, and, ultimately, through the ballot box.[2] They are all opportunities for "purposeful change" (as described in chapter 7), opportunities to influence community resilience with regard to the built environment.

The Built Environment and Community

The built environment strongly defines the community; in systems terms, we might say that the built environment provides the physical structure of the community's *identity*. (As discussed in chapter 9, identity is the essence of the system that we want to safeguard against disruption and help adapt to changing conditions by building the system's resilience.) In human systems, identity is very much bound up with the things we feel an emotional connection to. Individually, we may feel a connection to familiar locations (the neighborhood pizza shop), architectural favorites (that beautiful old firehouse down the hill), and travel paths (the route taken to work every day). As a community, we may feel shared connection to historic landmarks (the big war monument downtown), gathering places (the baseball stadium), civic institutions (the eastside library), and even major infrastructure (Highway 101, the L Train).

Of course, community identity is not just about how we think of ourselves. It is also about what we *value* about the community (see chapter 1), much of which is determined by the built environment. From the 1930s to the 1950s, the Rural Electrification Project brought electricity to hundreds of thousands of households across the United States, materially improving life and business in those communities. Today, some communities are investing in transportation infrastructure that enables people to forgo owning a car, like bicycle-share, bus rapid transit, and "shared streets."[3] In both cases, things that many people value as important parts of their community's identity (a modern lifestyle far from the bustle of the city; an urban lifestyle that is not dependent on driving everywhere) come from decisions that have been made about the built environment. The built environment's influence on identity is also palpable at smaller scales, like a city block; for example, what gets built on even a single lot—whether a large single-family home, a mixed-use building of stores and apartments, or a movie theater—can strongly affect how people feel about their immediate neighborhood, in part because it also influences what kinds of future development (or decay) might later occur nearby.

So, individual structures make up the built environment, and the built environment influences community identity. As noted at the beginning of this chapter, however, it does not necessarily follow that resilient individual structures lead to a resilient community. Why is that?

It is tempting to think of the resilience of the built environment in terms of individual structures having the right "resilient" or "sustainable" characteristics. For example, we might say that all the new buildings should be extremely energy efficient and be adaptable to multiple uses over time, or that all the city's bridges should be retrofitted to handle more powerful flooding caused by climate change. (Indeed, a lot of talk about the resilience of cities sounds like that.) That is a rather narrow view of the function of built structures in a community, however. If we legislate that all new housing stock must adhere to the strictest green building standards, but doing so forces developers to only build expensive housing that long-time residents cannot afford to rent or buy, that seems like a fairly exclusionary form of "resilience." Neither does it seem "resilient" if we allocate public funds to retrofit all the bridges with flood-ready designs but leave no money for needed improvements to the rest of our transportation infrastructure.

Individual structures do not exist in isolation, and the effects they have within urban space are very complex. To understand this complexity and its effect on resilience better, let us return to the idea of the built environment as a system or, better, a set of systems.

The Built Environment as a Set of Systems

The built environment, like any system, is composed of smaller-scale systems and components and is also nested within larger-scale systems. We know from systems literacy (chapter 7) that these relationships influence system behavior, and we know from resilience science (chapter 9) that behavior at one scale can influence the resilience of a connected system at a different scale. Because the ultimate goal is to build *community* resilience, where among all these scales and systems should we be acting, and how?

Imagine the scale of an individual building. Many new buildings now have "green" building features like natural ventilation, daylighting, water-conserving fixtures, adaptable design (i.e., spaces can be easily reconfigured), and on-site energy production. These features generally make a building more pleasant to be in and also build resilience; that is, they contribute to the building's capacity to continue serving its users through both short-term disruption and long-term change (because they provide flexibility, diversity, and other resilience-building characteristics).

Now imagine the scale of a city. Let us say that all the schools and libraries in a city produce all their own electricity. Energy self-reliance is obviously useful to those individual buildings, but taken together, those buildings' benefits turn into a *different* set of benefits at the larger city scale: they reduce the load on the electricity grid, and in the event of a blackout or an earthquake, they become invaluable resources to help the neighborhood self-organize its recovery. Or, let us say that all major new public buildings in a city are required to meet strict sustainability standards like LEED and Living Building Challenge.[4] At the individual level these buildings will be more efficient to operate and more pleasant to occupy, but taken together, at larger scales these buildings produce city-scale benefits like reducing demand for unsustainable materials, reducing load on utility systems (e.g., stormwater, sewage, electricity, and water), encouraging new markets for sustainable construction materials, building human capital (i.e., knowledge, experience) related to construction and building occupancy, and (thanks to location requirements near transit and bicycle infrastructure) reducing congestion and pollution associated with car travel.

Resilience, then, is happening at two different scales in each of these examples: the buildings are more resilient unto themselves, and they are also contributing to the resilience of the city as a whole. From a systems perspective, the individual structures are contributing to the *adaptive capacity* of larger systems, including the system called "the city." The resilience-supporting relationship works in the other direction, too, and more obviously: if transportation infrastructure, utility infrastructure, local design and construction knowledge, economic conditions, and cultural patterns are all supportive of buildings that are individually resilient, it is easier for such buildings individually to be constructed, maintained, and repaired.

Cross-scale resilience can also work in other ways. In the housing costs and bridges examples given earlier, what happened at the smaller scale—even though it was ostensibly conducive to sustainability or resilience—detracted from the resilience of the larger-scale system. From a systems perspective, the smaller-scale system is not supporting the *identity* of the larger-scale system. Imagine that part of a community's intentional identity is that it will always be an affordable, stable place where people and families can live their whole lives. As housing prices go up—thanks in part, for example, to a city policy requiring strict green building practices—it becomes harder and harder for the community to keep that identity. People who cannot afford to live in their neighborhoods anymore move elsewhere or become homeless; old neighborhood businesses disappear, and new businesses emerge to cater to the higher-income residents; and even local politics might change as the new residents get involved in decision making and elections. Ultimately, the identity of "affordable, stable, family-oriented community" is lost: the community did not have sufficient resilience to adapt to the changes caused by rising housing prices, until the point it crossed a threshold and took on a different identity.[5]

Resilience to What?

Now that we better understand what the built environment is and how it relates to the community as a whole in terms of resilience, let us briefly look at yet-larger scales and consider some of the more significant implications of the E^4 crises (described in part I of this book) for the built environment.

- **Energy.** Nearly three-fourths of total US oil consumption is used for transportation, a pattern of usage that is wholly determined by decisions about the built environment. Indeed, for more than a century we have invested trillions of dollars in constructing a built environment that assumes a steady supply of affordable petroleum to fuel our cars, trucks, ships, and airplanes.[6] This built environment is extremely energy-intensive by design, and it is not easily changed. The energy transition away from fossil fuels requires us to move to (renewably generated) electrified and low-energy transportation and to reduce transportation needs, in a matter of decades.

- **Environment.** We have paved over wetlands that supported biodiversity and regulated water flows, and have built entire neighborhoods within flood zones. We have built sprawling, inefficient suburbs instead of compact communities that could minimize travel, water use, and heating and cooling needs. Rising sea levels and extreme weather now put many communities at risk, and much of our existing infrastructure is unable to cope. As one headline put it, "California's Water System Built for a Climate We No Longer Have."[7]

- **Economic.** Our global, national, and local economies are all set up to require unending growth. Our built environment usually reflects this fact, from purposeful overbuilding to burgeoning infrastructure debt and maintenance backlogs, all of which assume future growth.[8] The end of twentieth-century-style growth will complicate those past decisions, and the new economy will have different infrastructure and buildings needs.

- **Equity.** We build infrastructure and buildings with a set of assumptions in mind about who will be able to use them and how. Transportation infrastructure can be a great equalizer (e.g., in New York City, nearly everyone—from rich to poor—rides the subway) or an excluder (e.g., many families were unable to escape New Orleans during Hurricane Katrina because they did not have a car[9]). Land use can empower (e.g., walkable neighborhoods, public parks) or disempower (e.g., gated communities only accessible to the wealthy). In addition, decisions about all aspects of the built environment already tend to exclude those without political or economic power. As inequality worsens, our approach to the built environment will need to change.

Resilience How?

Finally, to see what we can actually do with regard to the built environment to build community resilience, let us walk through each of the "Six Foundations for Building Community Resilience" introduced in chapter 1.

People

As discussed above, the concept of system identity is useful for understanding whether different scales of the built environment contribute to community resilience. In communities, identity can really only be determined by the community's members.[10] Although everybody cannot be involved in every decision about the built environment, it is important to ensure that decisions are in harmony with the identity that the community actually desires for itself.

One way to do so is to prioritize public participation in urban planning processes, such as by holding community workshops and visioning sessions and providing opportunities for residents, businesses, and other stakeholders to contribute to planning and design in meaningful ways. For example:

- As part of a three-year effort (2009–2011) to develop a vision and strategic plan for meeting livability goals, the City of Portland, Oregon, placed an unusually strong emphasis on public input, with "dozens of workshops and fairs, hundreds of meetings with community groups, and 20,000 comments from residents, businesses and nonprofits."[11]
- The Resilient Communities Project at the University of Minnesota connects communities with university faculty and students to work on sustainability and resilience initiatives. A key component of the project is the involvement of not just local government but a broad range of community stakeholders, including schools, places of worship, neighborhood associations, and businesses.[12]
- The Transition movement, which started in 2006 in England and has since spread around the world, supports community members to organize and collaborate on sustainability and resilience-building projects. The approach is particularly notable for its emphasis on relationships, local culture, and decentralized, collaborative leadership.[13]

Systems Thinking

Systems thinking includes concepts we have discussed throughout this book, such as scales, feedback, and identity. Ultimately, it is about understanding *complexity*. In a complex system, components interact and change both within the system and through influences outside the system, often unpredictably.

With regard to the built environment, one very clear example of such changing systems relationships comes from the late 2000s, when oil prices started rising beyond historic highs. Real estate developers in fast-growing cities like Las Vegas and Victorville, California, had been building suburban homes very far from urban centers, tapping a market of people who were willing to commute extremely long distances by car in order to afford cheaper, larger houses. At some point around 2008, the height of the oil price spike, demand for these houses suddenly plummeted in part because it had become much less afford-able to commute to job centers from such distant locations; some houses ended up being demolished.[14]

What happened was not just a simple issue of supply and demand but rather of a complex relationship between the built environment of far-flung suburbs and the highways that serve them, changing gasoline prices, and the economic dynamics of jobs, wages, and prices. Roads, houses, supermarkets, gas stations, and utilities had all been built as part of a system that, it turned out, depended on gasoline prices not crossing a certain threshold. Once that threshold was crossed, parts of the built environment went from being assets to liabilities. Systems thinking helps us recognize and manage such relationships.

Adaptability

Our built environment has not traditionally been very adaptable; once build-ings and infrastructure are in place, they can be difficult to change in response to new conditions. To achieve adaptability, our built environment will need resilience-building *attributes* like diversity and modularity as well as *processes* that cultivate adaptive capacity.

In recent years, examples of such attributes and processes have flourished across the country; indeed, adaptability is probably the most developed area of urban resilience thinking. Green infrastructure projects like stormwater-collecting bioswales are among the most cited examples of adaptation to build resilience, but virtually anything that reduces demands on infrastructure and provides multiple benefits—like bicycling or transit improvements that help reduce both car traffic and car dependency—can contribute to adaptive capacity.

The City of Scottsdale, Arizona, has taken adaptive infrastructure to very large scale with the Indian Bend wash, an urban waterway and flood zone that is designed to provide recreational space and wildlife habitat under normal condi-tions as well as purposefully flood and even sustain minor damage during heavy rains; the concept has been dubbed "safe-to-fail" as opposed to "fail-safe," the conventional standard for civil engineering.[15] Another approach is adaptable design, such as a parking garage conceived by LMN Architects in Seattle that is designed to be converted into apartments and offices at a later date when demand for parking has declined.[16]

To establish processes that lead to adaptability, institutional capacity is critical. The Rockefeller Foundation's "100 Resilient Cities" project has aimed directly at process by enabling cities to hire chief resilience officers so that resilience building becomes a regular city function and not just a series of ad hoc projects.

An essential part of adaptability is feedback. In systems thinking, feedback is how the system receives information about itself so that it can self-regulate; it implies a circular, iterative process. This issue is especially difficult with regard to the built environment because our processes for inhabiting it tend to be very linear: a parcel of land is zoned for a certain land use, and that zone might not change for decades, even if many other things about the neighborhood have changed. Architects design buildings, but they do not often return after the job is done to learn how occupants actually use their buildings. "Smart building" technology is creating opportunities for feedback in buildings, such as communicating statistics and automatically adapting to occupant behavior[17]—but that is just a start compared with what could be done throughout the cycle of planning, design, and management.

Transformability

When adaptation is not enough, transformation into a different kind of system is the next option. Transformation is a change of system identity, although the change does not have to be absolute. It involves changing some of the system's function and structure so that the system as a whole can build resilience in ways better suited to the changing reality.

Intentional transformation requires both options for change and capacity for change,[18] both of which a community can develop by allowing experiments—even bold ones—to take place. For example, green building practices have gone from the fringes to the mainstream thanks to real estate development teams that took risks with new design and construction practices, and thanks to communities that took risks with buildings that did not necessarily fit with existing regulations. What started in the late 1990s with local experiments in green building design and certification has blossomed into an international movement of countless practitioners and multiple established protocols (e.g., LEED-ND, EcoDistricts, and Living Community Challenge) for new types of sustainability-oriented development. The movement is slowly changing the architecture, planning, construction, and real estate development professions, and in the process, it provides options and capacity for transformation to communities that are ready to think differently about their built environment.

Sustainability

Resilience building is focused on stakeholders, system dynamics, and process; it does not necessarily incorporate all the environmental, economic, and social considerations prompted by sustainability. Resilience leaves the values of the system up to us, whereas sustainability helps us choose those values wisely. Sustainability gives us a frame for understanding how the planet works and how we affect it.

Thus, as we build the resilience of a community with regard to the built environment, we have to make a point of always referring to the insights of sustainability (see chapter 8). One of the important contributions of the Transition movement to community resilience building has been its clear focus on sustainability concerns like climate change and fossil fuel dependence, both in terms of how these global-scale issues have local impacts and in terms of how local actions in turn have global impact.[19] Sustainability provides a well-developed clarity of purpose for community-level initiatives that otherwise might lack both vision and a sense of importance. Other organizations, like the Urban Sustainability Directors Network and ICLEI, are invaluable resources for community initiatives and policies on the built environment that reflect sustainability values.[20]

Courage

The built environment is personal: we literally, constantly inhabit it. We live in our homes, travel on our streets, and meet daily needs in our neighborhoods.

It is indeed "our" environment. It is the setting for our community's culture, where we see and interact with other people. We invest ourselves in the relationships and places we find within our built environment; we might even literally invest money in acquiring part of it for ourselves.

It is no wonder, then, that decisions about the built environment can elicit strong feelings. Transportation infrastructure projects, whether a bike lane or a new highway, are notorious for inspiring protest from some segment of the community. The terms *NIMBY* (for "not in my backyard") and *LULU* (for "locally unwanted land use") suggest the difficulty of equitably configuring the community's built environment so that it works for everyone (or at least upsets as few people as possible).

We inhabit a built environment that was largely shaped in the twentieth century, but we are dealing with twenty-first-century challenges. That means that building the resilience of American communities will often involve making decisions—and almost invariably arousing opposition—about the built environment that are quite different from how things have been done in the past. It will require courage to envision what changes are possible and to work—even fight—to make them happen.

Conclusion

As the United States industrialized in the nineteenth and twentieth centuries, communities had to adapt their built environments to a quickly changing world. They redesigned streets to accommodate new types of motorized transportation, they regulated the construction of the huge numbers of new buildings needed by a growing urbanized population, and they started planning the use of land for a modern industrial economy that required greater efficiency and predictability. Importantly, these adaptations generally started as local initiatives but quickly spread nationwide as communities copied and adapted them to local needs.[21]

In the twenty-first century, communities must again adapt their built environments, but instead of adapting to the somewhat predictable needs of a growing industrial economy powered by energy-dense and seemingly limitless fossil fuels,[22] we must now adapt to the sometimes bewildering uncertainties generated by the E^4 crises. For example, should we plan for the physical needs and promises of a high-tech "green" economy, or prepare for the financial and social disruptions of the dying fossil fuel economy? Should we count on a widespread transition to 100 percent renewable energy and retrofit our cities for massive new fleets of autonomous electric vehicles, or transform our streets and land uses to make walking, bicycling, and public transportation the easiest ways to get around? Should we build levees against the rising seas, or start a decades-long effort to deconstruct and relocate endangered coastal communities?

As in the twentieth century, local leaders have been among the first to tackle such questions with grassroots initiatives, business ventures, and government policies. Communities everywhere should not only learn from these ideas, but should experiment and develop the resilience-cultivating actions that are best suited to their own unique built environments.

Notes

1. Although I am keeping with common usage by calling a community "resilient" here, it should be understood that resilience is better thought of as something to continually cultivate rather than something to achieve (see chapter 1).
2. The reality, of course, is different from community to community. One inspiring example of in-depth public participation in the land use process is Recode, a nonprofit organization in Portland, Oregon, that has worked to change city building codes to support deep green building practices such as on-site wastewater treatment.
3. National Association of City Transportation Officials, "Residential Shared Street," *Urban Street Design Guide*, accessed March 5, 2017, http://nacto.org/publication/urban-street-design-guide/streets/residential-shared-street/.
4. See http://www.usgbc.org/LEED/ and https://living-future.org/lbc/.
5. Although it is beyond the scope of this chapter to discuss, it seems that the process of community identity change as a result of gentrification also has some relation to the "release" phase of the complex adaptive cycle. As Brian Walker and David Salt describe it in *Resilience Thinking: Sustaining Ecosystems and People in a Changing World* (Washington, DC: Island Press, 2006), 77: "Resources that were tightly bound are now released as connections break…. The loss of structure continues as linkages are broken, and natural, social, and economic capital leaks out of the

system." Compare this view with the gentrification effects of long-time residents selling their homes, social relationships dissolving, community culture and memory disappearing, and, soon, the "capital" of urban space being repurposed for new homes and new businesses as new relationships and cultures form.

6. See Daniel Lerch, *Post Carbon Cities: Planning for Energy and Climate Uncertainty* (Sebastopol, CA: Post Carbon Institute, 2007).

7. Lauren Sommer, "California's Water System Built for a Climate We No Longer Have," *KQED Science*, February 27, 2017, https://ww2.kqed.org/science/2017/02/27 /californias-water-system-built-for-a-climate-we-no-longer-have/.

8. For example, see the writing of Charles Marohn of Strong Towns on "The Growth Ponzi Scheme" at https://www.strongtowns.org/the-growth-ponzi-scheme/.

9. Laura Sullivan, "How New Orleans' Evacuation Plan Fell Apart," NPR, September 23, 2005, http://www.npr.org/templates/story/story.php?storyId=4860776.

10. See "Why Communities?" in chapter 1, "Six Foundations for Building Community Resilience."

11. City of Portland, "About the Portland Plan," accessed March 7, 2017, http://www .portlandonline.com/portlandplan/?c=56527.

12. See the Resilient Communities Project website at http://rcp.umn.edu/. The model of this project was originally developed at the University of Oregon as the Sustainable City Year Program, https://sci.uoregon.edu/scyp-0.

13. See http://transitionnetwork.org. For an illuminating look at the overlaps between the transition movement's approach to resilience building and the approach of the resilience science community, see My Sellberg et al., "Improving Participatory Resilience Assessment by Cross-Fertilizing the Resilience Alliance and Transition Movement Approaches," *Ecology and Society* 22, no. 1 (2017): 28, https://doi .org/10.5751/ES-09051-220128.

14. See Warren Karlenzig, "The Death of Sprawl: Designing Urban Resilience for the Twenty-First-Century Resource and Climate Crises," in *The Post Carbon Reader: Managing the 21st Century's Sustainability Crises*, ed. Richard Heinberg and Daniel Lerch (Healdsburg, CA: Watershed Media, 2010), http://www.postcarbon.org /publications/cities-the-death-of-sprawl/.

15. Kelsey Wharton, "Resilient Cities: From Fail-Safe to Safe-to-Fail," Arizona State University website, July 21, 2015, https://research.asu.edu/stories/read/resilient -cities-fail-safe-safe-fail.

16. Aarian Marshall, "It's Time to Think about Living in Parking Garages," *Wired*, November 2, 2016, https://www.wired.com/2016/11/time-think-living -old-parking-garages/.

17. However, care must be taken that the opportunities and efficiencies gained by technology do not decrease resilience by making systems too complex and brittle.

18. Acceptance of the need for transformation is also required. See Brian Walker and David Salt, *Resilience Practice: Building Capacity to Absorb Disturbance and Maintain Function* (Washington, DC: Island Press, 2012), 101.
19. My Sellberg et al., "Improving Participatory Resilience."
20. See http://usdn.org and http://icleiusa.org/.
21. For example, the use of zoning codes to separate conflicting land uses (like factories and residences) emerged from a handful of communities in the early 1900s and went on to dominate American city planning for most of the twentieth century. By the end of that century, a "New Urbanist" movement had emerged to adapt planning practice in light of the problems unwittingly created by single-use zoning.
22. Consider that, in the one hundred years from the launch of Ford's Model T (the first car truly available to the American middle class) in 1908 to the start of the Great Recession in 2008, the inevitability of long-term nationwide economic growth and long-term availability of oil to power transportation and coal (and, later, natural gas and nuclear power) to generate electricity could generally and quite safely go unquestioned by communities (not to mention the long-term stability of the climate).

CHAPTER 18

Conclusion: Where to Start

Asher Miller

AMERICANS (AND MANY PEOPLE elsewhere in the world) are struggling to understand and respond to a dramatically shifted political reality
following the 2016 US general election. For those concerned about the climate
crisis, environmental protection, social justice, and other so-called progressive
causes, these are worrisome days indeed.

If we have learned anything from this book, it is that it would be foolish
to predict what the coming years will bring: the complex and dynamic interactions of so many systems simultaneously going through profound shifts can
lead to unpredictable results. That said, some things seem safe to bet on. We
are likely to experience more discontinuity, if only as a result of inputs already
baked into the system; among them are higher atmospheric concentrations
of carbon dioxide and the decline of conventional fossil fuels. Also, the need
to radically reduce human impacts on the biosphere will only increase as the
global growth- and extraction-based economy strives to support more people
consuming more resources. Finally, it is a very safe bet that investing heavily in
local and regional resilience will be a no-regrets strategy. At minimum, it will

improve the well-being and social cohesion of local communities; more likely, as discontinuities become a common feature of the coming decades, building resilience will literally save lives.

If, like me, you have read the chapters of *The Community Resilience Reader* with a mixture of alarm, excitement, confusion, and clarity, then welcome to the rest of the twenty-first century! The truth is that unless we choose to live in ignorance (which is tempting, but if you have gotten this far, then it is also largely impossible), we are going to have to navigate the future through a flurry of contradictions. Here are five that come to mind.

1. **We must live in this world while building the next.** This challenge is one of the biggest I personally encounter, and it is one that many of my friends and colleagues share. I spend much of my time living like a hypocrite: driving a (partially) gasoline-powered car; eating food that was not grown in my bioregion; using natural gas-powered electricity and heat; wearing clothes that were manufactured far away by people I do not know in unenviable conditions, with petrochemical inputs embedded in every phase of their life cycle; and so on. It is true that many of my daily choices can be improved upon or are the result of laziness, but the truth is also that I—and you—live in a fossil-fueled, extraction- and consumption-based system. We have to be thoughtful and judicious in where we invest our time, energy, and resources for change. Doing so may entail accepting certain hypocrisies and unsustainable choices—and being mindful of them as such—as trade-offs for freeing up the time and effort needed to change the conditions that reinforce those unsustainable choices.

2. **We have no time to waste, yet we must take our time.** Some of the challenges we face are truly dire; if we do not act boldly now, we may not be able to mitigate or even *adapt* to them later. This contradiction is perhaps most evident in the context of climate change, wherein rapidly approaching tipping points will create unstoppable, reinforcing feedback loops. The writer and climate activist Bill McKibben has said, "We have to adapt to that which we can't prevent, and prevent that to

which we can't adapt."[1] We must also avoid jumping at false, incomplete, or unsustainable solutions out of panic. Are single-occupancy electric vehicles truly sustainable in the long run? What are the possible risks of rushing out so-called negative emissions and carbon capture technologies? Are they even scalable? When viewed with a systems lens, it seems clear that building truly just and sustainable resilience comes down to dramatically shifting human behavior, values, and numbers, which by necessity require relationships, modeling, education, and therefore time. That is particularly true in the case of building *community* resilience.

3. **We have to simultaneously oppose and propose.** Unfortunately, not everyone understands that we need to transition away from an economy that is dependent on globalization, resource extraction, fossil fuels, debt, and perpetual growth. In fact, there are many—including those who hold a tremendous amount of political and financial influence—who want to double down on these very things. (Donald Trump's "America First" rhetoric earned him the votes of millions disaffected by globalization, but nationalism is not localism; nor was he a champion of renewable energy and conservation.) Policies that reinforce our unsustainable path, especially those that include large-scale infrastructure and long-term investment, simply have to be opposed outright. The climate and social justice movements have grown their resistance efforts over recent years and by all appearances intend to continue to do so. Efforts like resistance to the Keystone XL and Dakota Access pipelines, even if not always victorious, remain highly important. Opposition can only be successful if the right alternatives are being proposed and implemented, however.

4. **We must act both locally and globally.** Many people concerned about issues like the climate crisis or global justice correctly point out that even the most sustainable and equitable community is deeply vulnerable to national and global forces like climate change, war, and human rights abuses. Thus, we must dedicate time and resources to advocating and organizing for the right regional, national, and international policies.

The opposite is equally true, though. If we spend all our time championing top-down policy solutions in capitals far from home without winning the hearts and minds of our neighbors, our victories will be politically compromised or fleeting. In addition, much of what is required to build a truly sustainable and resilient world is by necessity organized around relationships, individual and collective values, and the practical experience of living within the biophysical capacity of our environment, all things that almost by necessity are grounded in the small and local.

5. **We must have a clear vision and strategy while putting a premium on experimentation, feedback, and adaptation.** Since 2003, Post Carbon Institute has been tracking and supporting efforts to relocalize and build community resilience, efforts that were usually driven by the passions and concerns of small groups of individuals. The more motivated these individuals were, the more they wanted to do something, *anything*, and so they naturally sought to take action in ways that aligned with their own personal interests and skills. These efforts often failed to scale up or survive for more than a few years, however. We have found that the most successful local efforts are ones in which participants take the time to build relationships, assess the resilience of their community, identify the best areas for engagement, and facilitate people-driven visions and planning. A clear vision and strategy should not be written in stone, though; after all, truly resilient systems (and communities) are ones that are dynamic and have tight feedback loops, diversity, and an ability to adapt and transform.

Navigating these contradictions is hard work, but it is necessary; otherwise, our impact will be incomplete, superficial, or temporary. That is not to say that each and every one of us must personally engage in all these levels, in all these ways, at all times. Doing so would be impractical. It is nonetheless incumbent on us to ensure that work on each of these levels is, in fact, happening in the communities where we live.

So, when my colleagues and I at Post Carbon Institute are asked the inevitable question, "Where do I start?," the answer is usually three-fold: *Think in systems. Collaborate with others. Find your passion.* There is no one-size-fits-all blueprint or solution for doing any of it. All communities are unique, and you are unique. We have, however, found one starting step that can focus systems thinking, facilitate collaboration, and draw on one's own talents and passions: organize people in your community to design and implement *a community resilience assessment.*

Before you begin, keep in mind that a community resilience assessment—if it is not just an academic exercise and is intended to lead to meaningful action—has to be undertaken with the consent and involvement of the community and should harness the expertise and insight of community members. So, at the very earliest stages of the assessment, you will need to start talking to people. In fact, forming or joining a team to design and conduct the assessment—one composed of people who reflect the economic, political, and ethnic diversity of your community—is highly recommended.

A community resilience assessment aims to answer three essential questions:

1. *Resilience of what?* What, really, is the community you are interested in? What is its boundary? Is it a bioregion? A county? Your city? Your neighborhood? Your school? What are that community's interactions with natural systems? What are its resource flows, dependencies, and impacts?

2. *What defines the **identity** of your community?* The identity of an ecosystem may arise from climate, topography, soil types, and key species and their interactions. Communities are largely human systems, however, so you might need to engage in many conversations or undertake a formal survey to get an idea of what makes your particular community unique and what people want to see happen (i.e., persist, change, or fade away) as the community adapts and transforms itself over time.

3. *Resilience to **what**?* What are the most likely foreseeable disturbances, both short-term and long-term? Are there particular uncertainties regarding resource flows or climate? What are the vulnerabilities not only of the community system as a whole, but of the community's many subsystems—the

areas covered in chapters 11 through 17 as well as things like transportation and the local economy—and their respective components?

A community resilience assessment also aims to identify three key dynamics:

1. *The functions of social and political systems.* How is the community governed? Who makes decisions and how? Who are the stakeholders? Who is often left out? The answers to these questions help you determine who should be involved in the assessment and who you should be talking to, people you might otherwise not have considered. Among other things, the assessment should seek to reveal how adaptable the governance system itself is. Building community resilience will likely require action on the part of the governance system, and it may also require change in its design, composition, or rules.

2. *Likely cross-scale interactions.* Every system is composed of subsystems, and every system is part of a larger system. That is certainly true in a community. Are the community's subsystems approaching critical thresholds? Are changes in larger systems outside the community likely to spill over to affect or overwhelm it?

3. *Existing and potential allied efforts.* What are the *opportunities* available to build sustainability and adaptability? Who are potential allies for resilience-building projects? Who in the community is already working on sustainability and resilience issues generally, and who is working on the key vulnerabilities that you have identified?

The goals of a resilience assessment are to provide the community with a clear picture of its identity, strengths, and vulnerabilities and to identify the most opportune areas for resilience-building action. Synthesize and share your findings, ideally by presenting clear and actionable recommendations for projects and policies that the community can implement. If you have conducted a truly people-driven community resilience assessment, your recommendations will be received not only with interest, but also with a sense of ownership on the part of the community.

Ultimately, a community resilience assessment should lead to the development of a resilience action plan and concrete, practical, and inspirational projects. In addition, by the end of the assessment phase, you will likely have become a better systems thinker, have formed and strengthened new relationships within the community, and have discovered where you are called to serve.

At the end of chapter 16, Mike Lydon observes how neighborhood-scale projects, when multiplied across a city, "collectively embody important resilience-building functions." The same is true for community resilience building in general. Any single community that aims to build its resilience will not thrive for long if many other communities do not do the same; we are all far too interconnected for "lifeboat" strategies to work. When multiplied and scaled up, however, community-scale efforts can start to build the resilience—and influence the sustainability—of the higher-level systems we care about and depend on: our regions, our country, and ultimately our world.

Notes

1. McKibben has expressed this notion many times in various forms over the years. One early instance is in Maureen Nandini Mitra, "Ready or Not," *Earth Island Journal*, Autumn 2011, http://www.earthisland.org/journal/index.php/eij/article /ready_or_not/.

Contributors

Sarah Byrnes is the public housing training program manager at the Mel King Institute in Boston, where she works with residents of public housing and their advocates to enhance participation in the oversight of their housing developments. Previously, she worked at the Institute for Policy Studies, where she founded the New England Resilience and Transition Network and was one of the leaders of the Jamaica Plain New Economy Transition initiative. Byrnes has collaborated with many grassroots groups around the United States to build community and enhance resilience. She has degrees from Boston College and Harvard Divinity School and lives in the Roslindale neighborhood in Boston, where she is a leader in the grassroots group Roslindale Is for Everyone (RISE).

Chuck Collins is a senior scholar at the Institute for Policy Studies where he coedits Inequality.org. His newest book is *Born on Third Base: A One Percenter Makes the Case for Tackling Inequality, Bringing Wealth Home, and Committing to the Common Good* (White River Junction, VT: Chelsea Green, 2016). He is coauthor, with Bill Gates Sr., of *Wealth and Our Commonwealth: Why America*

Should Tax Accumulated Fortunes. His previous books include *99 to 1: How Wealth Inequality Is Wrecking the World and What We Can Do About It.* He is cofounder of the Jamaica Plain New Economy Transition, a local Transition movement initiative working to build community resilience. He is a father, cyclist, gardener, part-time Vermonter, and anti–fossil fuel activist who mostly lives in Boston. Collins is a board member of Post Carbon Institute.

Rosemary Cooper has been helping communities, nonprofit organizations, and professionals strategically advance their efforts in sustainable community planning, green economic development, next-generation transportation, and sustainable consumption for more than twenty years. She is currently a senior associate with One Earth, a "think and do tank" cofounded by Bill Rees whose mission is to transform consumption and production systems so that they are healthy and just within Earth's finite limits. Cooper coauthored the 2015 *Local Governments and the Sharing Economy Roadmap* and was a signatory to the breakthrough 2014 *Eugene Memorandum: The Role of Cities in Advancing Sustainable Consumption.* She teaches sustainable consumption at the British Columbia Institute of Technology in Vancouver and is passionate about advancing consumption and production innovations that foster lasting prosperity. Cooper has a master's degree in environmental studies (planning) from York University and a certificate in urban design from Simon Fraser University.

Denise Fairchild is president and chief executive officer of Emerald Cities Collaborative, a national nonprofit organization of business, labor, and community groups dedicated to climate resilience strategies that produce environmental, economic, and equity outcomes. She and Al Weinrub are coeditors of *Energy Democracy: Advancing Equity in Clean Energy Solutions* (Washington, DC: Island Press, 2017).

Joshua Farley is a fellow at the Gund Institute for Ecological Economics and professor of community development and applied economics at the University of Vermont. He is coauthor with Herman Daly of *Ecological Economics: Principles and Applications* (Washington, DC: Island Press, 2003; 2nd ed., 2010), which helped define the then-emerging field of ecological economics. His broad research interests focus on the design of economic institutions capable of balancing what is biophysically possible with what is socially, psychologically, and ethically desirable. He has previously served as the executive director of the University of Maryland's International Institute for Ecological Economics. Farley is a fellow of Post Carbon Institute.

Richard Heinberg is senior fellow of Post Carbon Institute and is regarded as one of the world's foremost advocates for a shift away from our current reliance on fossil fuels. He is the author of thirteen books, including some of the seminal works on society's current energy and environmental sustainability crisis. His writing has appeared in such publications as *Nature*, *Wall Street Journal*, *American Prospect*, and *Yes!* magazine, and he has been quoted and interviewed countless times for print, radio, and television. Heinberg has delivered hundreds of lectures to audiences in fourteen countries, from local city councils to members of the European Parliament, and has appeared in many documentaries, including Leonardo DiCaprio's *11th Hour*.

Leena Iyengar is director of Tune Into Earth, a sustainability consulting firm based in Geneva, Switzerland. She has worked for more than fifteen years in environmental management, conservation, and sustainability with national governments and nongovernmental organizations, including the World Wide Fund for Nature (WWF), Global Footprint Network, and the United Kingdom's Natural Resources Institute. Much of her work has involved assisting scientists and technical teams in developing communication material for environmental organizations and outreach campaigns. Iyengar helped develop and coordinate the United Arab Emirates' Ecological Footprint Initiative and was lead editor and project manager of the WWF's flagship publication, *Living Planet Report 2014*.

Daniel Lerch is publications director of Post Carbon Institute, serving as lead editor and manager of the institute's books and reports. He is the author of *Post Carbon Cities: Planning for Energy and Climate Uncertainty* (2007)—the first major local government guidebook on the end of cheap oil—and was the founding chair of the Sustainable Communities Division of the American Planning Association and a founding codirector of the City Repair Project. Lerch has delivered more than one hundred presentations to audiences across the United States and abroad and has been interviewed for numerous media outlets. He has worked with urban sustainability issues for more than twenty years in the public, private, and nonprofit sectors.

Mike Lydon is a principal of the Street Plans Collaborative, an international award-winning planning, design, and research-advocacy firm based in Miami, New York City, and San Francisco. With Tony Garcia, he is the recipient of the 2017 Seaside Prize and coauthor of *Tactical Urbanism: Short-Term Action for Long-term Change* (Washington, DC: Island Press, 2015), named by Planetizen as one of the top ten planning books of the year. He received a master's degree in urban planning from the University of Michigan and lives in Brooklyn, New York.

Asher Miller is executive director of Post Carbon Institute. Previously, he served as partnership director at Plugged In, international production coordinator at Steven Spielberg's Shoah Foundation, ghostwriter for a Holocaust survivor, and consultant for a number of other nonprofit groups. He currently serves on the board of Transition US, the hub of the Transition movement in the United States.

Stephanie Mills is an author, lecturer, and longtime bioregionalist. Her books include *Epicurean Simplicity, On Gandhi's Path*, and *In Service of the Wild*. Since 1969, Mills has written prolifically; spoken widely; edited periodicals; kept a salon; participated in countless local, national, and international conferences; and served on the boards and advisory committees of dozens of ecologically oriented organizations. Since 1984, she has lived in Northwest Lower Michigan where, along with ongoing writing and public speaking, she helped organize Great Lakes Bioregional Congresses, build her dwelling, and start a local currency. More recently, Mills was awarded an honorary doctorate by her alma mater, featured in the PBS documentary *Earth Days*, and received an Arthur Morgan Award from Community Solutions. She is an elder of the Human Nature School and a member of the Neahtawanta Research and Education Center board. Mills is a fellow of Post Carbon Institute.

William Rees is the originator and codeveloper of ecological footprint analysis. A human ecologist and ecological economist, he is professor emeritus and former director of the University of British Columbia's School of Community and Regional Planning in Vancouver, Canada. Rees has authored or coauthored more than 150 peer-reviewed papers and book chapters as well as numerous popular articles on humanity's (un)sustainability conundrum. Active across disciplines, Rees is a long-term member of the Global Ecological Integrity Group, a founding member and past president of the Canadian Society for Ecological Economics, and founding director of the OneEarth Initiative. In 2006, he was elected to the Royal Society of Canada, and in 2007, he was awarded a prestigious Trudeau Foundation Fellowship. He is the recipient of both the 2012 Boulding Prize in Ecological Economics and a 2012 Blue Planet Prize. Rees is a fellow of Post Carbon Institute.

Margaret Robertson, ASLA, teaches at Lane Community College in Eugene, Oregon, where she coordinates the sustainability degree program. She is the author of *Sustainability Principles and Practice* (London: Routledge, 2014; 2nd ed., 2017) and *Dictionary of Sustainability* (London: Routledge, 2017).

David Salt has been writing about science, scientists, and the environment for much of the last three decades. He created and then produced *The Helix* (Australia's best-loved science magazine for young people) for more than a decade, served as communications manager for the Commonwealth Scientific and Industrial Research Organisation (CSIRO) Division of Wildlife and Ecology, and was the inaugural editor of an Australian version of the popular science magazine *Newton*. More recently, Salt has written and edited books on farm forestry and agri-environment policy. He currently edits two research magazines, *Decision Point* and *Science for Saving Species*, and is based in Canberra at the Centre of Excellence for Environmental Decisions at the Australian National University. With Brian Walker, Salt coauthored *Resilience Thinking* (Washington, DC: Island Press, 2006) and *Resilience Practice* (Washington, DC: Island Press, 2012).

Scott Sawyer is sustainability director at the Vermont Sustainable Jobs Fund and the lead author, editor, and designer of Vermont's *Farm to Plate Strategic Plan*. His work has included researching, analyzing, writing, editing, evaluating, and designing for a variety of renewable energy, forest products, and food system projects and programs, including Vermont's Farm to Plate Initiative, the Community Energy Dashboard, the Renewable Energy Atlas, and the Vermont Bioenergy Initiative. Sawyer has a PhD in sociology from Washington State University, where his dissertation was titled "The Politics of Reliability: A Sociological Examination of the State of Vermont's Response to Peak Oil and Climate Change."

Howard Silverman teaches applied systems thinking in the MFA in Collaborative Design program at Pacific Northwest College of Art. Specializing in hands-on workshops that elicit critical and creative thinking through the use of systems and design techniques, he has taught in innovative undergraduate and graduate programs around the United States. Formerly, he was senior writer and analyst with the Portland, Oregon, nonprofit organization Ecotrust, where he worked in numerous areas (food systems, fisheries and forestry, green building, climate and energy) and learned from the use of numerous approaches (scenario planning, spatial planning, market design, life cycle assessment, participatory processes). He is a partner in the scenarios, research, and design consultancy Pattern Labs and writes at solvingforpattern.org.

William Throop is professor of philosophy and environmental studies and director of the environmental studies program at Green Mountain College. He was provost at Green Mountain College for twelve years, during which time he helped build the sustainability focus of the college and led the creation of its graduate programs. At the national level, he served on the board of directors of the Association for the Advancement of Sustainability in Higher Education

(AASHE) for six years and as board chair for his last two years. He has also served on the editorial boards of *Restoration Ecology* and *Environmental Ethics*. His PhD work at Brown University focused on philosophy of science and epistemology, but his recent publications have been on ethical issues in ecological restoration and sustainability education. He is currently working on a book project titled *Flourishing amid the Age of Climate Change: Finding the Heart of Sustainability*.

Brian Walker has been one of the leading proponents of resilience theory and practice in the past two decades. He is currently an honorary fellow at Commonwealth Scientific and Industrial Research Organisation (CSIRO), Australian National University visiting professor, and a fellow in the International Beijer Institute for Ecological Economics in Sweden. Walker was chief of Australia's CSIRO Wildlife and Ecology (1985–1999), chaired the Global Change and Terrestrial Ecosystems Project of the International Geosphere-Biosphere Program (1990–1997), and was director of the international Resilience Alliance (2000–2010). He is a fellow of the Australian Academy of Science and of the Australian Academy of Technological Sciences and Engineering and a foreign member of the Royal Swedish Academy of Agriculture and Forestry. He has a long list of scientific publications and has served on the editorial boards of five international journals. With David Salt, Walker coauthored *Resilience Thinking* (Washington, DC: Island Press, 2006) and *Resilience Practice* (Washington, DC: Island Press, 2012).

Al Weinrub is coordinator of the Local Clean Energy Alliance (LCEA), the San Francisco Bay Area's largest clean energy coalition. The LCEA promotes the equitable development and democratization of local renewable energy resources as key to addressing climate change and building sustainable and resilient communities. He and Denise Fairchild are coeditors of *Energy Democracy: Advancing Equity in Clean Energy Solutions* (Washington, DC: Island Press, 2017).

Rebecca Wodder is a nationally known environmental leader whose conservation career began with the first Earth Day. As president of the national advocacy organization American Rivers from 1995 to 2011, she led the development of community-based solutions to freshwater challenges. From 2011 to 2013, she served as senior advisor to the US secretary of the interior. Previously, she was vice president of the Wilderness Society and legislative assistant to Senator Gaylord Nelson. In 2010, she was named a Top 25 Outstanding Conservationist by *Outdoor Life* magazine. In 2014, she received the James Compton Award from River Network. In her writing and speaking, Wodder explores how communities can enhance their resilience to climate impacts via sustainable, equitable approaches to rivers and freshwater resources. She serves on the boards of River Network, the Potomac Conservancy, and the Nelson Institute for Environmental Studies at the University of Wisconsin–Madison.

About Post Carbon Institute

Post Carbon Institute envisions a transition to a more resilient, equitable, and sustainable world. It provides individuals and communities with the resources needed to understand and respond to the interrelated ecological, economic, energy, and equity crises of the twenty-first century. Visit postcarbon.org for a full list of its fellows, publications, and other educational products.

For supplementary content and resources for this book, visit
postcarbon.org/resilience

Index